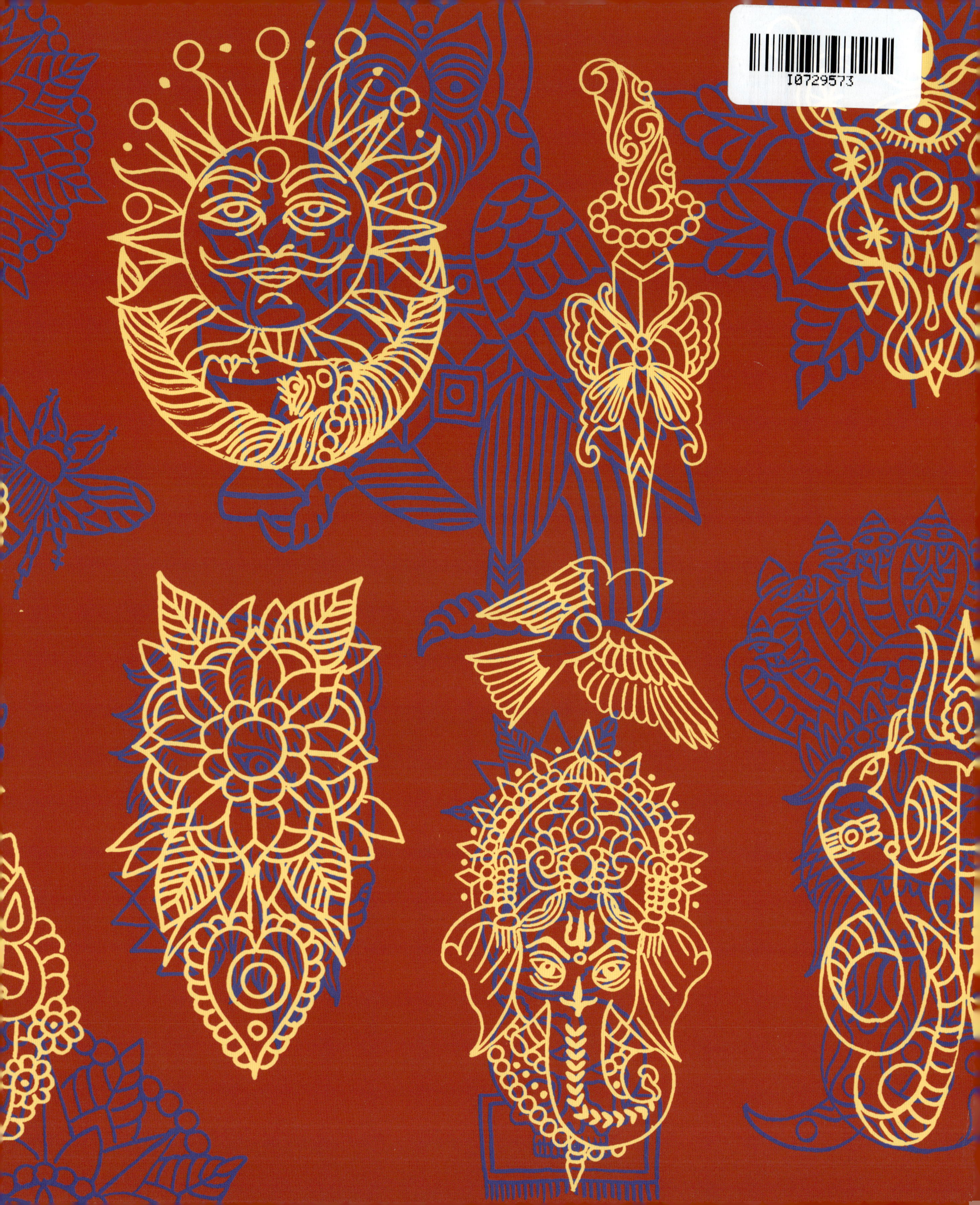
I0729573

Published by Featherproof Books and Mandible Projects
www.featherproof.com
www.mandibleprojects.com
Chicago, Illinois

Second edition
10 9 8 7 6 5 4 3 2 1

Library of Congress Control Number: 2021941460
ISBN 13: 978-1-943888-28-3

Edited by Ben Fasman and Tim Kinsella
Photographs by Laura Ferrara, Ryan Lowry, Autumn Spadaro, Sara Stadtmiller, Chris Strong and Mitchell Wojcik
Design and layout by Field of Grass

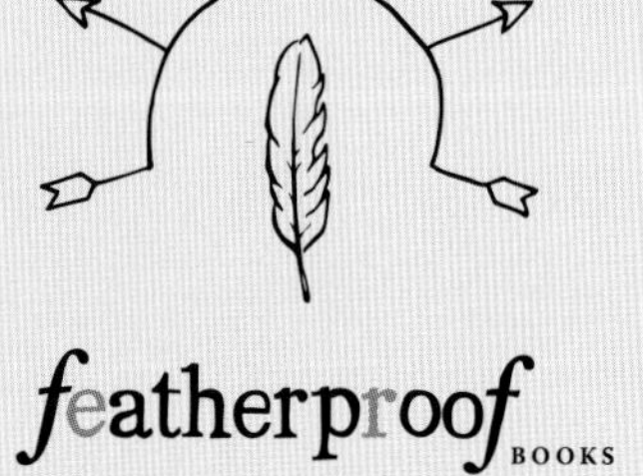

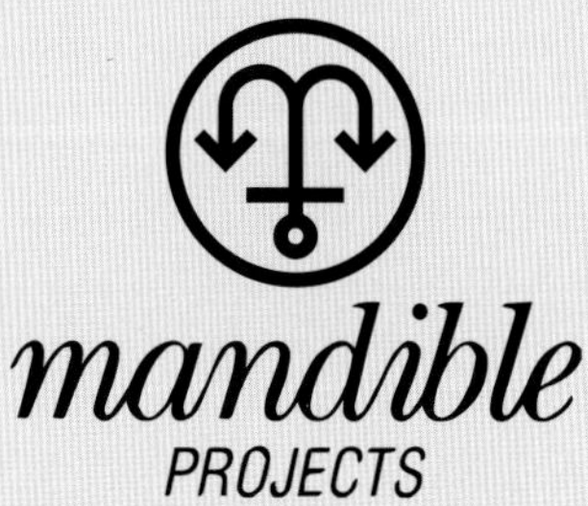

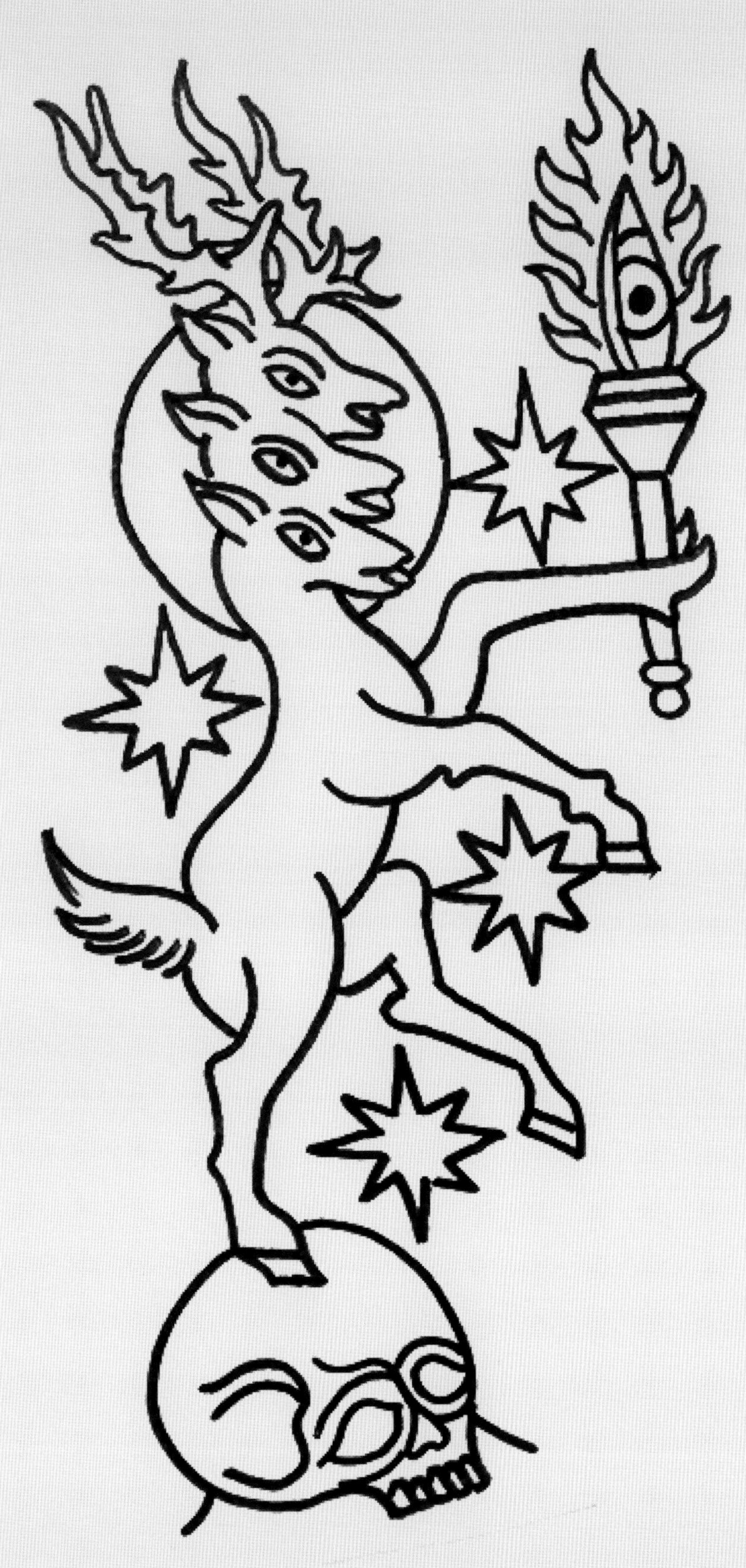

THE
INBORN
ABSOLUTE

THE ART OF
ROBERT RYAN

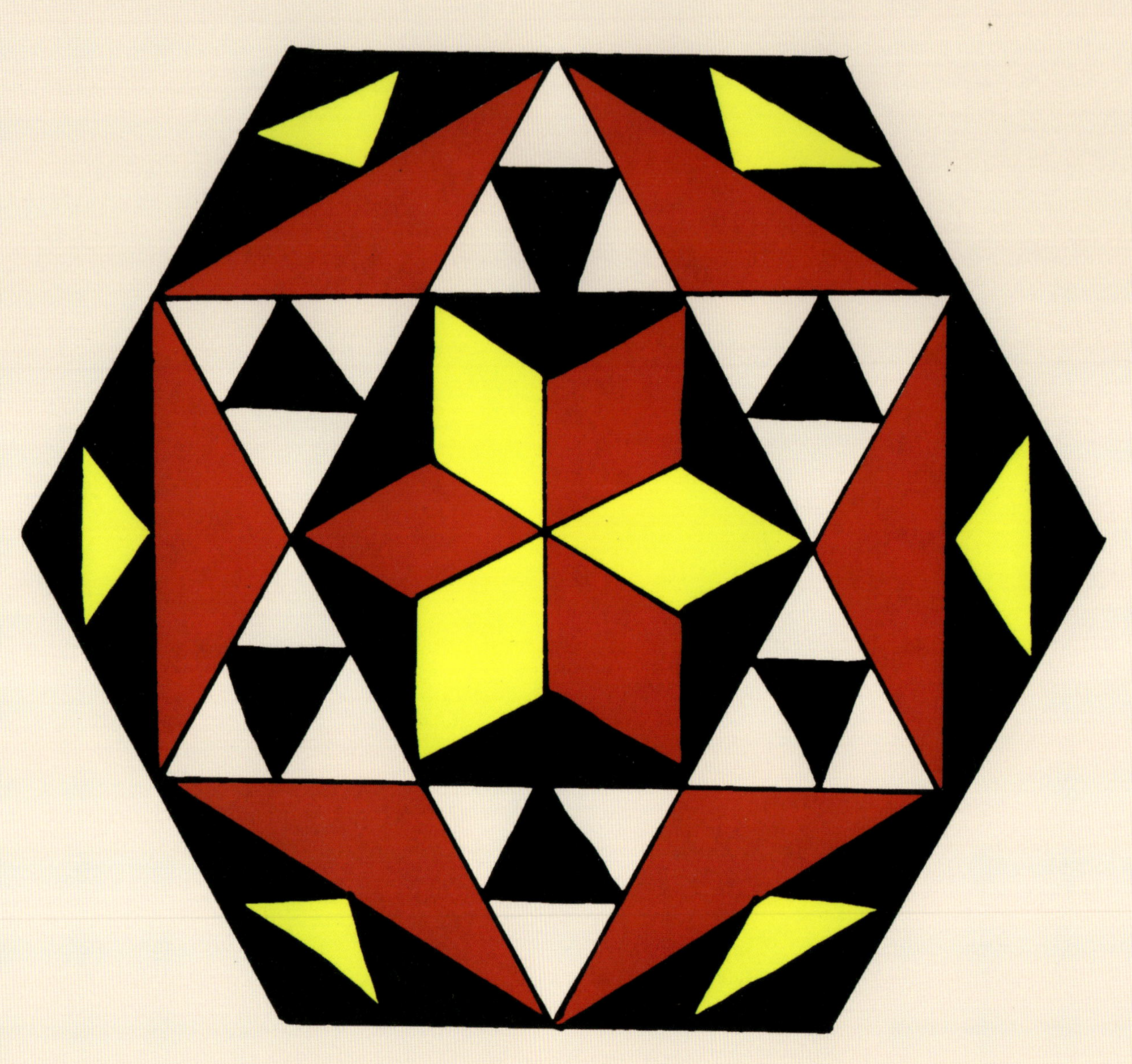

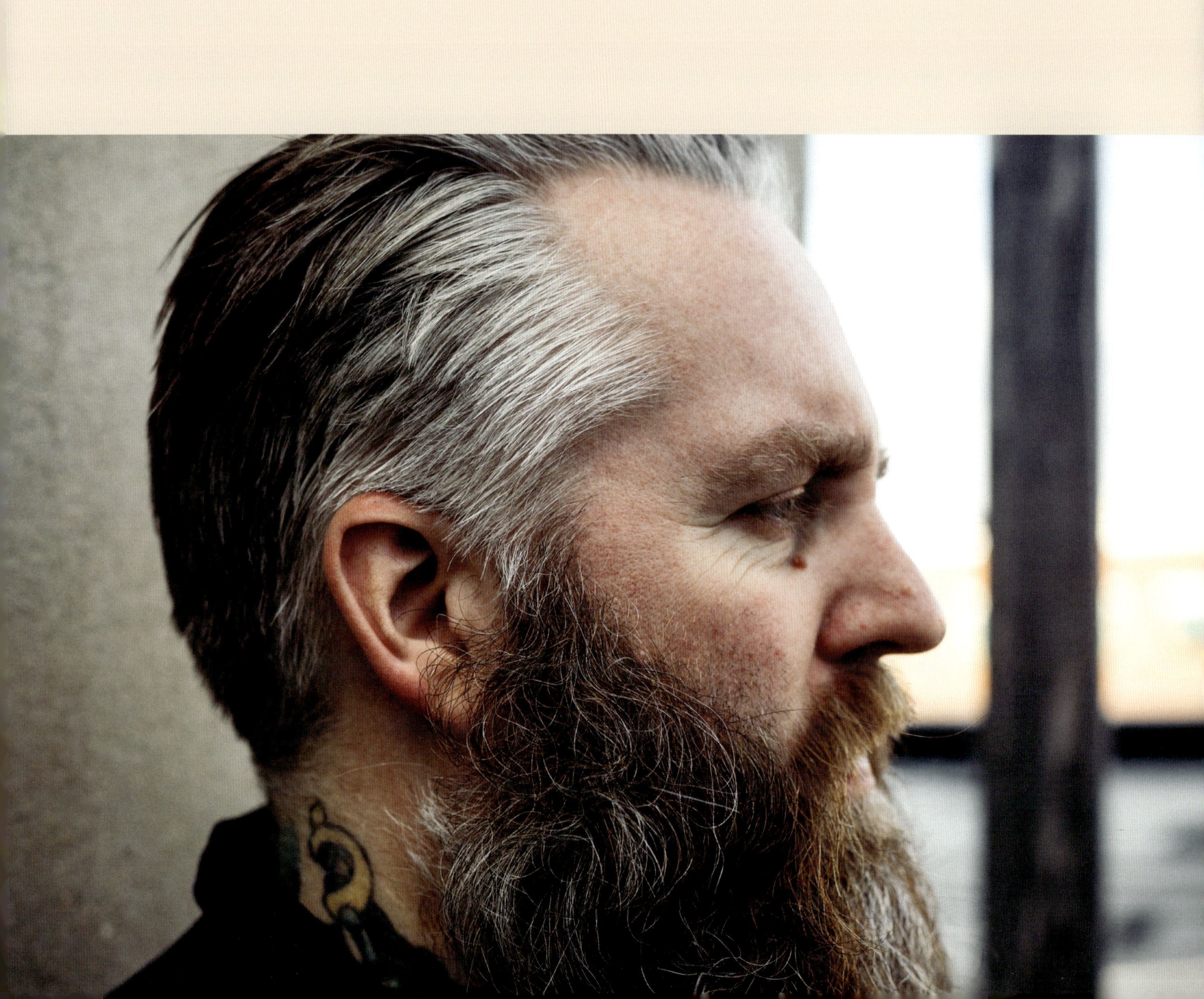

The paintings I am sharing in the following pages are distillations of distant cultures, esoteric cults, and ancient technologies. Most of these aspects are expressions of stories taught to me by shamans, sadhus, magicians, and fakirs. It was a path perfectly mapped out and swept clear for me by the grace of the divine.

By my early twenties, I began my tattoo apprenticeship. The craft of tattooing taught me an entirely new visual codex. It was a mixed bag, all the directions and social strata sharing in the use of power animals and psychological insignias being used to act out existential struggles and triumphs from the sacred to the profane. The practice of becoming a tattooer means becoming well versed in thousands of encoded designs and learning how they may apply to the wearer. When boiled down past its seemingly commercialized and trendy aspects, tattooing is one of the most ancient practices known to mankind. My introduction to the elders of the tattoo community took me into the realms of the unknown: the language of carnivals and the underworld, the passing down of hidden information, the protection of the craft, and the meeting of true outsiders. These people were practicing a medium scoffed at by most, limited in its own tools and form, yet complexly thrilling and incredibly sophisticated on historic, aesthetic, and spiritual levels. These were the first of many wizards I would have the fortune of meeting.

Many years later, working with ayahuasca tied everything together for me. The ancient practice of tattooing, the esoteric occult mysticism, and my connection to the Eastern traditions of Sanatana Dharma, as well as my deep love for song were all contained in the powerful visions from the mother vine. It reinvigorated my spiritual path all while connecting everything I had learned from so many extraordinary teachers. Within the next year, my painting and tattooing took a more focused route. I began to visit sacred places in India, Nepal, and Peru. I met holy men who lived in caves, cremation grounds, and rivers. I dieted plants with curanderos in the deep jungles of the Amazon and hiked through the mountains with shamans in Cuzco. In each one of these steps, I would hope to bring back some of the essence of the mystery, beauty, and wonder contained within the teachings I was receiving. I hope that you enjoy these paintings and that they spark something in you in the same way the subject matter has affected me. Please accept my humble offerings.

Robert Ryan
Asbury Park, New Jersey
November 2015

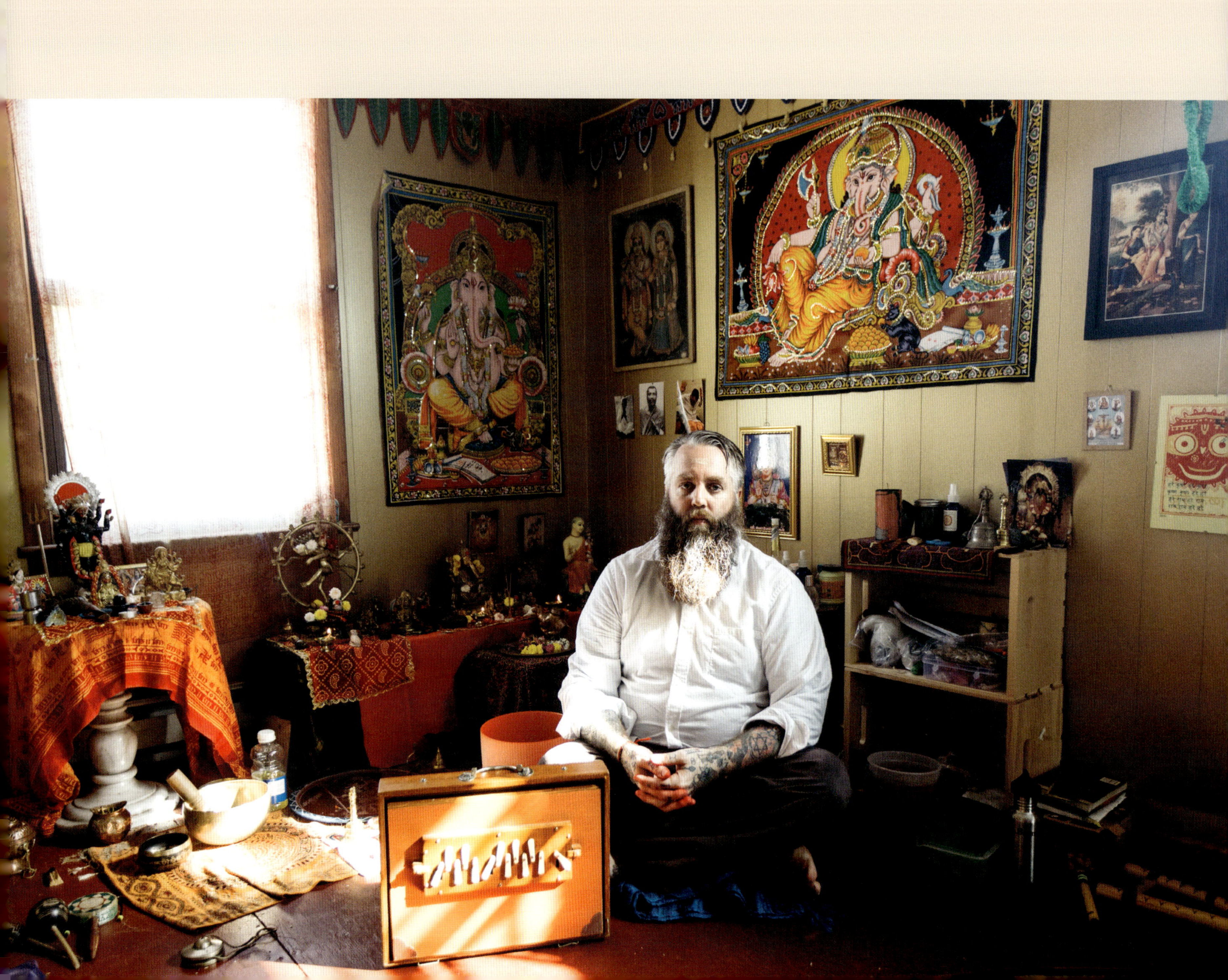

THE SURFACE AND BELOW

Under the tangled cables and tumbling tumbleweeds, the crumpled plastics and commercial jingles that make up this land, there slithers something altogether different, in what Greil Marcus called the old, weird America. Some stark-eyed sailor probably picked it up from shamans and warriors, dropping it off at each new port. Its fangs are a soldered needle, its venom ink.

Sure, many American artists wandered the disappearing landscape, romantic surveyors making the "before" for all those postindustrial "afters," but not all artists easeled in the wilderness or portraited a hundred corpulent rich people tickled to their ribs with food. A few of them found company with soldiers and sailors, weirdos and freaks, outcasts and castaways, and forged a tradition in American art worn in the flesh.

All those they tattooed brought with them their own unusual spirits and dreams, scattered ideas growing like wildflowers in the cracks of the concrete—strange beliefs, spiritual visions, occult traditions. In the simple lines of a sailor's steady hand on a shaky ship, the ink in their skin mingled with their souls, the bright bold enthusiasm of the American personality with the mystical animals and sacred geometry of a land that beaconed to all the fervid and strange across a wide world. All that indigenous spirituality, both homegrown and imported, that refused to disappear under one imperial monotheism or another found shape in the screaming eagles and circling snakes, in the warriors' prayers and buxom pinups.

Tattoos have gone mainstream to be sure, but that's because we live in less repressive times (though surely the semiotics of illicit power beam from every screen). But tattoo's traditions, born in parlors and prison camps, free ports and arcane ritual certainly, survive.

They find no shapelier form than in the dancing brush and needle of Robert Ryan. In his pictures, written on paper and skin, Ryan gathers all these traditions drawn from a thousand sailors' visions of Eastern temples and steeped in the practice of a thousand tattooers before him, from all of us searchers' quest for meaning across a continent. From beneath the surface of America, from beneath the surface of reality, Ryan mines mystic possibility and gives these traditions new life and new power.

Andrew Berardini
December 2015

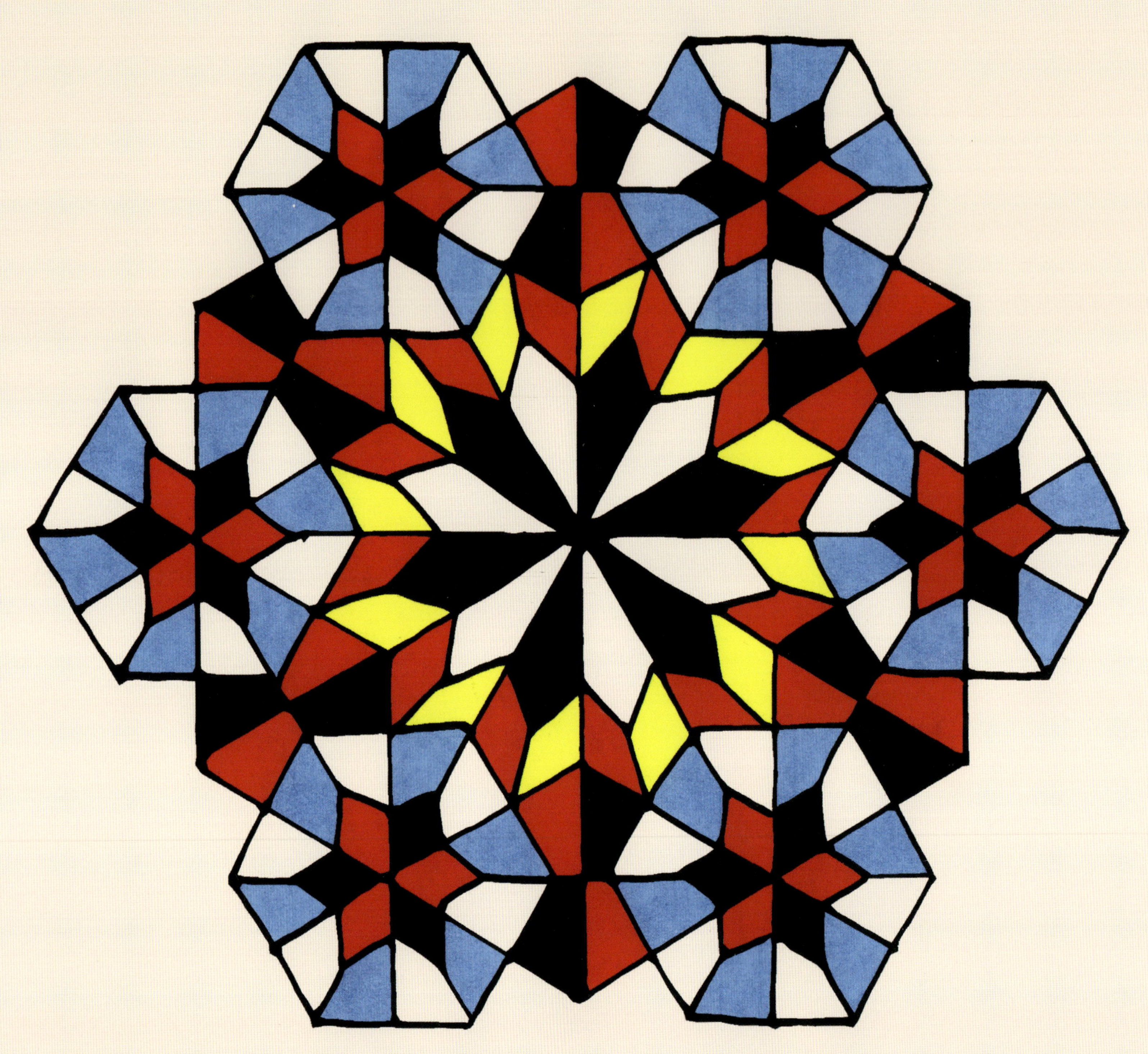

INTENTIONAL AND INEVITABLE:
Robert Ryan and Freddy Corbin

This conversation between Robert Ryan and Freddy Corbin took place over a few weeks in the summer of 2015. Freddy is a fellow world traveler and living legend in the tattoo world.

fc Did you grow up around art and music? What was the spark that led you to the four spokes in the wheel: art, music, tattooing, and your practice or path?

rr I grew up in what at the time seemed like a pretty basic suburban home situation in Point Pleasant, New Jersey. My folks both worked a lot, so I was left to figure out a lot of things on my own. Luckily my grandparents lived just a couple houses away, and my grandfather was a big inspiration to me. He was a retired police chief of forty years in a small town, so he knew everyone and he didn't have that cop attitude at all. People really liked him; he was very well respected and a fair guy who was always helping people. He was a Freemason of a high degree and quoted Shakespeare and collected cool art and antiques. His house was filled with amazing stuff. The house itself he bought from Oona O'Neill, who was the daughter of the playwright Eugene O'Neill and was the wife of Charlie Chaplin, so you could imagine the vibe of the place. My grandfather liked folk art, especially the Pennsylvania Dutch stuff. It was from him that I first learned about signs. They owned a farm out in Pennsylvania, and we traded with the Amish and Mennonites, and they would always talk about "the signs." Like if a beehive was hanging low in the spring, it would be a hot summer, and fascinating things from folk remedies to divining rods. So between his esoteric Masonic leanings

and his connection with fringe religious folks that were connected to the land in rural Pennsylvania, I think that's what sparked my interest in symbolism and spirituality expressed through visual modes. I also learned that there was a holistic approach to healing and treating problems.

Music came into my life a little later. I started skating and surfing when I was twelve, and I remember hearing Suicidal Tendencies, JFA, the Ramones, and Youth Brigade at a backyard half-pipe and being floored. I already had my Devo moment, when I realized there was more to music than what I had perceived, but this stuff was raw, and it resonated on a whole new level. The music was visceral, but so was the look, the album covers, flyers, all of it. My friends and I all started bands. A local scene was already occurring a little bit, but going to New York City for the first time to a Sunday matinee at CBGB was a huge revelation. The Lower East Side in 1987 was such a powerful and hectic scene. It became a weekly routine to go to shows to meet and become friends with more people outside my school and my hometown. That was really liberating for me. So I got turned onto the Cro-Mags singing about Krishna, the Bad Brains singing about Jah Rastafari and Youth of Today singing about not eating meat. Vegetarianism made a lot of sense to me. I always loved animals and had a hard time dealing with their suffering, so in 1988 I stopped eating meat.

A few weeks after I took that plunge, I was hanging out at the boardwalk in my town with a bunch of punks and this guy came up to me and said, "You're under arrest … for smiling," and he handed me a sticker of Jagannath that read "SMILE! Chant and be happy." I didn't understand it all, and he began to tell me about Krishna. I knew Hare Krishnas didn't eat meat, and the Cro-Mags were cool, and I heard Ray from Youth of Today had dropped out and joined them, so I started asking him all these questions about it. The guy was a good talker and asked me if I wanted to chant with him. That was where I first learned the Maha Mantra, and he gave me my first set of japa beads. I owe that guy so much. A few weeks later I went to the vegetarian feast at the Radha Govinda temple in Brooklyn, and the place was breathtaking: the music was great, the paintings were fantastic, the smells and the food were amazing! That's where all of this really began for me. For a few years I tried to go the way of a Brahmachari—a celibate student—but it was tough to do as a teenager. By nineteen I was back to fucking and smoking weed, but the seed was planted. I had my heart melted by Krishna, and I would never be the same. That is all around the time I started working at my good friend Mike Schweigert's first tattoo shop. I was a floor guy, helping out however I could. I was so enamored by the tattoo world. Mike was so respectful of the history even though he was new to it as well.

fc That's an amazing story in itself. It seems like a bunch of synchronistic events molded you as a young person. Punk shows in the '80s were so free of boundaries! So scary and exciting! I can definitely relate to that. With punk I felt like I had found my tribe, and finding tattooing was some weird extension of that. Learning about your grandfather makes so much sense, especially seeing so many symbols in your artwork today. Not just copying them from a book, but knowing the roots and what they actually mean. You're very lucky to have these experiences. And I can also see a lot of your grandfather's qualities in you! I'd like to know about your early beginnings in tattooing, but also how you started consciously incorporating these loves and inspirations into your tattooing.

rr I have been tattooing for eighteen years. It took me a long time to actually start tattooing because I had no confidence in my drawing skills, let alone my ability to put a tattoo on someone. I was just planning on being a helper. At that point, I just wanted to play music. Mike had a business partner at this shop where I started out. He was a professional wrestler named Handsome Jimmy Shoulders. After a year of me coming there, Mike dissolved his end of the business. He and I were playing in a band called Fireball Head at the time, and we moved into this house in Red Bank, New Jersey. It was this old house that our roommate Aryn decorated in a really elaborate, psychedelic way. In one room the walls and even the ceiling were covered in orange fur. The fur was a prop from a Monster Magnet video where the band was playing on a giant orange furry crucifix. That was when I really started going deep with mushrooms and LSD. Mike was just tattooing out of the house, and I took a job working at a vegetarian restaurant with a Turkish cook named Ty, who had come to the US in the early '70s. He was another guide for sure; we would smoke a lot of hashish in the kitchen, where he would tell me all kinds of stories about Turkey and we would listen to a lot of great music. One day Mike and I just went around to all the local tattoo shops, just out of curiosity. We ended up meeting Gene Bernardo, who was the president of the mother chapter of The Breed Motorcycle Club. He had a really heavy reputation and was feared by everyone. When we went into his shop, he was really cool to us and we bullshitted with him for hours. By the time we got back home, there was a message on the answering machine from Gene offering us both jobs. So I started helping around the shop a little, but really I started running marijuana for him. His buddy Vito, who lived upstairs from him, was underboss for Pussy Russo (who was the guy they based the character Big Pussy on in The Sopranos). Vito was the one who was getting all the weed. I would go to his pizza place and pick up three pounds a week and run it all over the local area by train. I did that for a while, until it got too hot. Gene offered me and Mike a situation where we could open a new shop and run it for him, and staff it, and that's where I pretty much started my apprenticeship. That was early 1994.

That was right around the time I met Dan Higgs. Dan is the guy who has inspired me the most. I loved Lungfish, and I had started seeing his work here and there, maybe just 10-15 photos total. I had just seen Lungfish for the first time a few days before and was walking down Second Avenue when I saw Dan talking to a bunch of hobos on a street corner. I asked him if he was tattooing in NYC and got an appointment at East Side Ink with him two days later. I started getting a lot of tattoos from him, and he really encouraged me to start tattooing. It was like getting a blessing from the Dalai Lama to become a monk. A year or so later, he came to work with us about every three months. Dan was very helpful and encouraging. He pushed me to go outside tattooing for my inspiration but to still stay rooted in its foundation. So that's when I really started integrating the Eastern stuff into my work. Tom Yak started working with us as well, and he is a Krishna devotee, as are some other old friends of mine, so I have always been blessed to have the association of other spiritual aspirants around me who helped shape what I do now.

fc Fucking great! It's so cool to find all these paths converging. That is why I love port towns. San Francisco, New York, Baltimore, New Orleans: they're all melting

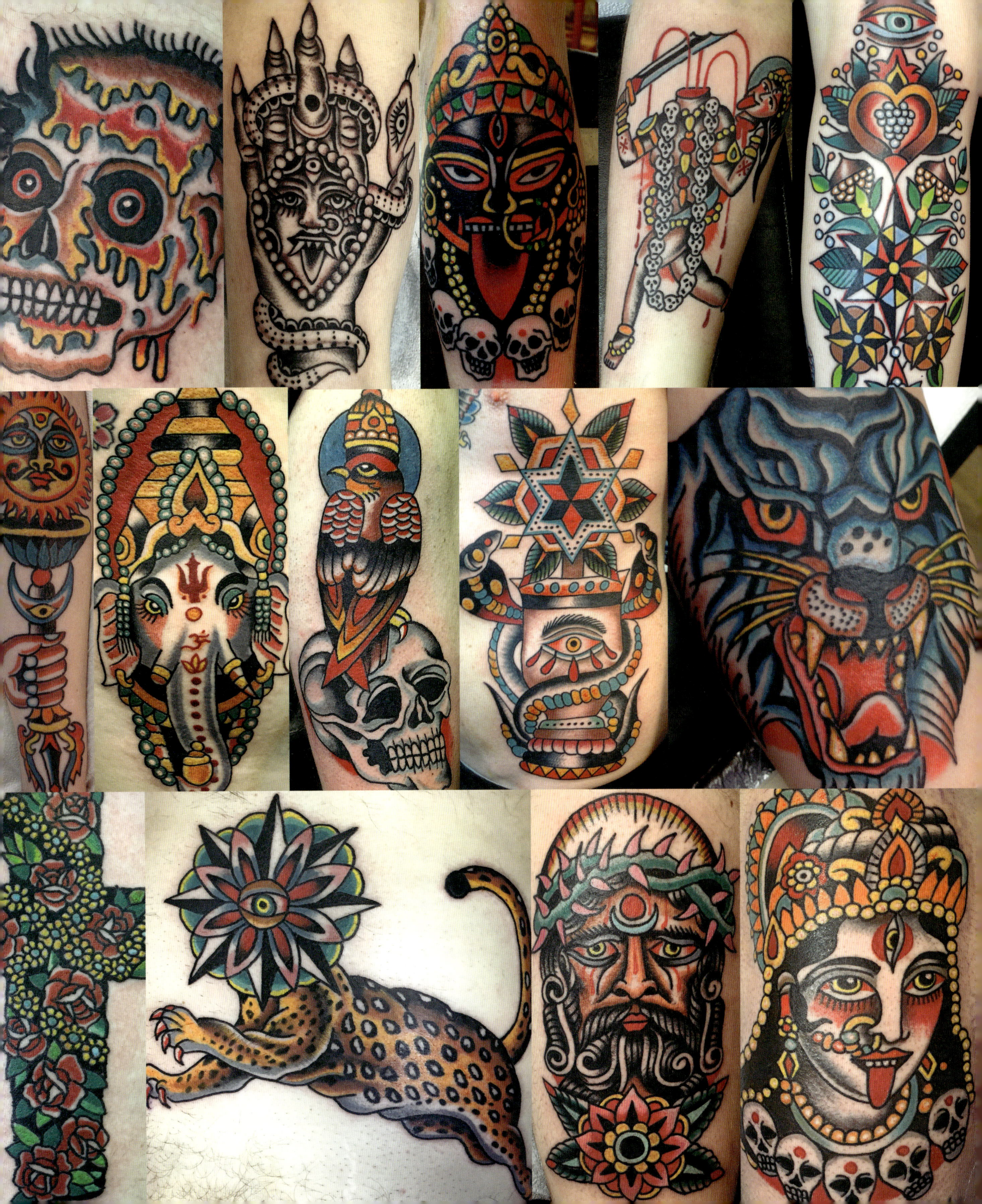

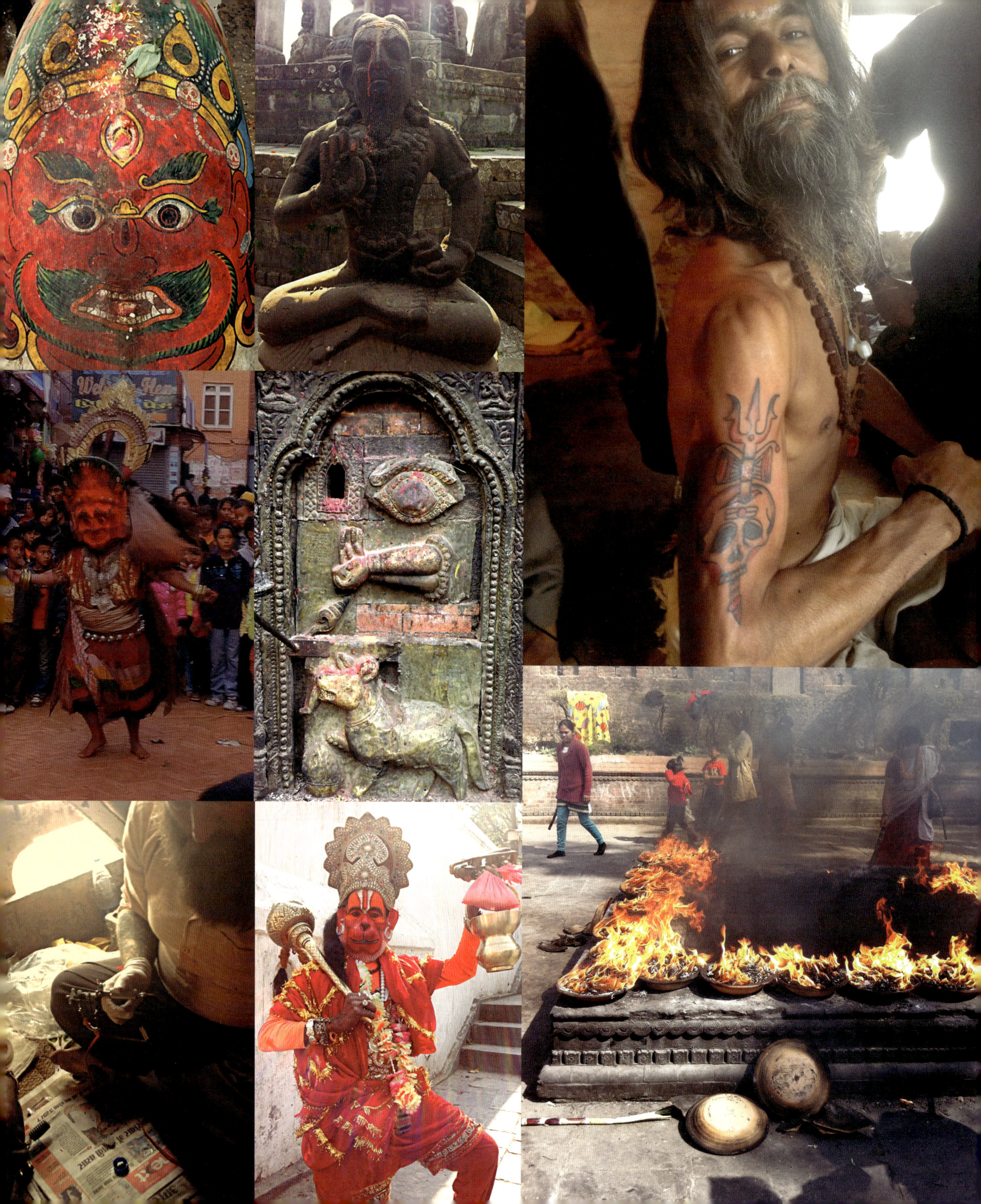

pots of cultures from around the world. Dan always said very kind things about you before we had met. Your work emulated Higgs-style tattooing, but your style also developed when you went to India. Dan's work was this completely new approach to traditional tattooing. A lot of people tried to emulate that. But your work obviously now has this heavy Krishna-Indian folk geometry. I've always really loved how you manage to take images that are at the very least a century old—and some even ancient—and do something completely different with them.

Can you talk about how you got into traveling, and how it affected your art?

rr Dan's work was such an inspiration to me and it still is. I love the way he distilled things. He took the limitations of a tattoo and made it an aesthetic strength. His approach to art, music, and life was a spark for me. Daniel has a level of integrity and understanding that is so unique in our world today. I consider him one of my strongest teachers. Having Higgs as a foundation for the fundamental approach and watching the way he would take any image and apply it through the Americana tattoo filter helped me a lot in my approach to tattooing and painting deities. It made it approachable for me. It also had the same level of respect and love. He showed me to not be abusive of or trite with your art and that your output can be purely devotional. I had been tattooing about ten years, and the traditional tattoo look was really starting to become more popular. Dan had stopped tattooing, and everyone was beginning to ape his look hard. It was a true study in the element of soul to me. You started seeing people trying to incorporate the esoteric and occult in their work, and it would just look off. It was like all the elements were there, they had the same references, same vocabulary, but they weren't alive. It was because the work wasn't being done. The initiation wasn't there. You can't make psychedelic art without having a psychedelic experience. You can't make devotional art without devotion, and you surely can't have expression without something to express.

So around 2004 I started moving away from a lot of the usual elements and started working more with mandalas and yantras and abstractions. I also started incorporating sacred geometry into more of my work. That's also when I started doing my Easter Christ series that began with me taking LSD and painting crucifixion scenes every Easter. I had taken a long break from psychedelics, and through Christ I was finding my way back. In 2007 I got an email from Howie the Cosmic Commander. I hadn't talked to him in years. He had read something I had posted online about how important it was for us as a species to become symbol literate to break the bondages of sexism, racism,

and tyranny, to take our symbols back from those who were using them to oppress us. Howard had just had been turned onto ayahuasca through Theo Jak. So I get a message from him saying, "We need to talk." I thought someone had died or something terrible had happened. I reached out, and he came to my shop the next day and read me the riot act about how I needed to start working with the plants! Within a month, I was signed up for my first ceremony. It was a revelation, to say the least. Everything up to that point made perfect sense. Every single step of the path was gilded; every experience was quantified; every heartbreak and mistake and neglect was forgiven and absolved. It was a true initiation. So Howard and I started doing every ceremony we could. After my third was when we sat with a shaman named Don Diego. Toward the end of the ceremony he started chanting the Gayatri mantra, and I was split in half! To hear that in a ceremony was a truly religious experience. I knew that he was the guy I would continue to work with.

So I sat with Diego a lot during that first year, maybe ten ceremonies. I could feel purification happening; I could feel my heart opening. My life was staring to fill with song. My panting and tattooing became so much more focused. I started to shed a lot of useless things from my life. I began chanting again, meditating, learning mantras and studying. I started looking toward India. I was actually having visions of it. In a ceremony, Don Diego did a blessing on me, and after he closed the ceremony he called me over and said, "I saw your trip to India. It's going to be amazing; you're going to meet so many different important people and you're going to visit many holy places." The next morning I booked a flight to New Delhi. I went to Mathura, Vrindavan, and Varanasi for a month. I had no idea where I was going or what I was doing, but I was guided the entire time. My first morning I went to the place where Krishna was born. I visited the temples of the Goswamis in Vrindavan, bathed in Radha Kund, took a twenty-four-hour train ride to Varanasi, and went straight to the oldest cremation grounds in the world. When I rounded the corner along the Ganga to get to Manikarnika, I realized that it was the place I had returned to in every ayahuasca vision that I had. I began to cry. I met a young street kid, and he brought me inside the Kali temple at the cremation grounds. There was a sadhu sitting inside, and I felt a chill go down my spine when he looked at me. The boy said, "He is a real holy man, a true baba." Later that afternoon, I saw the same man chasing away a monkey from a tea stand he was running. He looked up at me and we locked eyes again, and he motioned me over and invited me into his small hut. He prepared me a chillum and began writing things down in English. He explained that he was not speaking; he was fasting from talking. I went back and sat with him in silence for the next three weeks.

I have been back to Varanasi six times since then and always visit him. He now speaks. His name is Oshu Baba.

fc Dan was definitely a role model for me as well in terms of righteousness, integrity, and intention. I was so young when we were hanging out. A lot didn't hit me until later how heavy it was. LSD—the Christ consciousness. Howie! God bless his soul. I truly miss Howard. So you're working with plants, doing ceremonies in and taking trips to Varanasi. I guess you'll be turning into a rainbow being next. On a serious note, I can really see the cumulation of people and events in your life and where your artwork and tattooing has evolved. I find it new and beautiful, full of life and the wonders of mysticism, imagination, and devotion; it's truly dynamic in all the right ways. I feel honored to get to know more of your life story. A great new chapter in our friendship and brotherhood. It's been a blessing to participate in this project with you, Robert. You bring a lot of positive energy. You have a great perspective on life and art! And I am one of your biggest fans.

rr Thank you, Freddy. It means a lot coming from you. You have been a huge inspiration to me on this path. Seeing your work when I was younger had a deeply magical effect on me. It feels crazy to be talking about this on the second anniversary of Howard leaving this plane of existence. He brought me to the plants, which have been such a huge part of my life. Cosmo was one of my guides: the cosmic clown, the trickster. His life was surrounded in chaos. I physically watched him transform in front of my eyes. He found peace, love, and understanding before he died. He was a gnarly, tattooed, gold-toothed, North Philly loudmouth Jewish wrestling manager. He would scream and yell at you in your face, like Dennis Hopper in Apocalypse Now. Yet he found calm and beauty through ayahuasca and meditation. He turned all that chaotic energy and fervor into being an amazing father to his children. I would sit next to him in ceremonies and watch him lose it. Deep in the jungle, covered in tears, vomit, and his own shit, screaming and blabbering like a baby. It sounds terrible, but he was working through his blockages and his weakness. It was such a testimony not only to the power of the medicine but the strength of the human will to find its true self. He is a really important spirit in my life.

There have always been these people put in my life by the grace of the divine. The first heavily tattooed person I saw lived next to my high school. His name was Fred Clousten, and he was Thom DeVita's assistant. DeVita taught Nick Bubash to tattoo, Nick helped Tux Farrar learn, Tux taught Dan Higgs, and Dan helped me get my start in tattooing. I eventually became close friends with Freddy Clousten and he brought DeVita to our shop. That day one of the magical circles was completed for me. Every moment in this life is perfect. No mistakes exist. Of course there are things we might wish we had done differently, or outcomes from these chains of circumstance we had hoped would turn out more to our liking, yet have we ever really had any say in any of it? When you open your heart and spirit to this world and get out of your own way, so many truly beautiful things can happen to you. Even the hard lessons, especially the challenges, can all be transmuted from copper to gold. Through love, surrender, and devotion, anything can be achieved in this life.

I think I should say something about puja because you and I did a puja ceremony for Howard in your shop when he passed. That was really special for me to be with you, honoring our brother who had just passed. I know how excited he would have been about it. By making puja you are showing reverence, love, and respect for the divine. You are connecting with the holy and when you make a puja in someone's name, you are helping connect them as well. You are honoring your friends, family, loved ones, and God, but most importantly, you are honoring the self. Each ingredient in this ritual is an aspect of our own spiritual development, the unmanifested becoming manifest. For someone that isn't familiar, it can seem strange: seems like it's just worshipping a rock. But through intention, experience, and vibration, it becomes an entirely different thing. These ancient rituals—much like ayahuasca and even tattooing—connect us with our earliest attempts to express divinity. Rooted in what is ancient, and through lineage and respect for those who came before us, we maintain their purity. Currently there are tattoo shops on every city block and all over television; you can drink ayahuasca with a "shaman" who has never dieted in isolation in the jungle and buys his medicine online, and you can pay a Brahman to wave a coconut around your head and utter some meaningless mantras. Unfortunately this is a symptom of our age. Yet that does not disqualify the purity, integrity, and magic that can be received when these rituals are done with love. I think it actually gives them even more power! I'm so honored to have been blessed enough for the ascended masters who have made their way into my life and all the people I have ever learned from. I love you all.

Om Namah Shivaya.

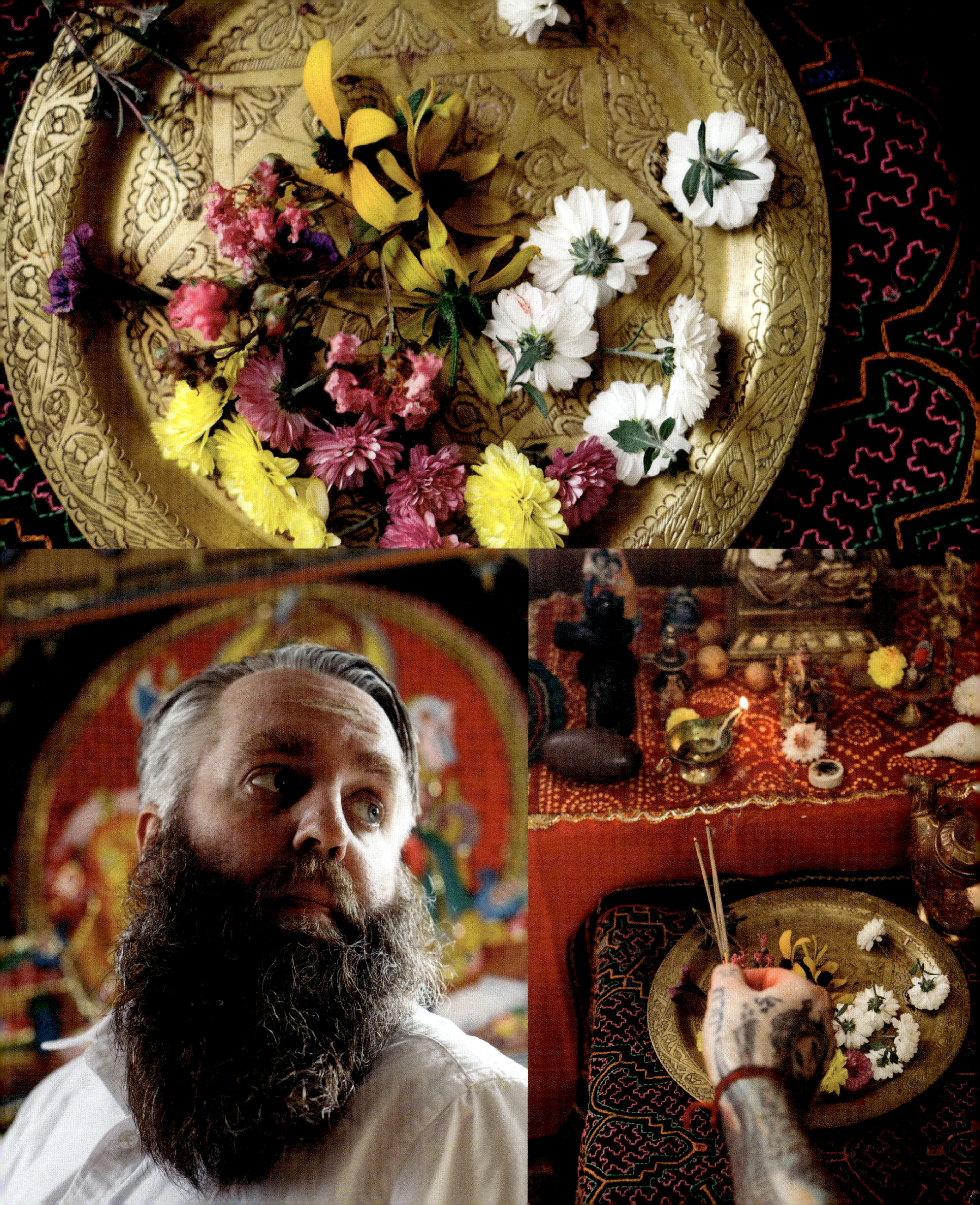

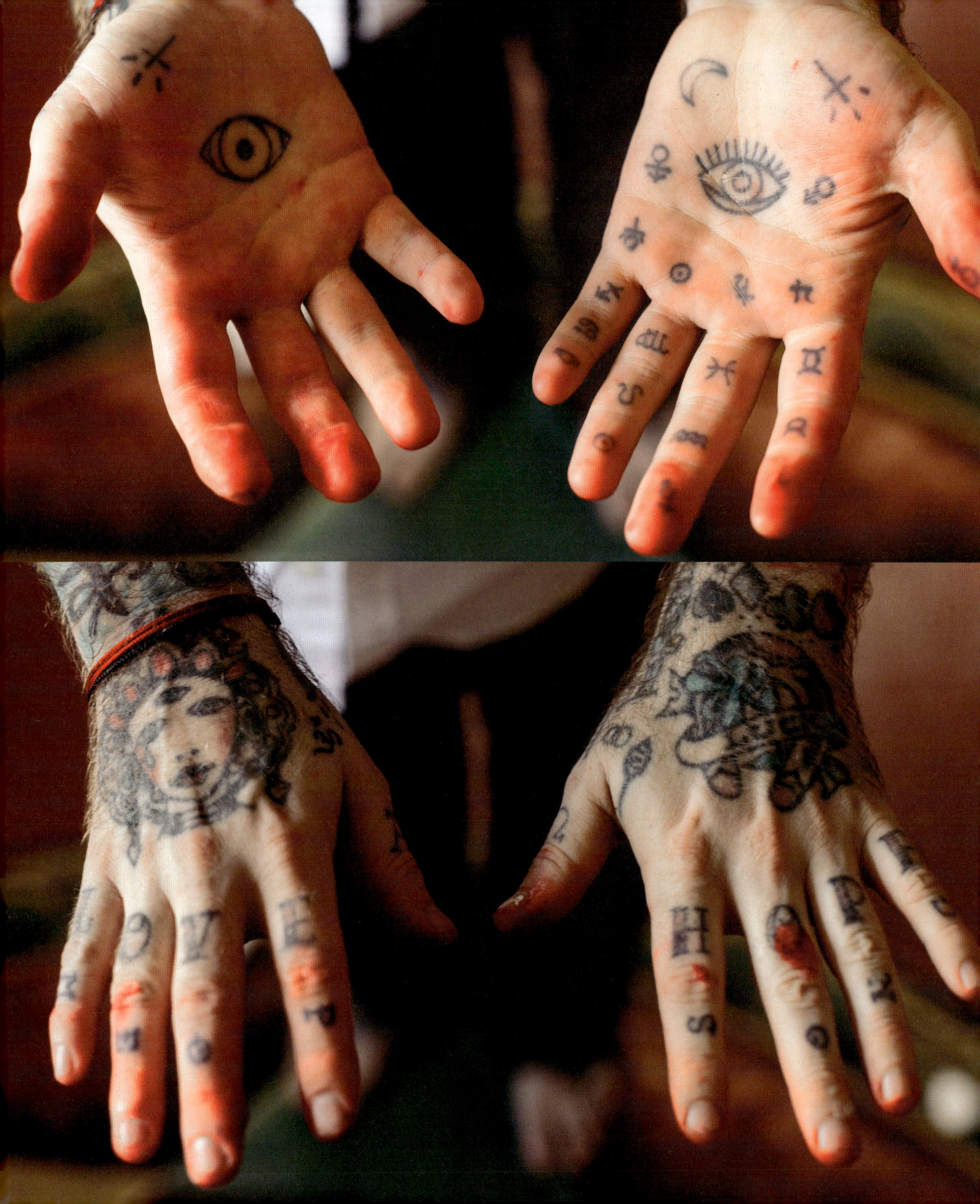

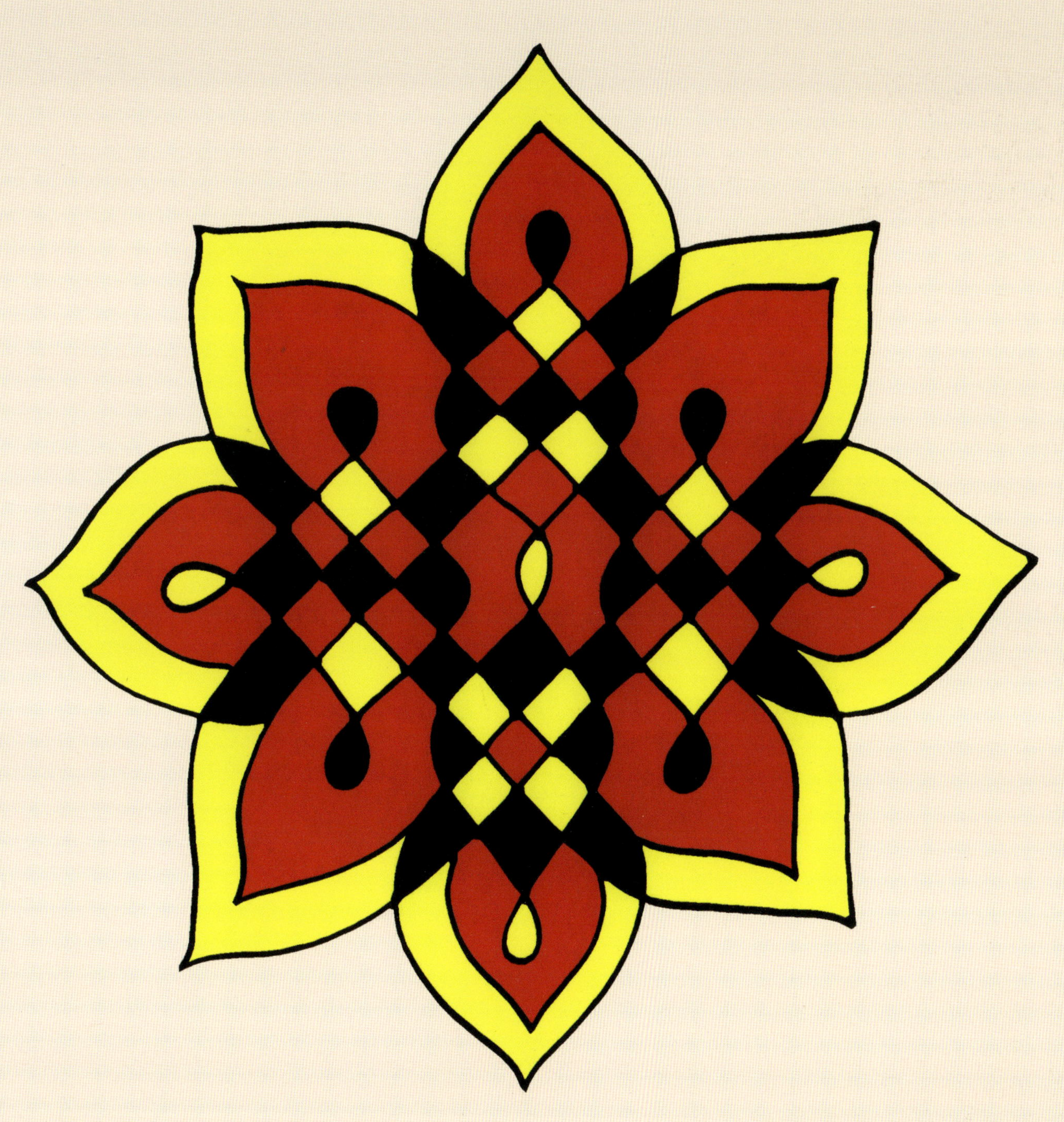

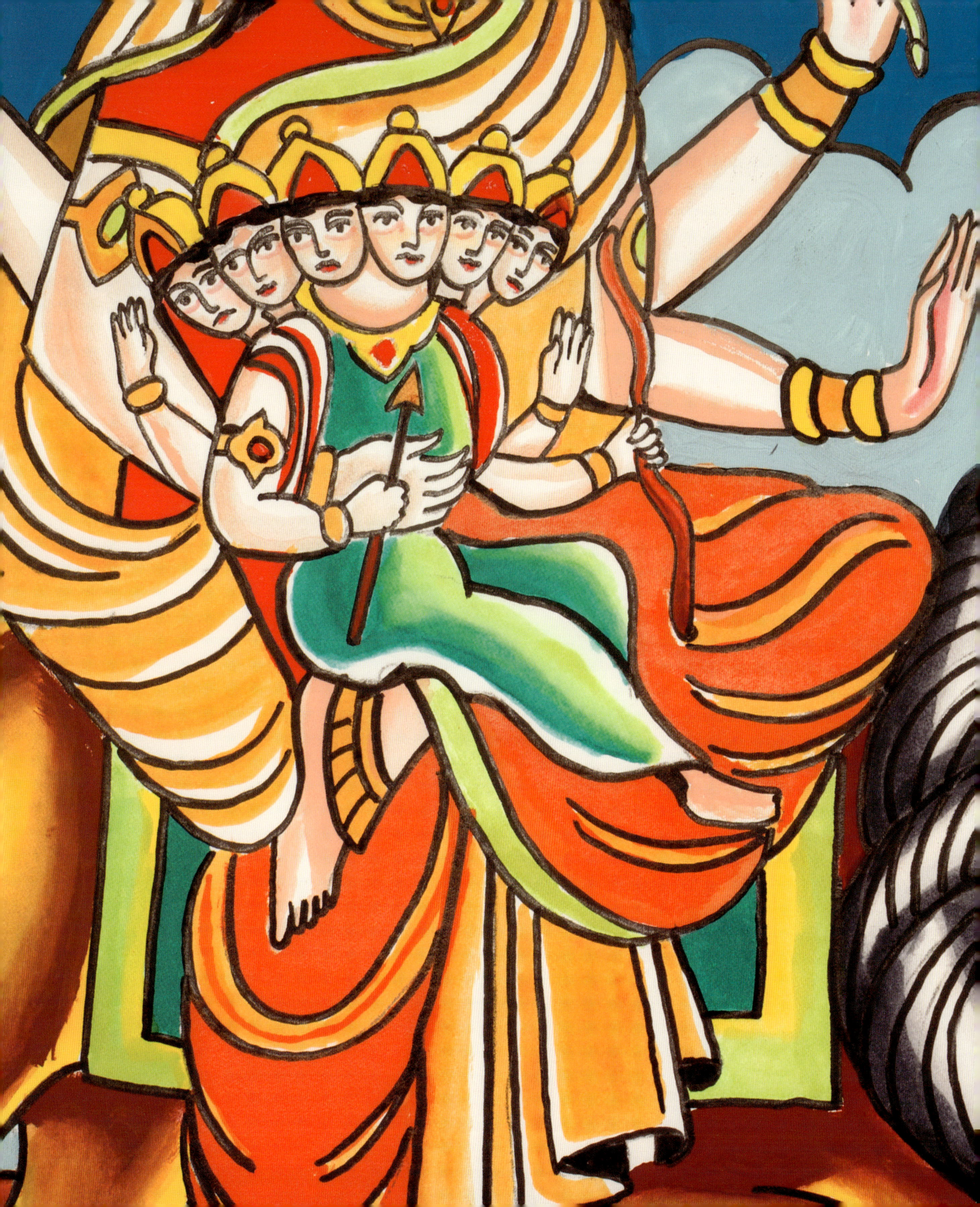

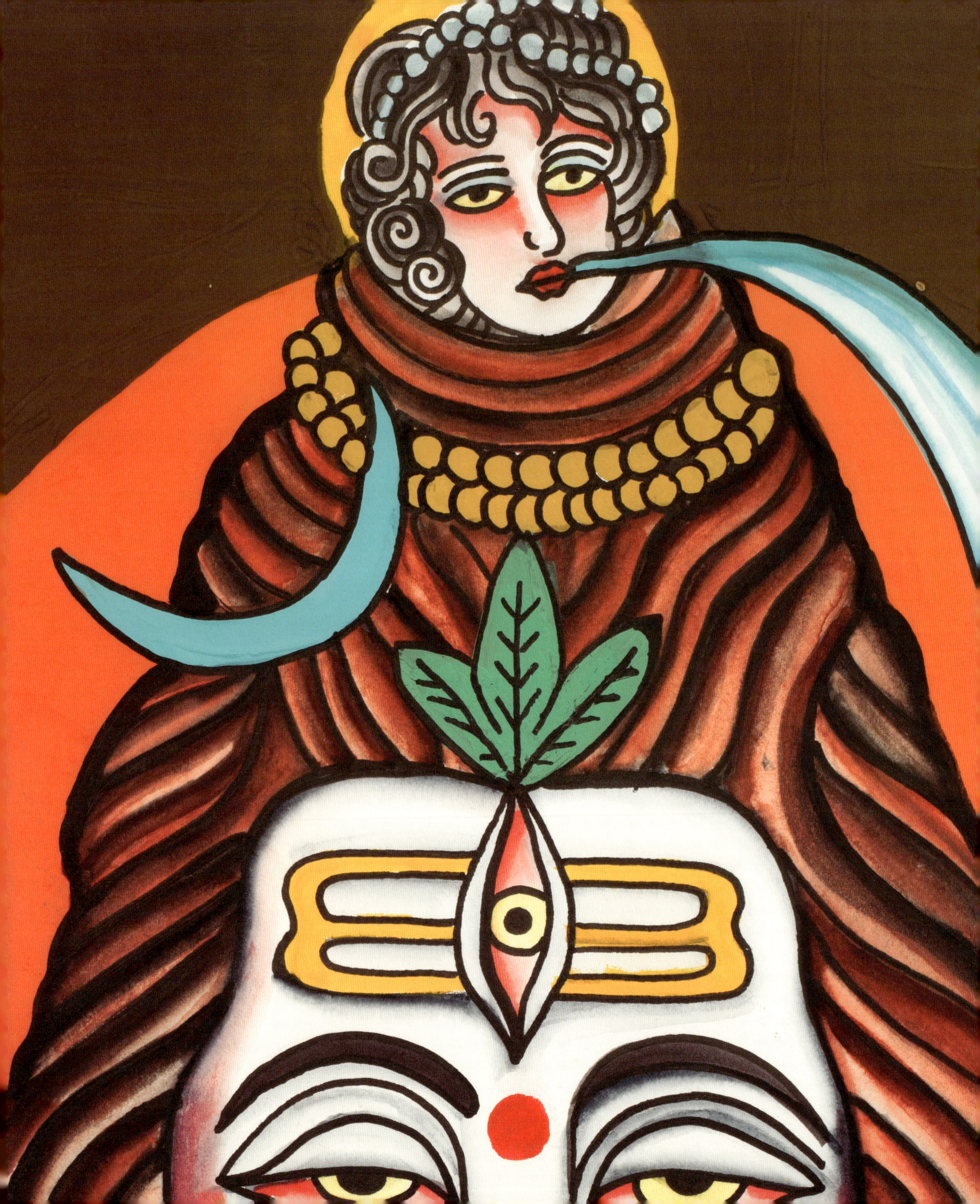

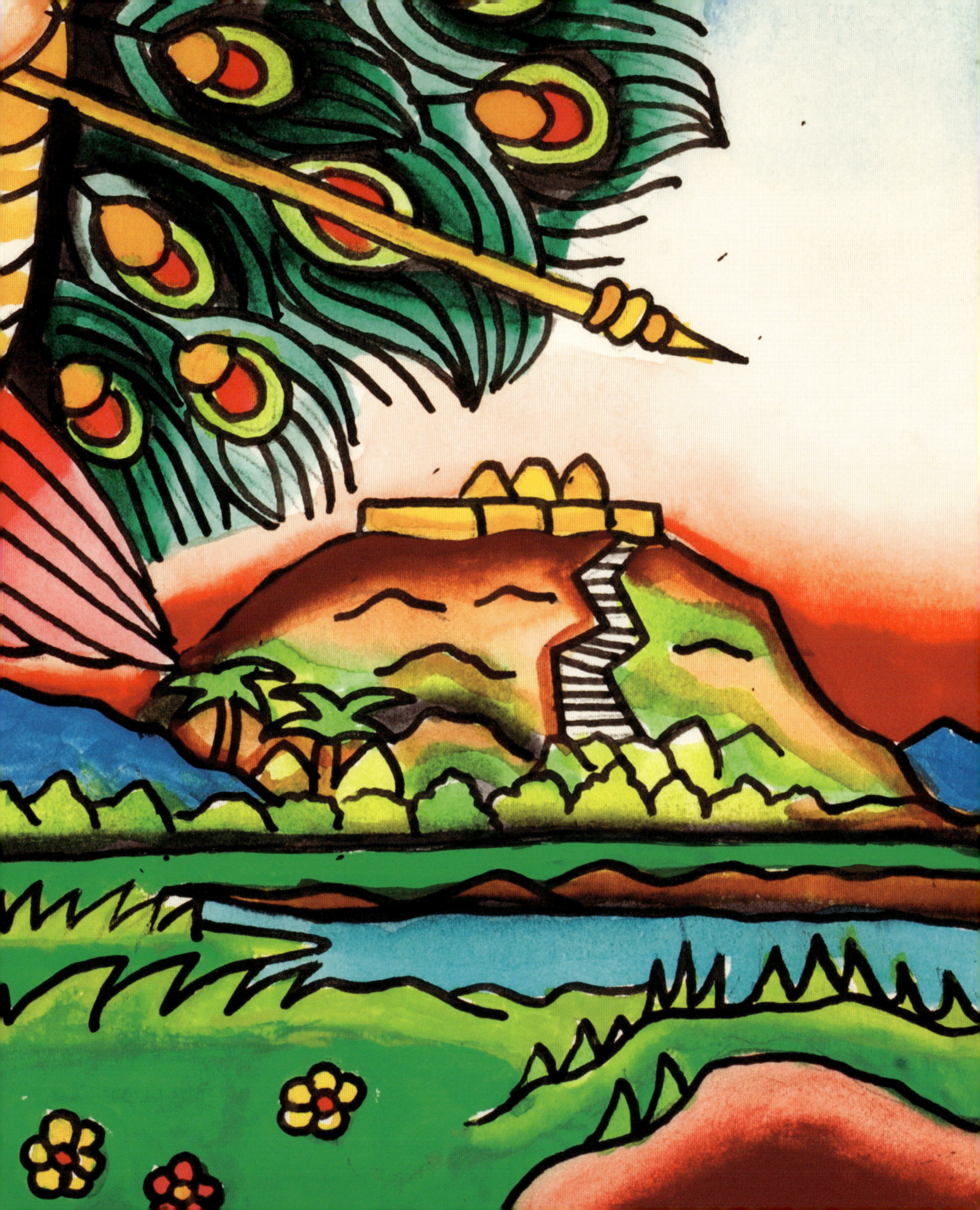

ROBERT RYAN
PAINTINGS 2011-2015

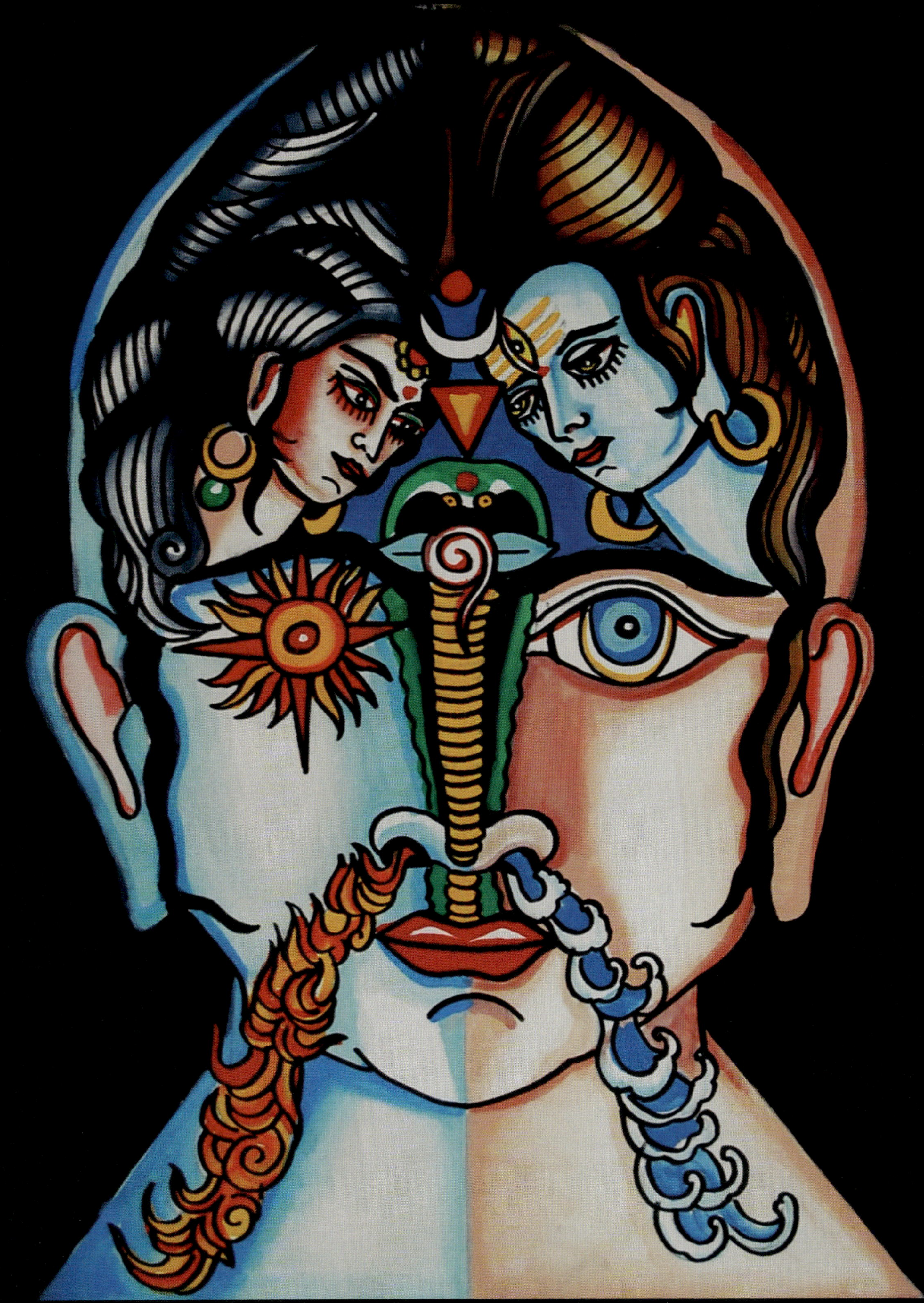

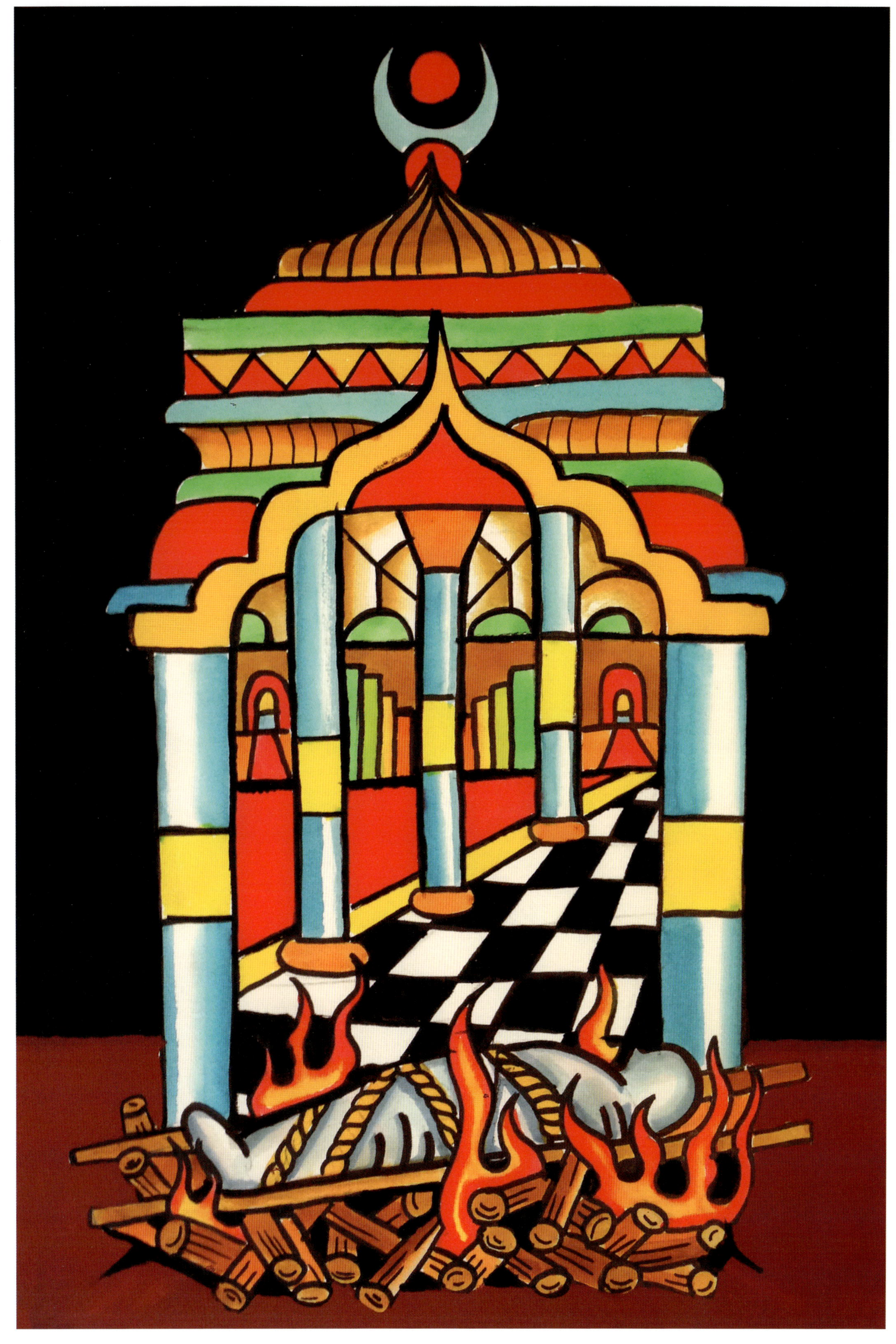

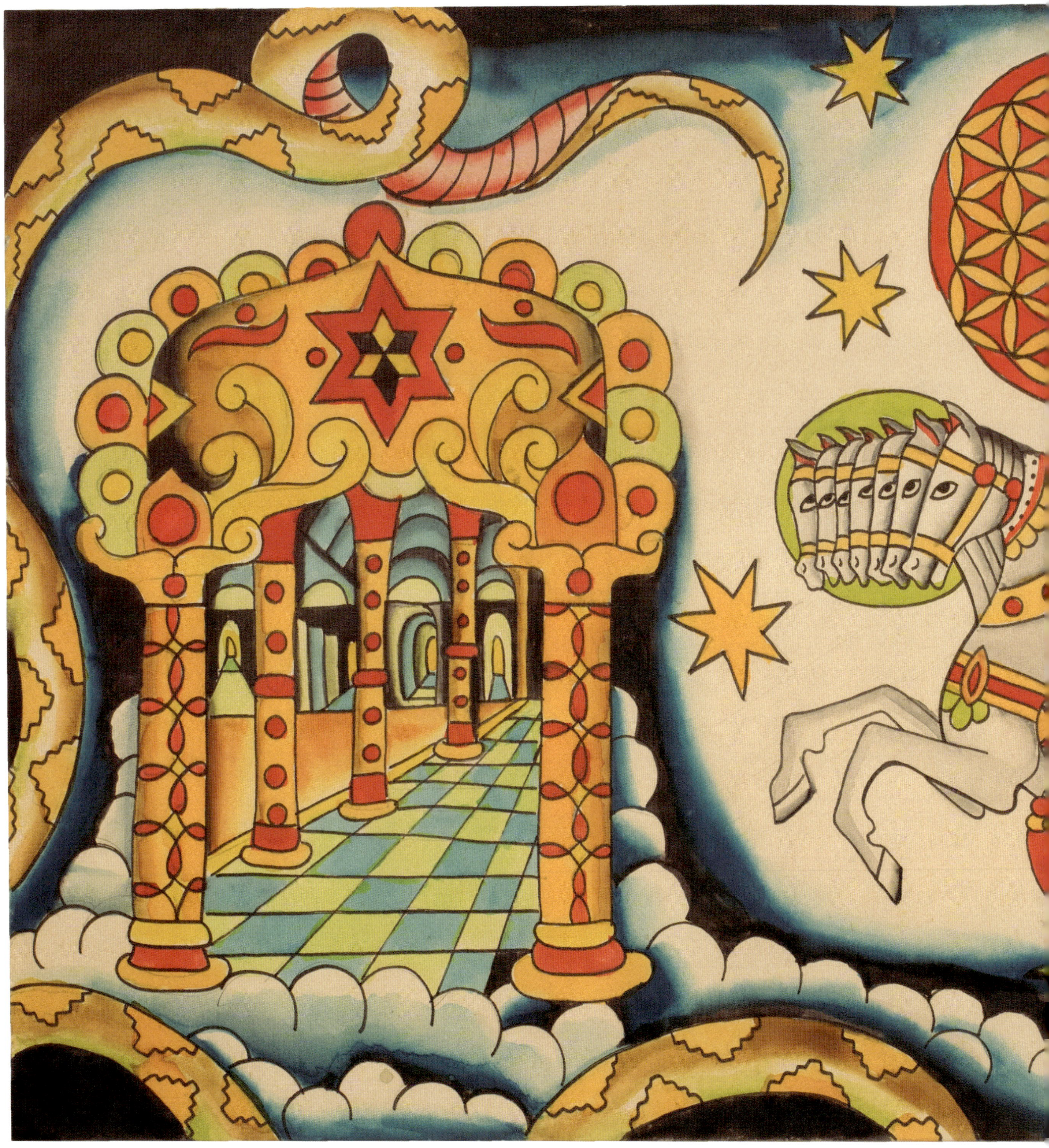

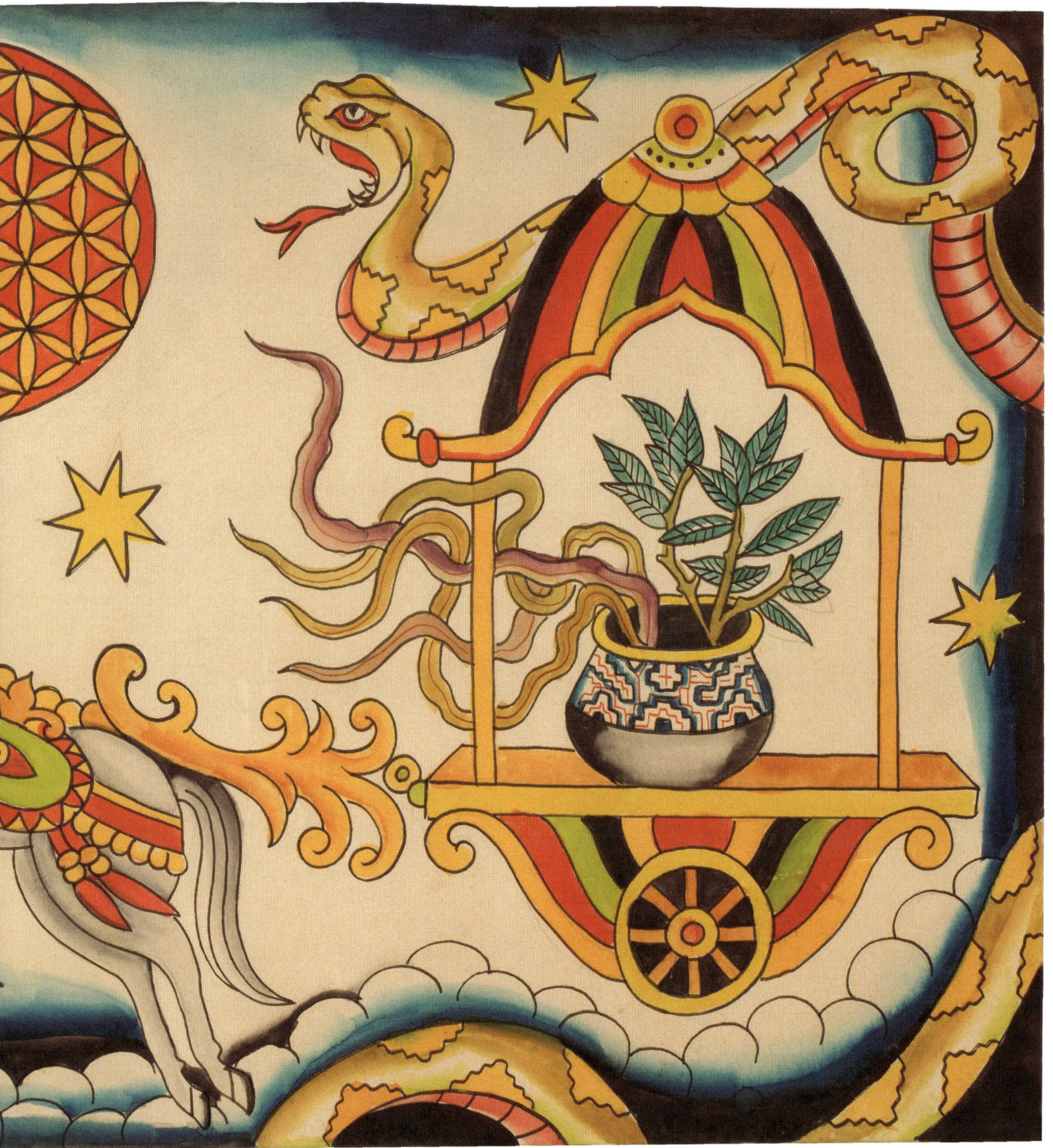

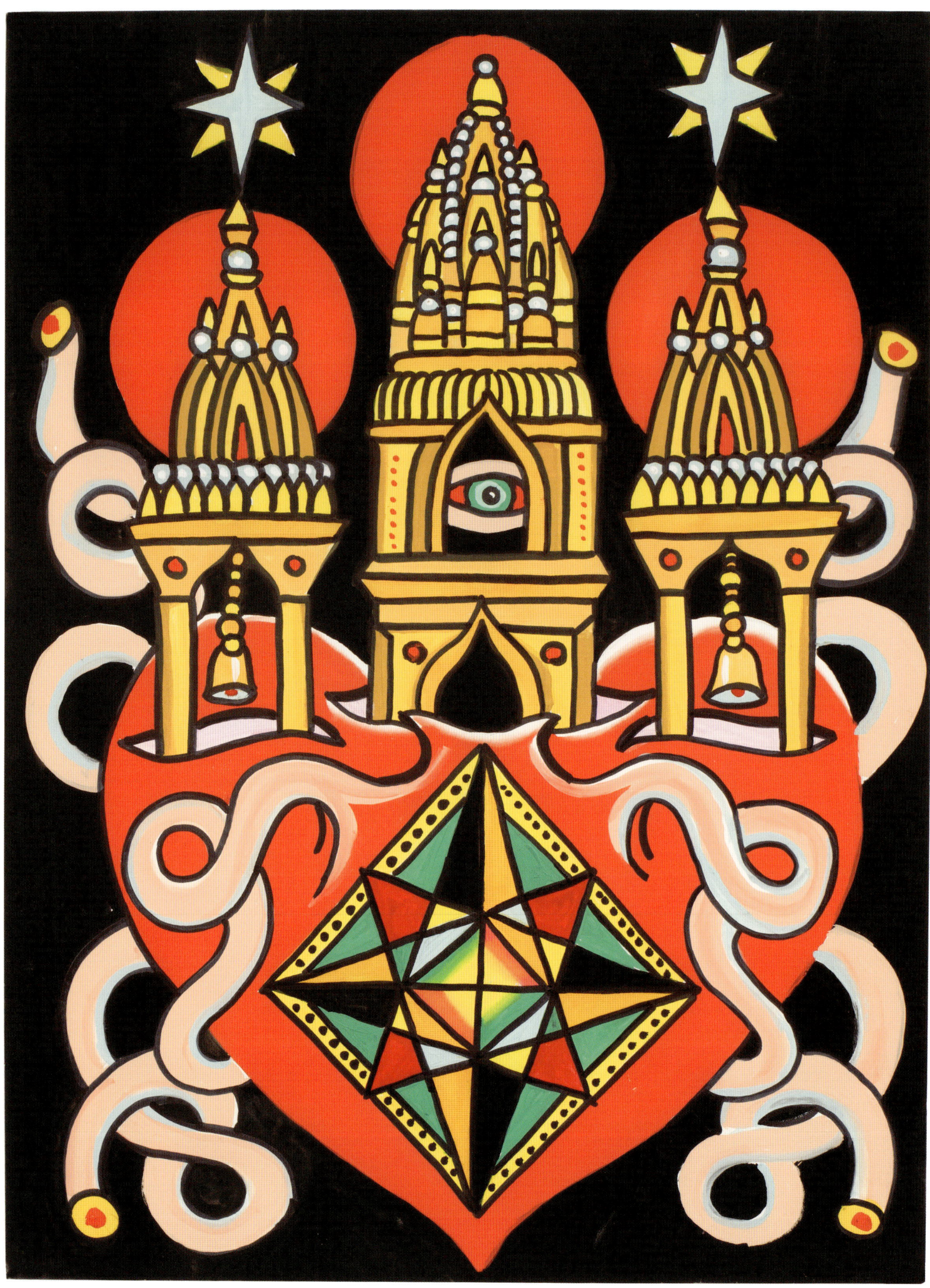

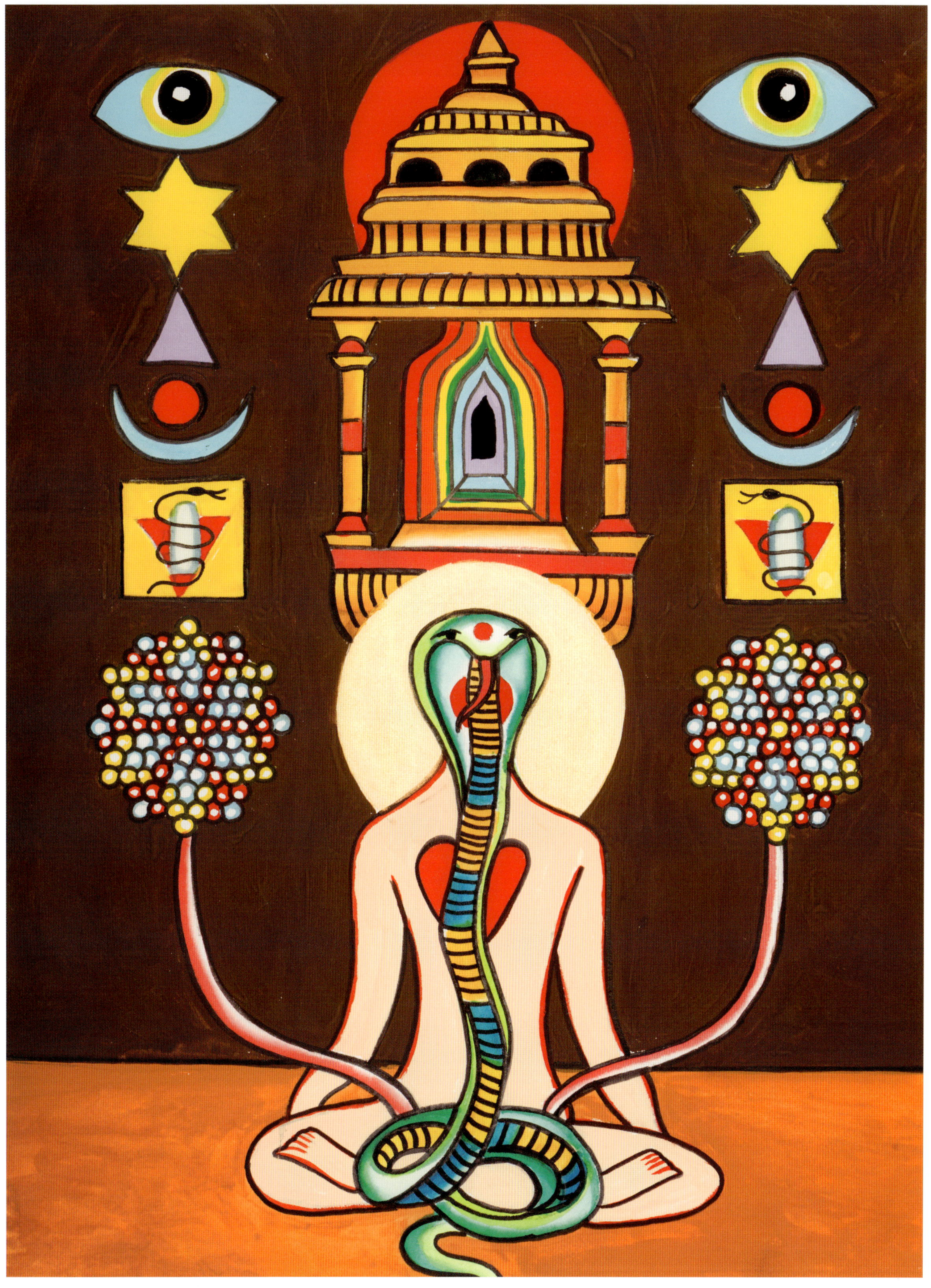

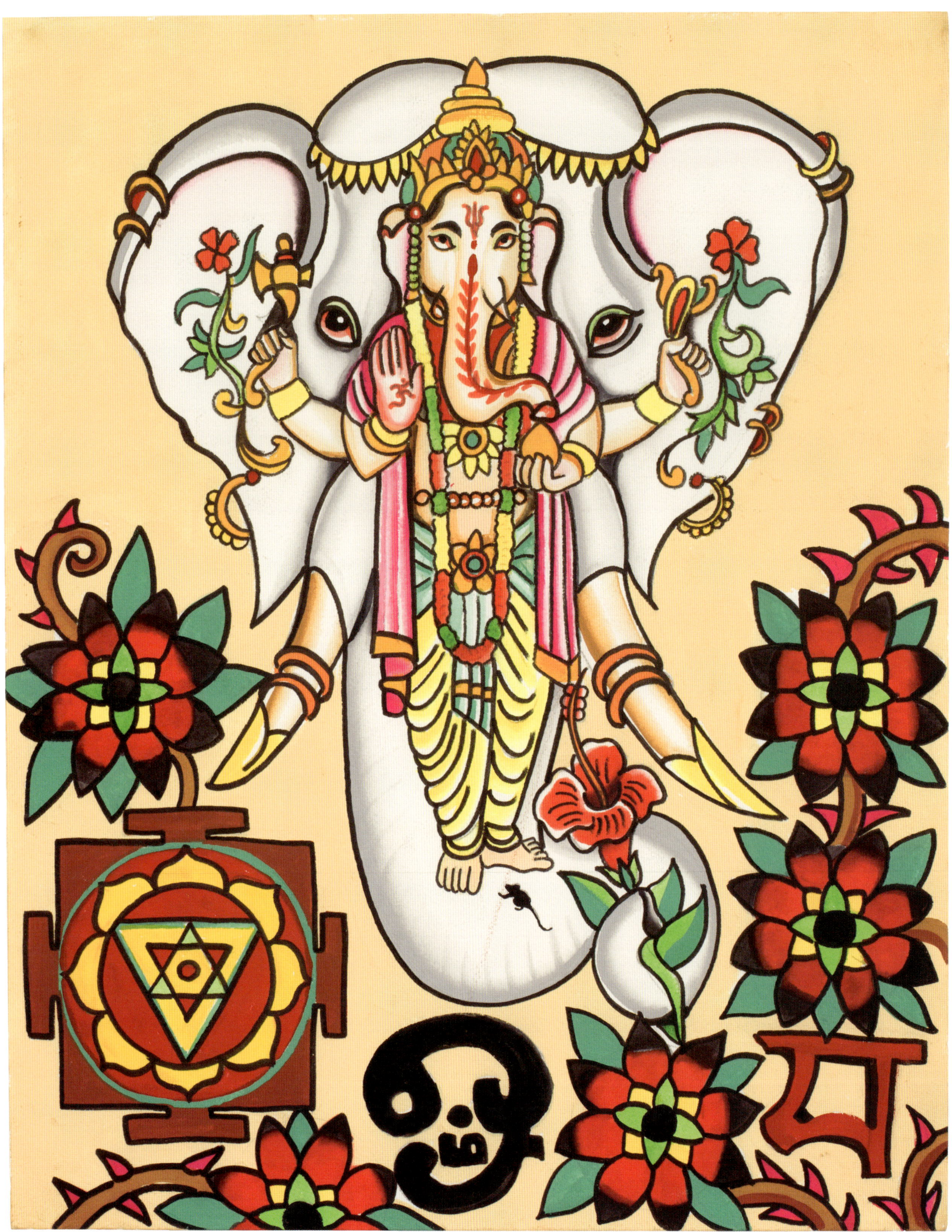

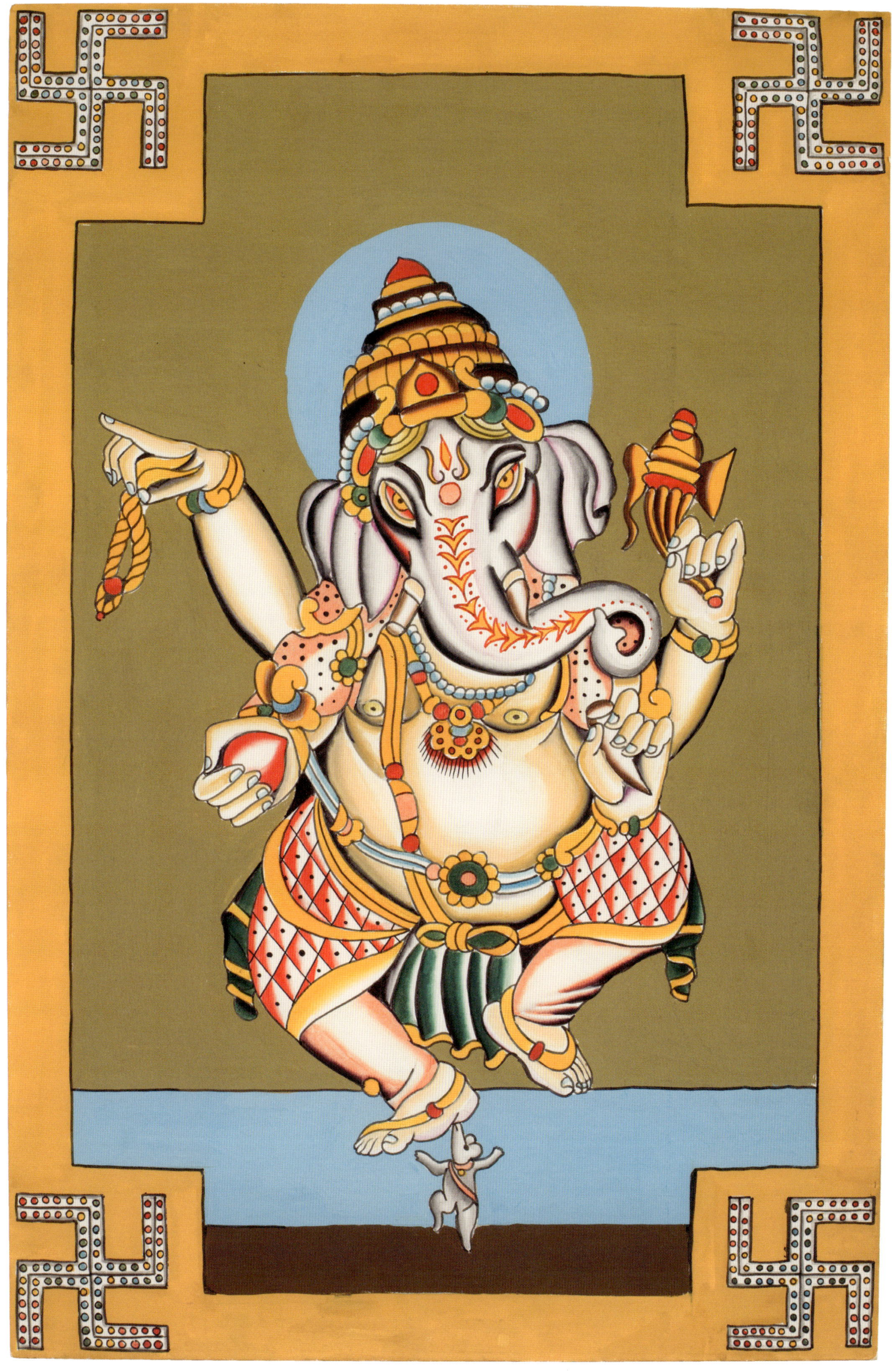

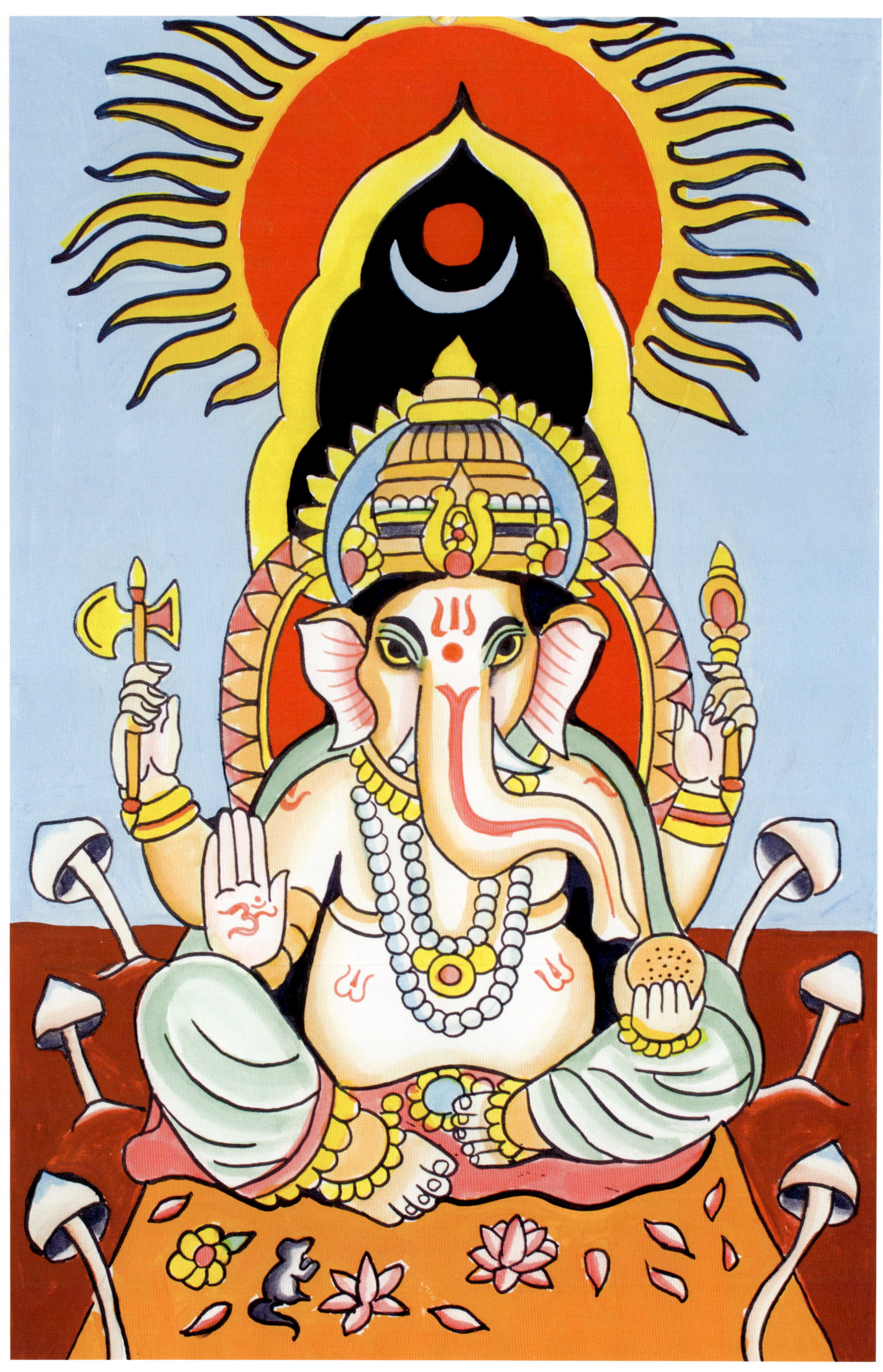

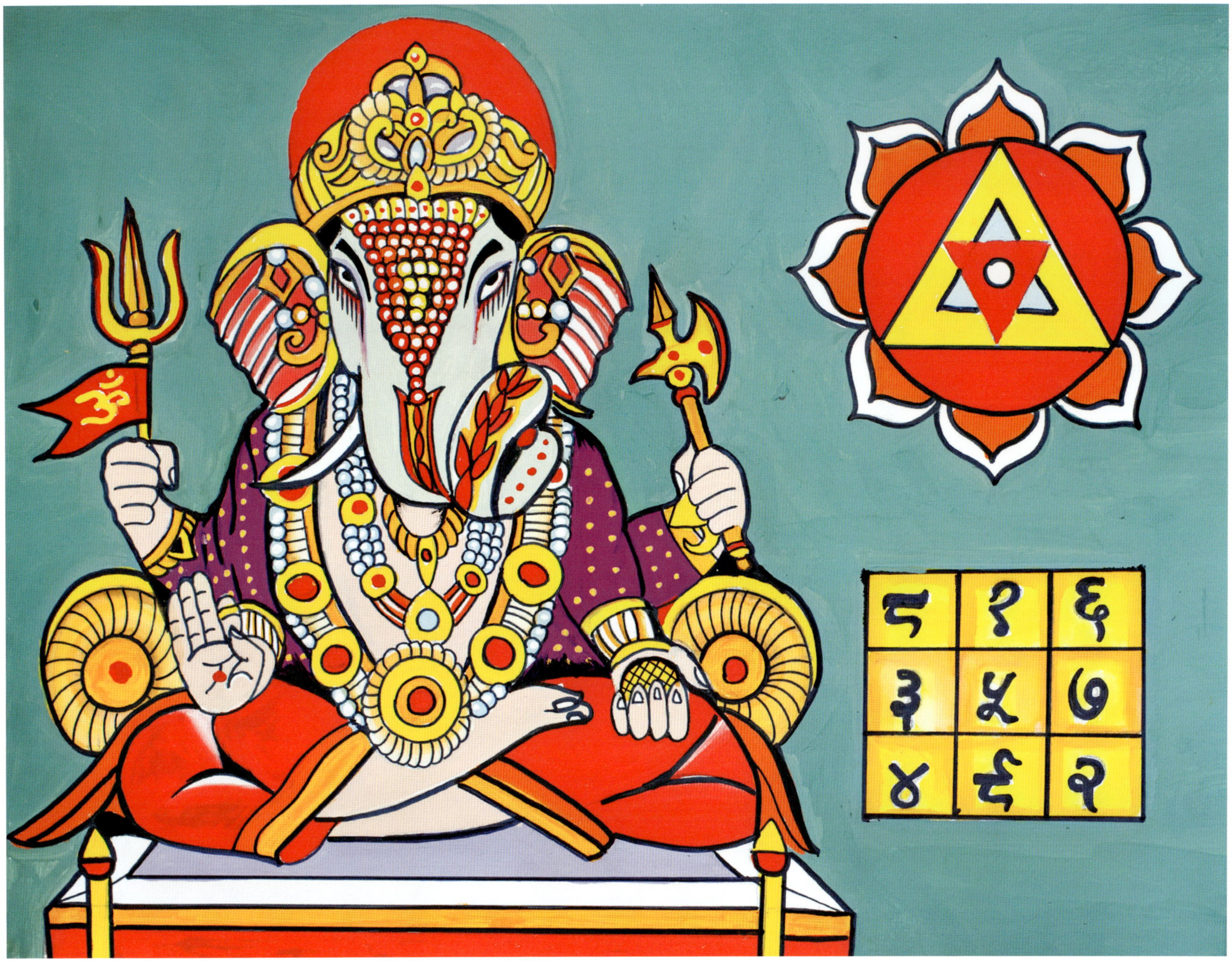

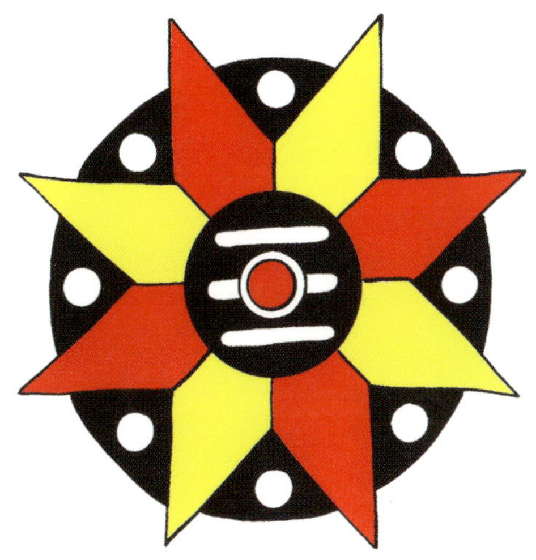

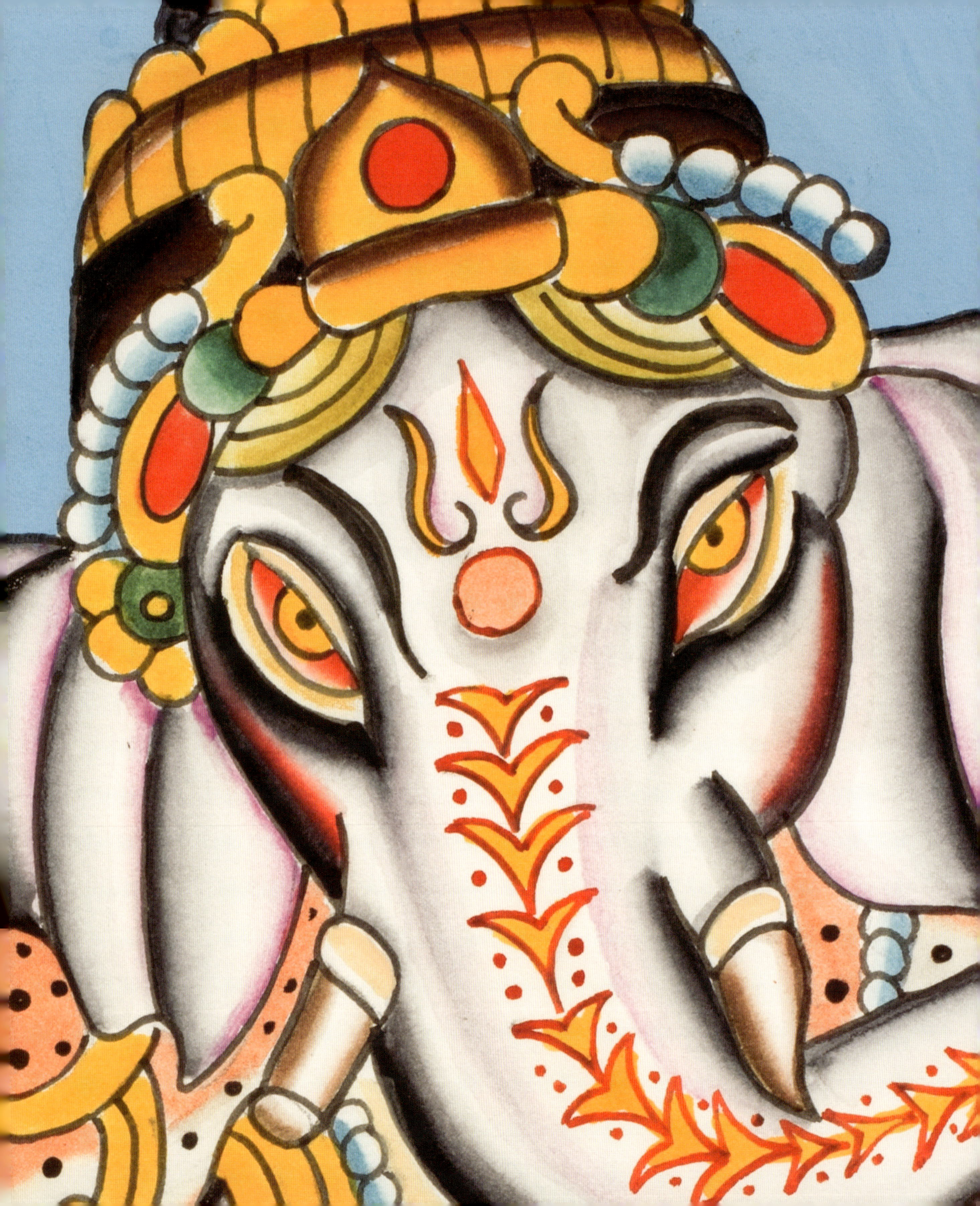

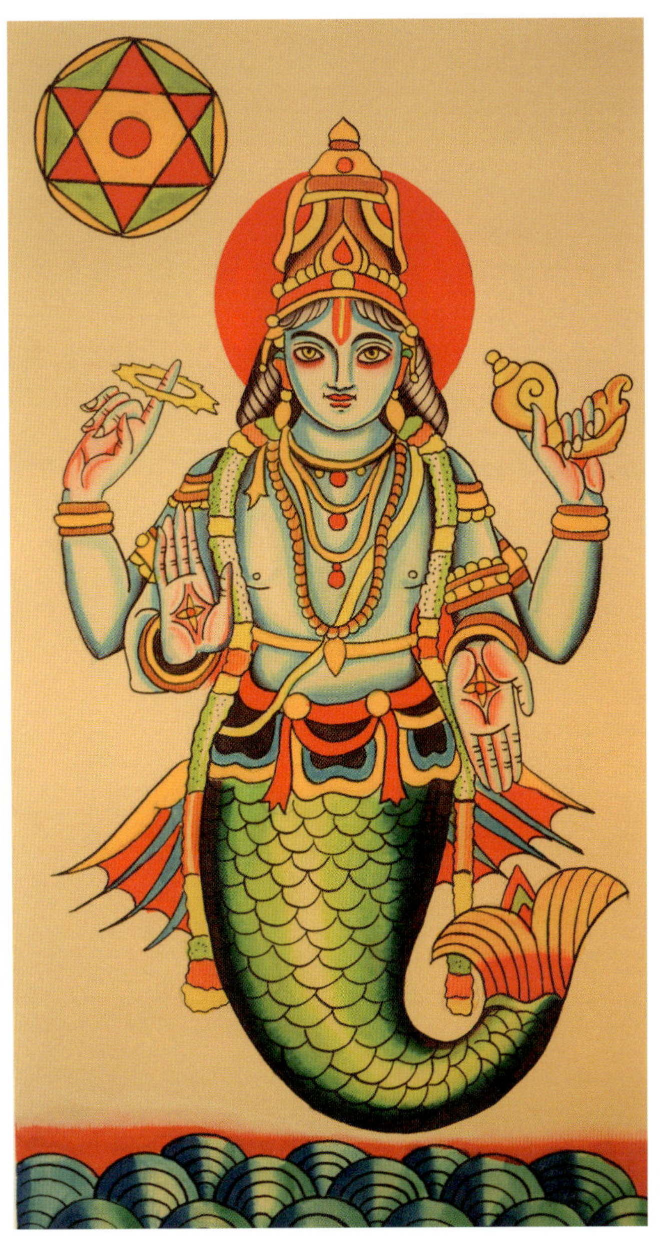

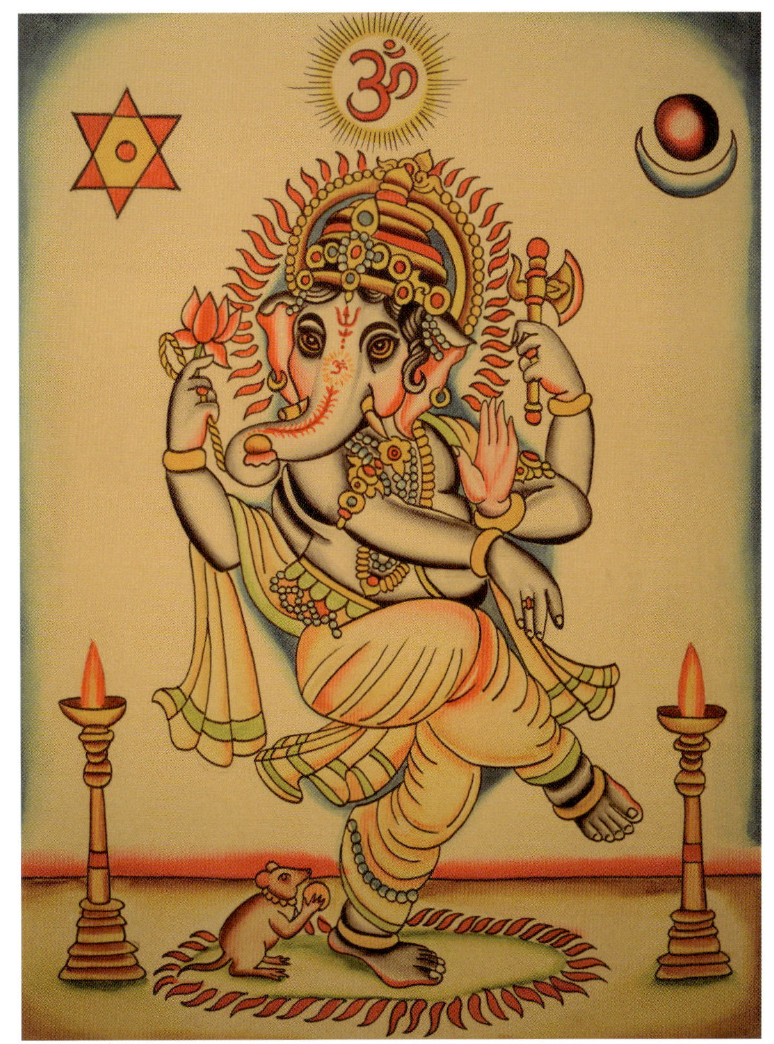

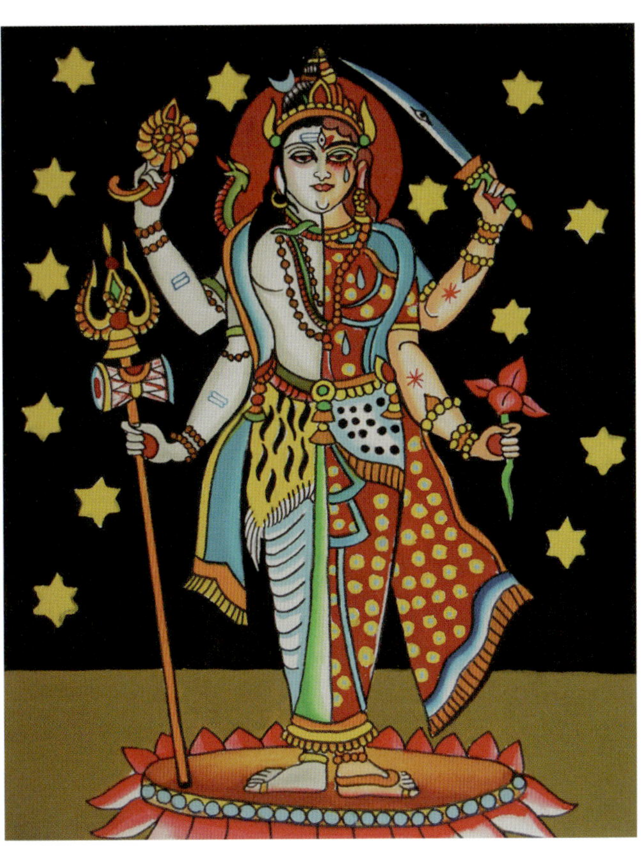

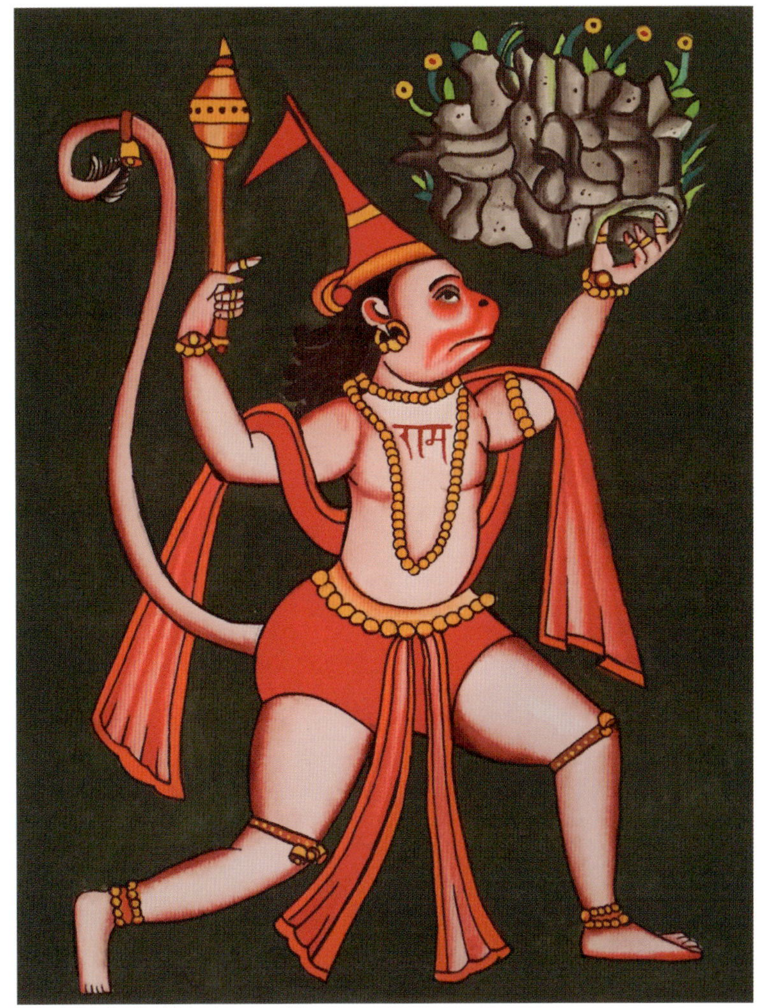

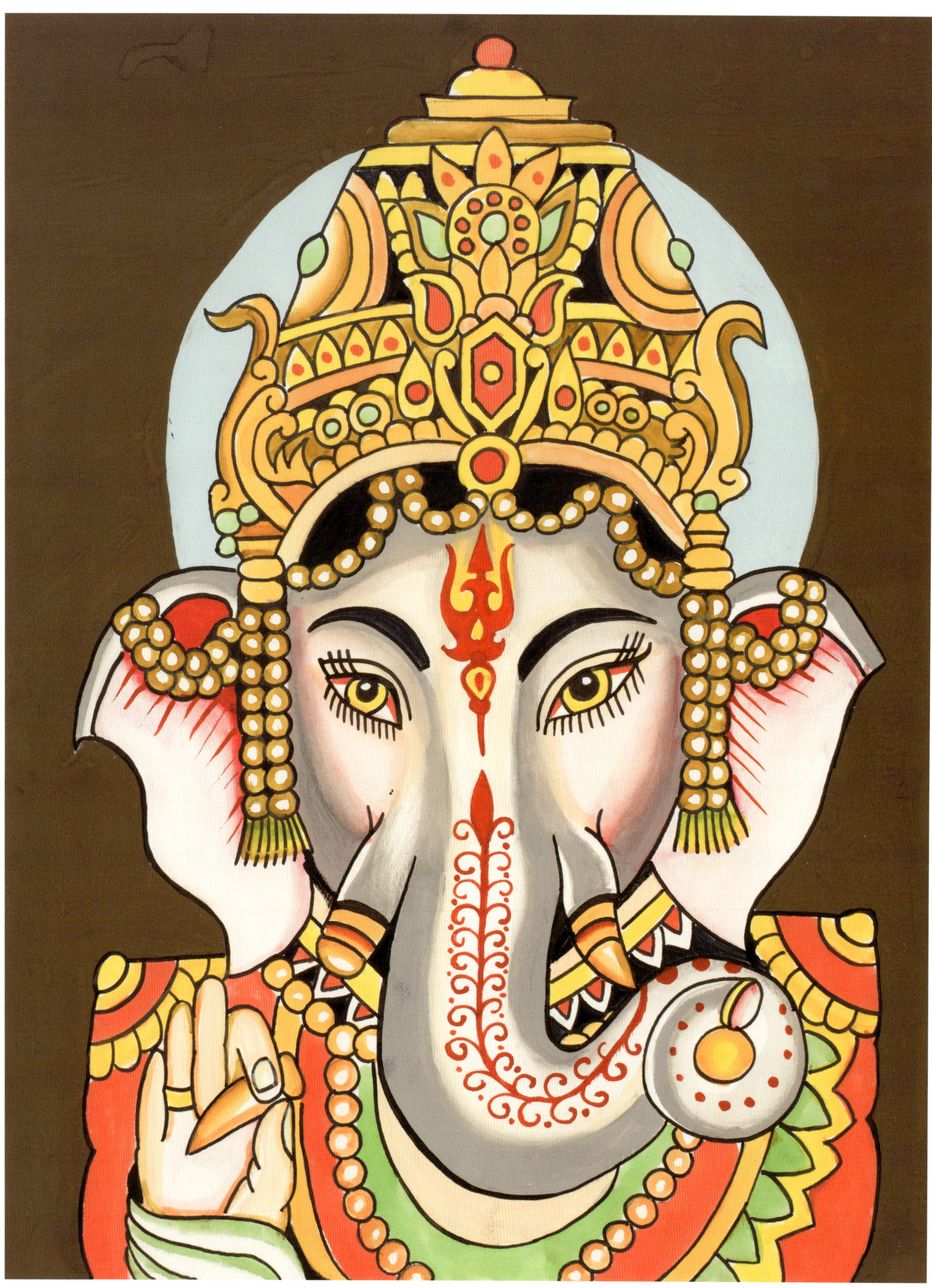

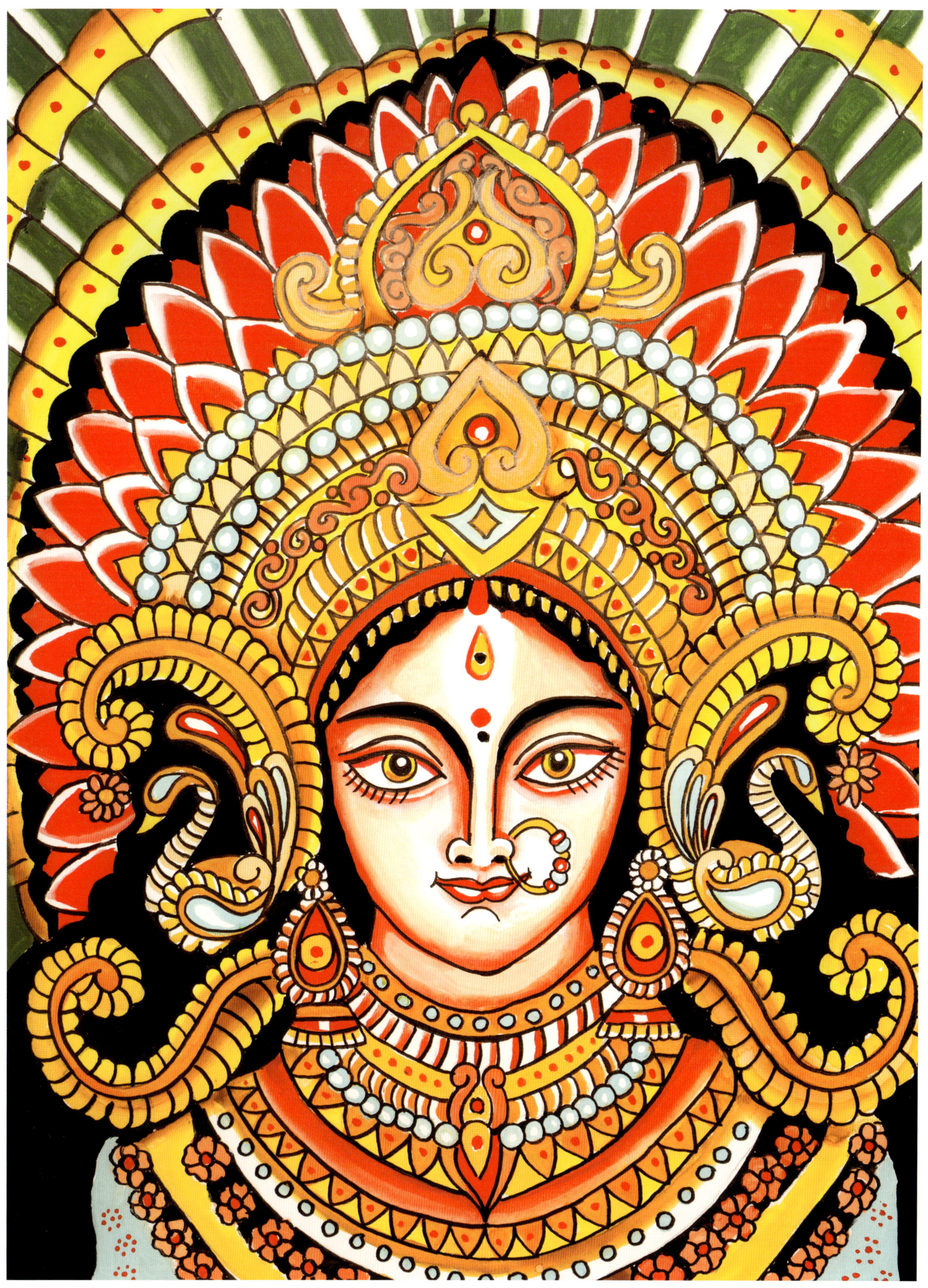

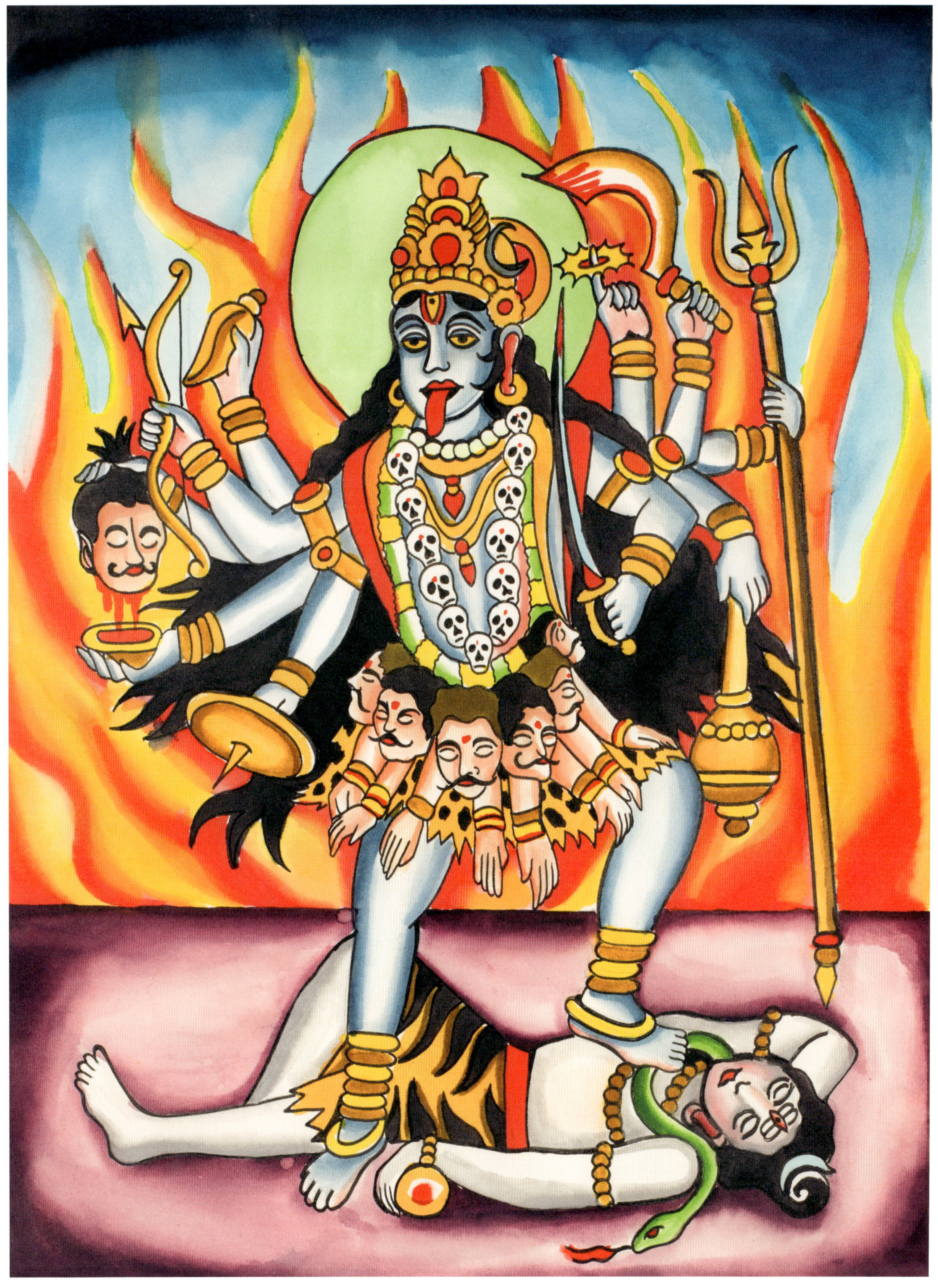

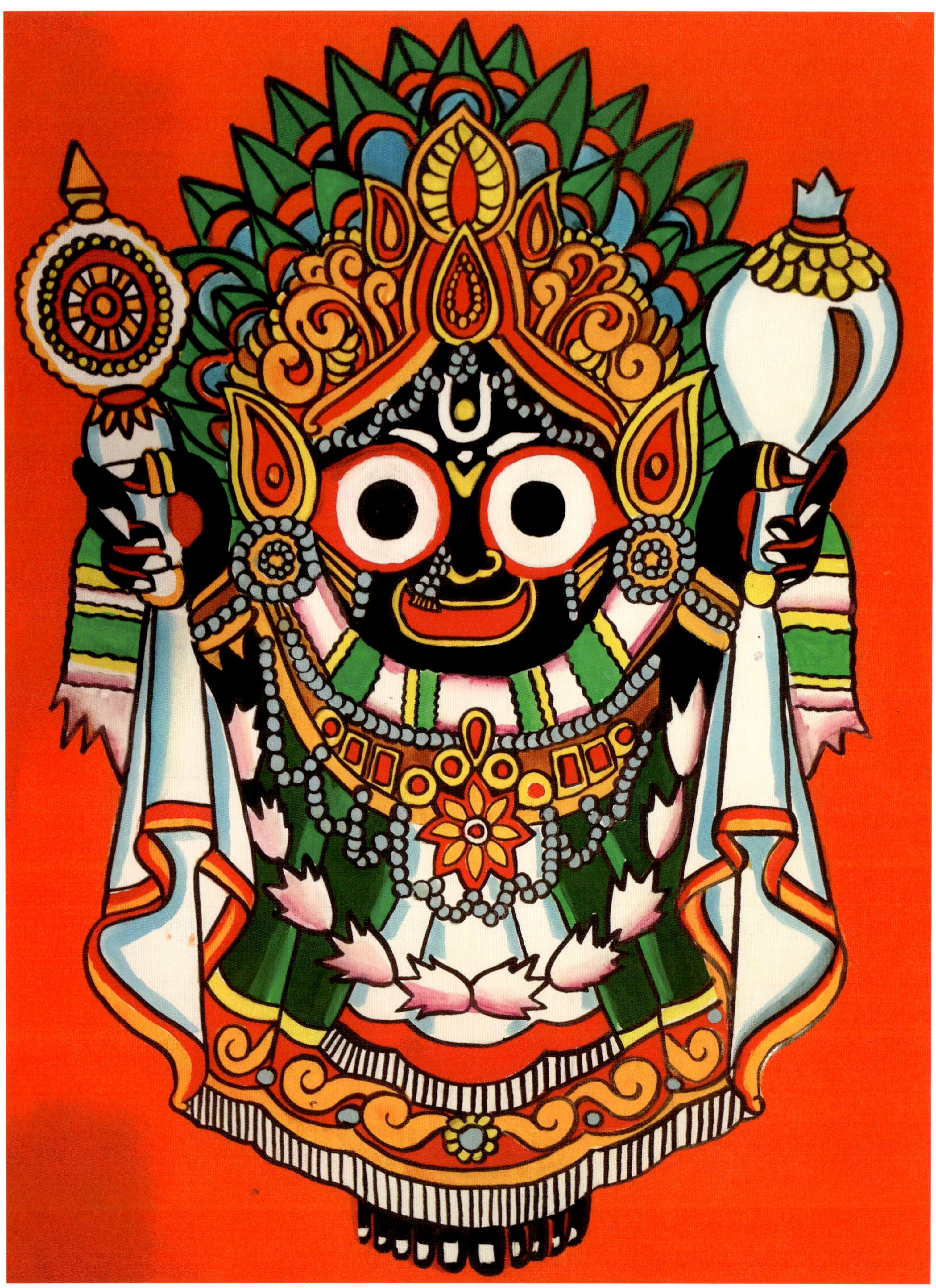

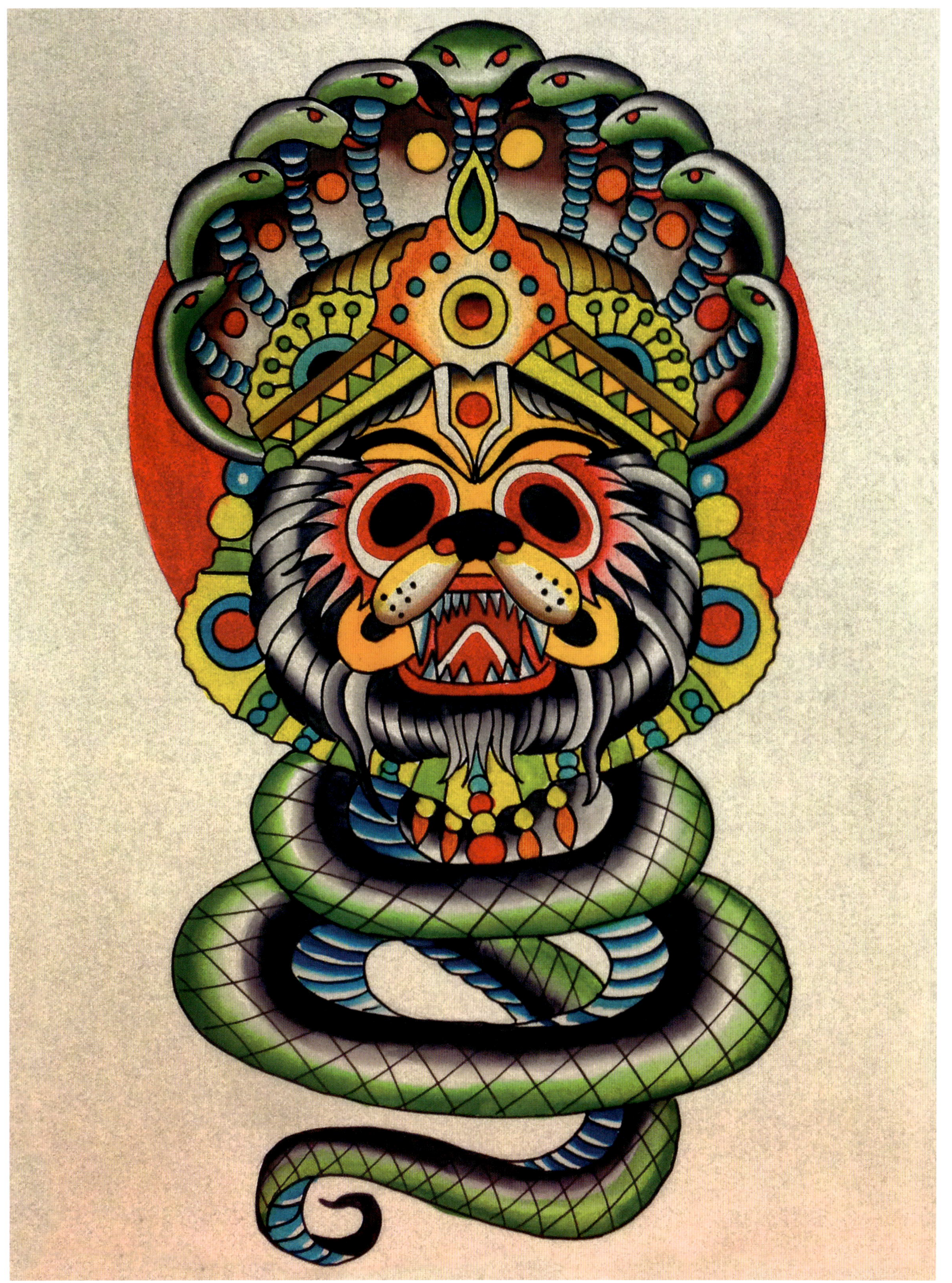

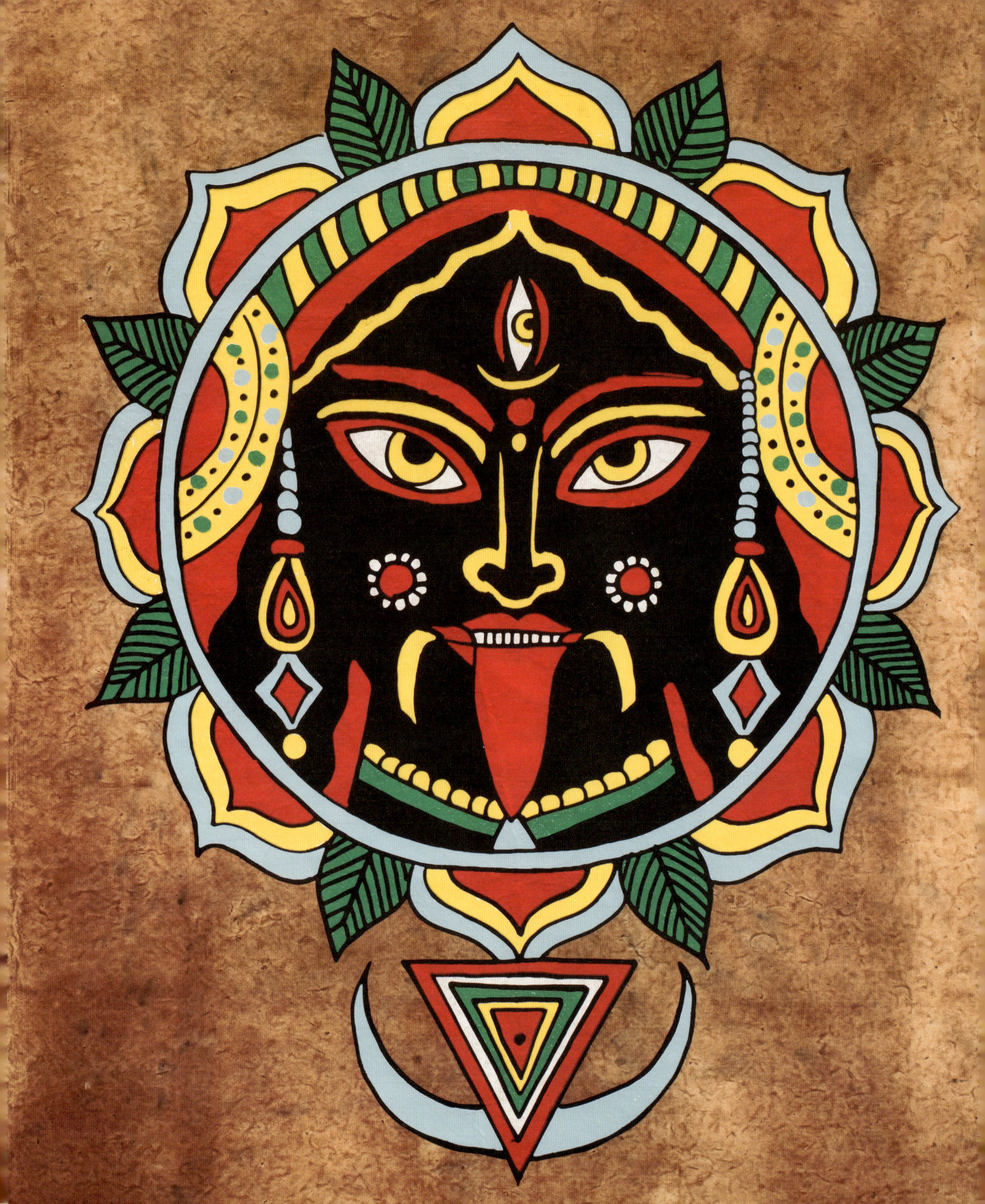

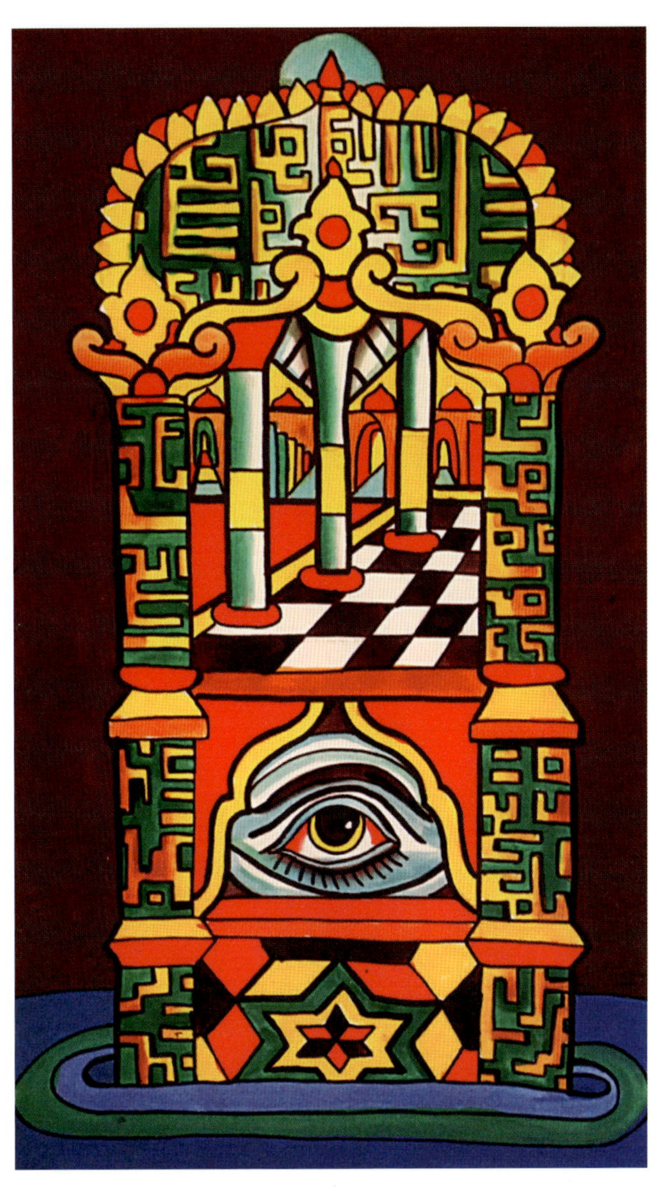

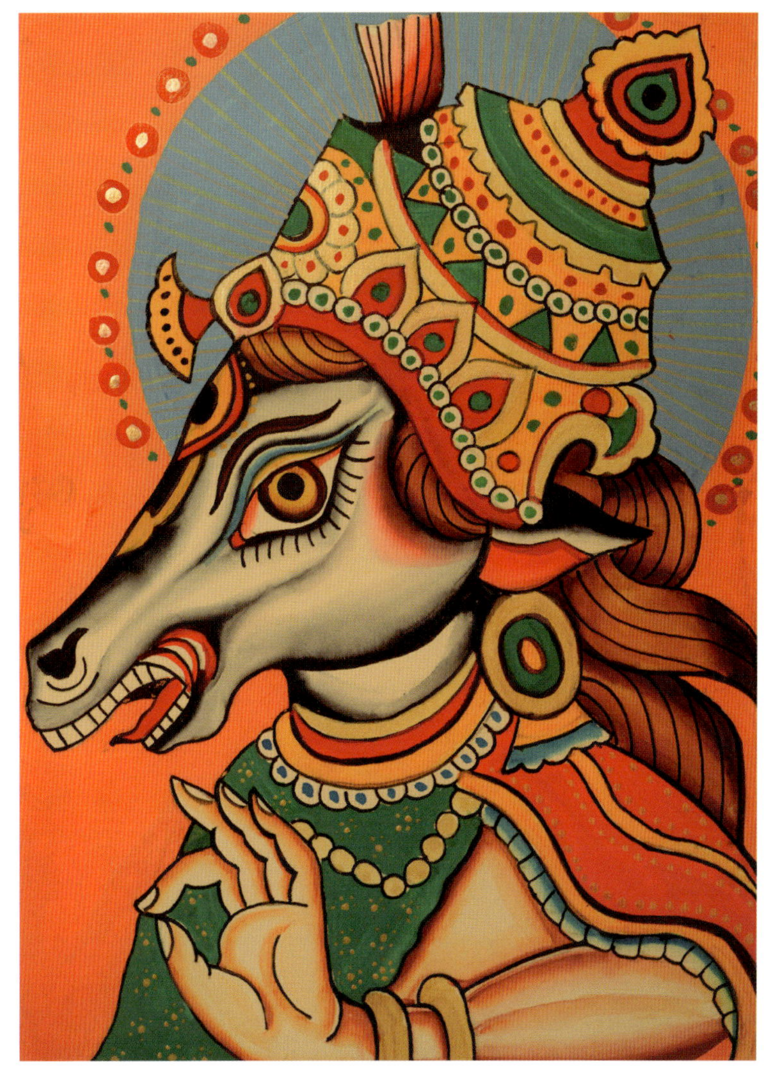

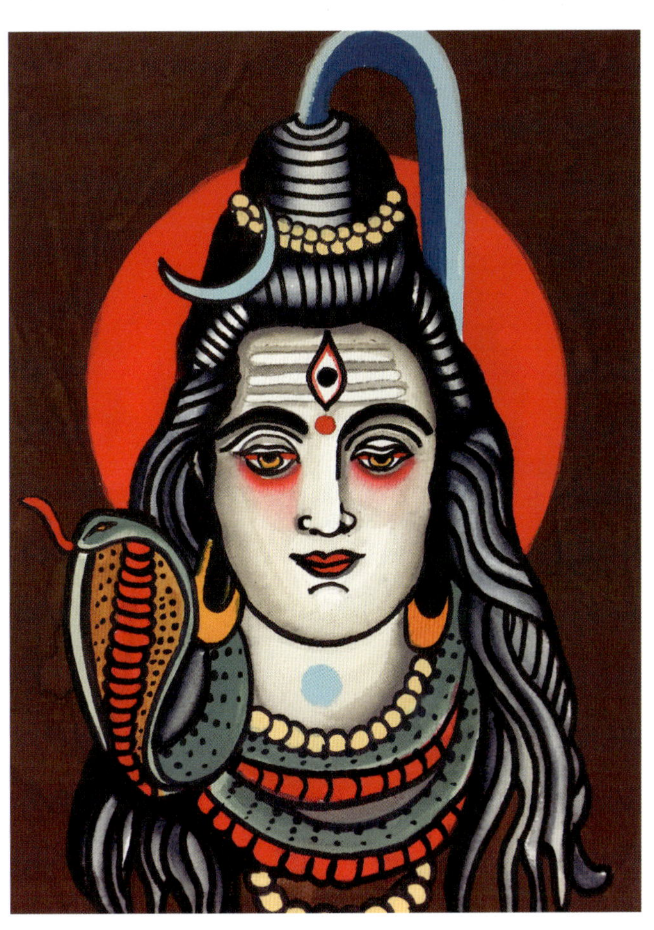

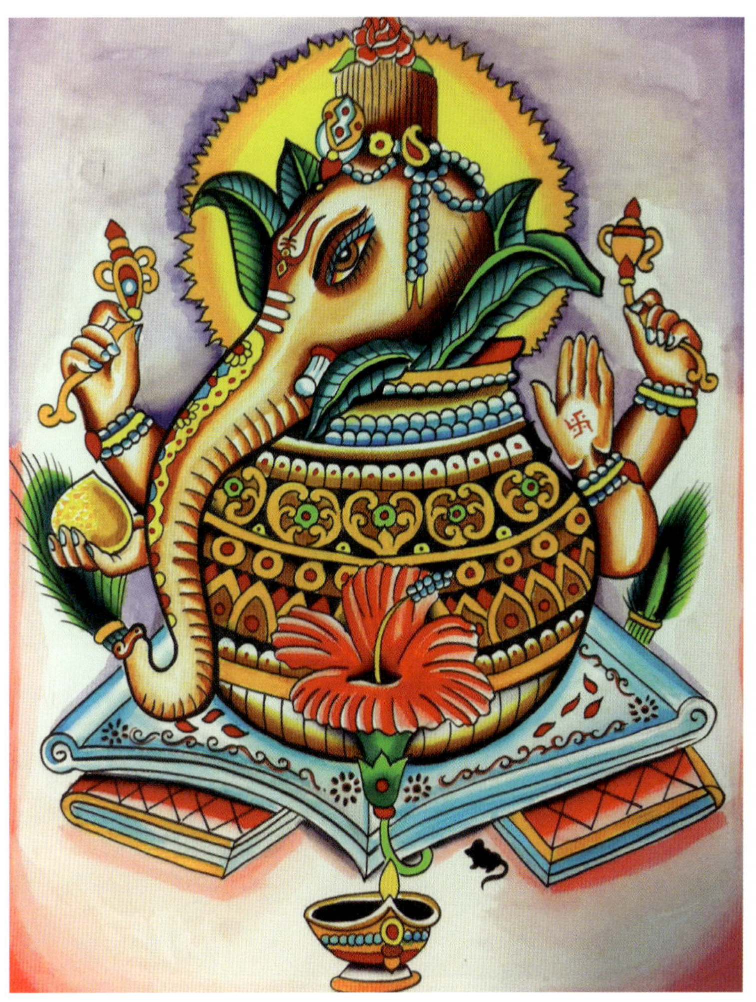

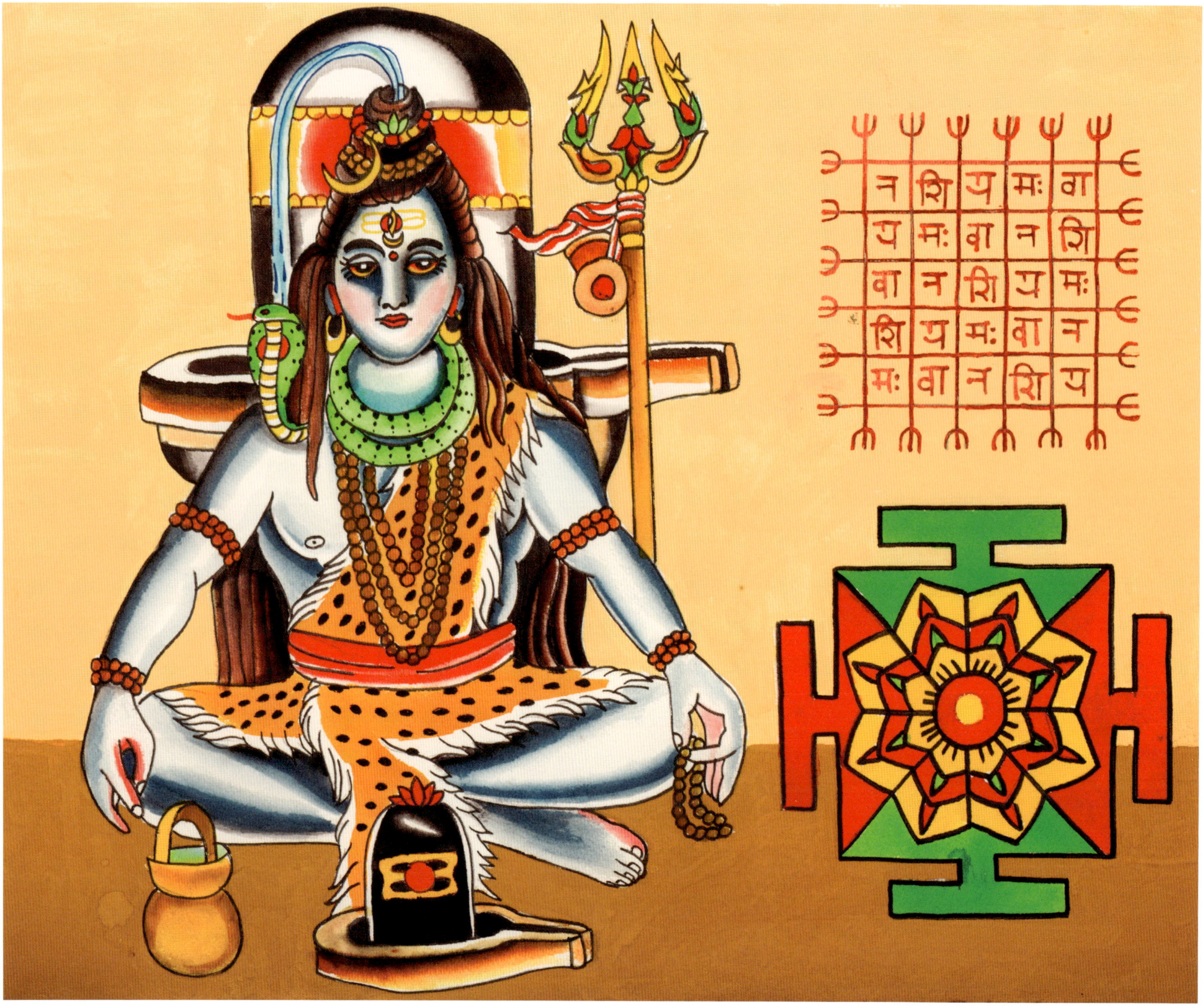

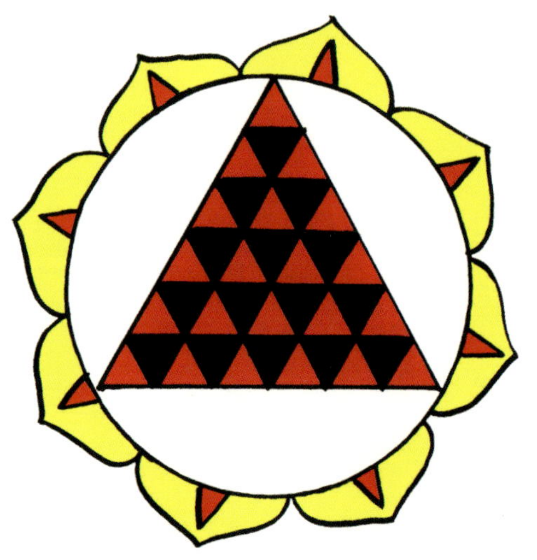

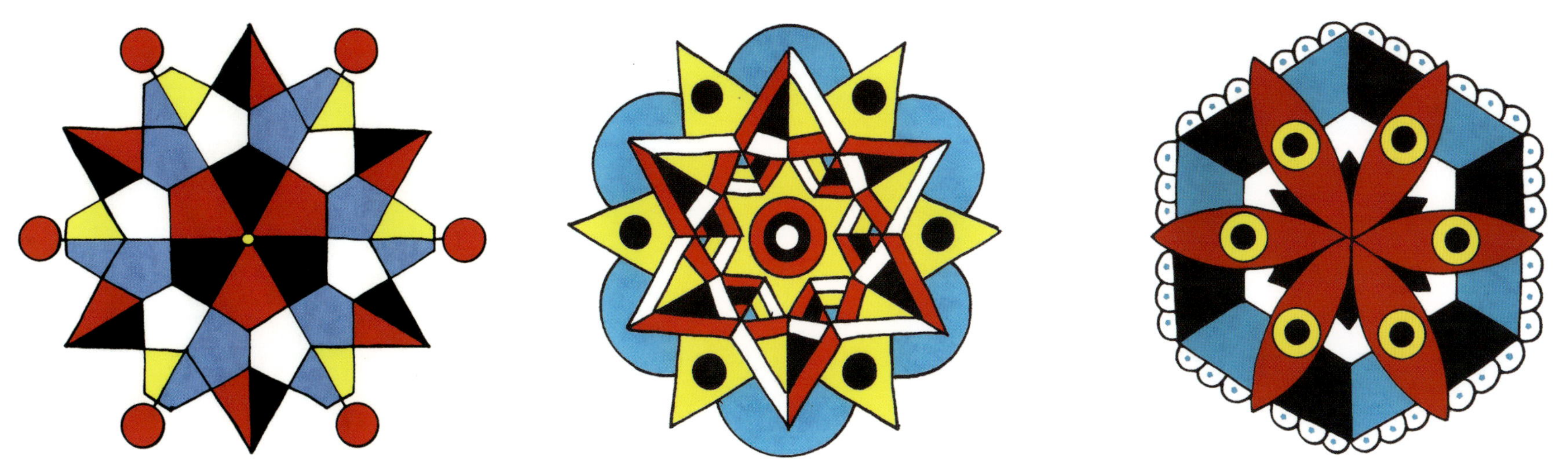

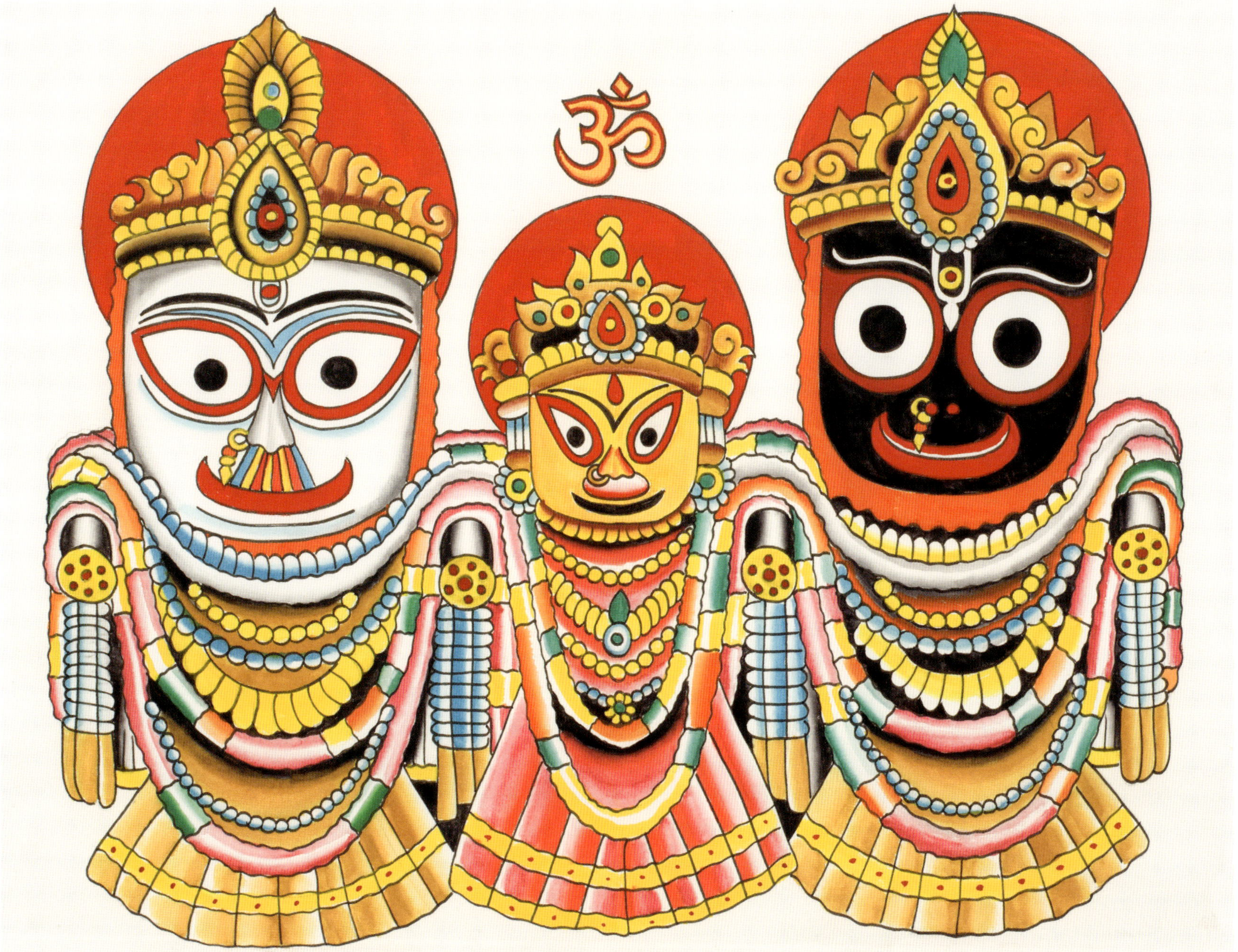

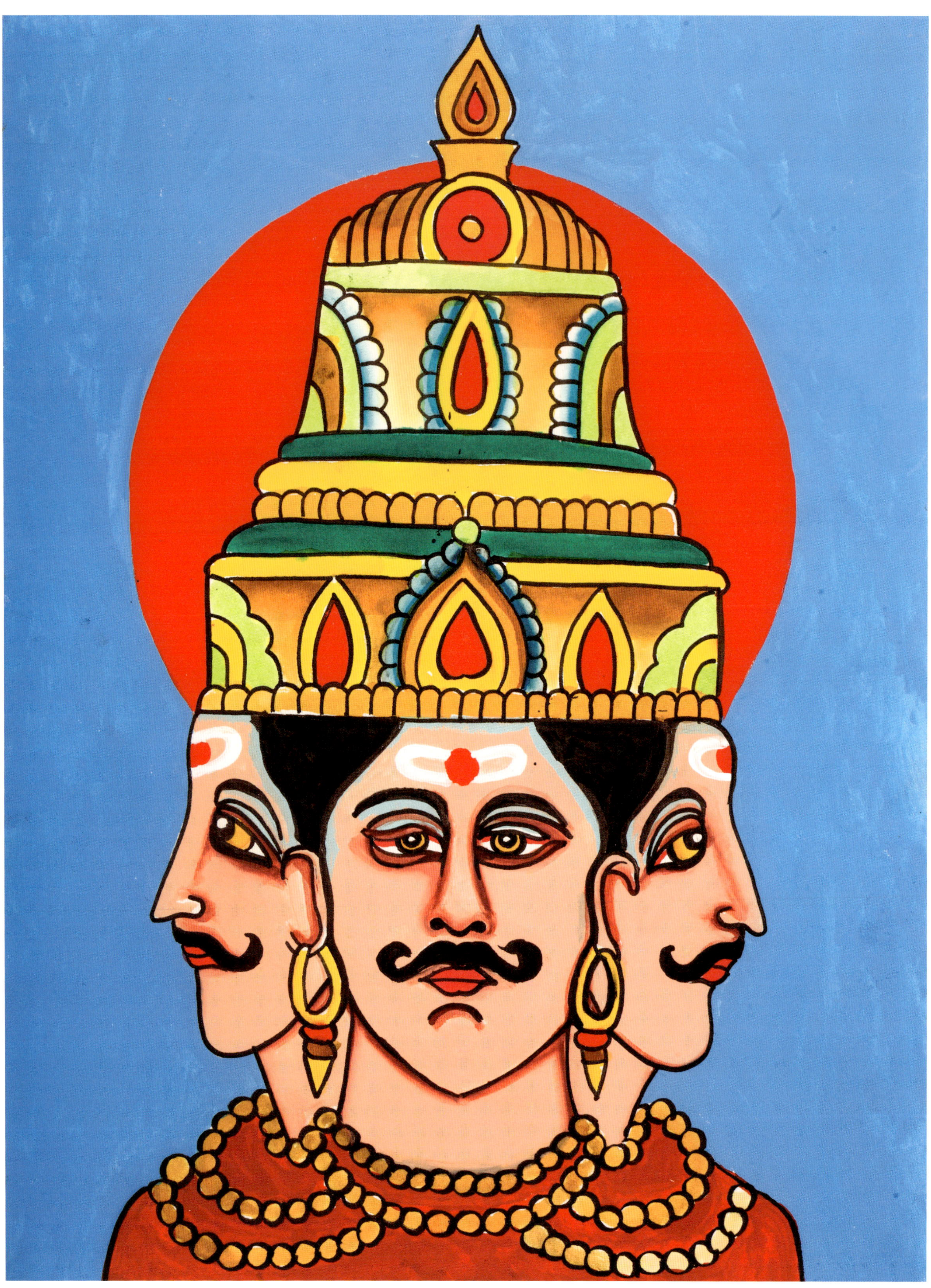

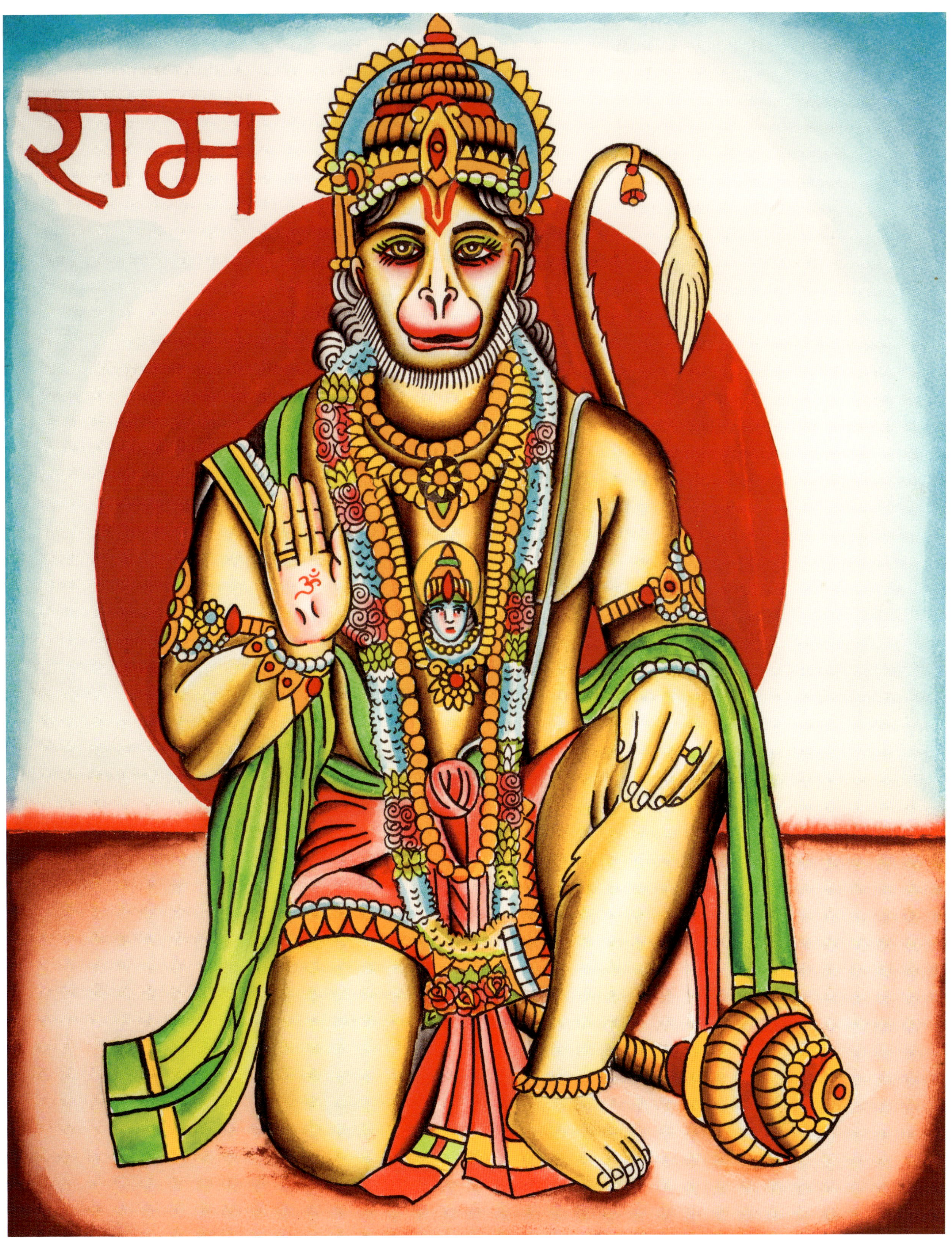
राम

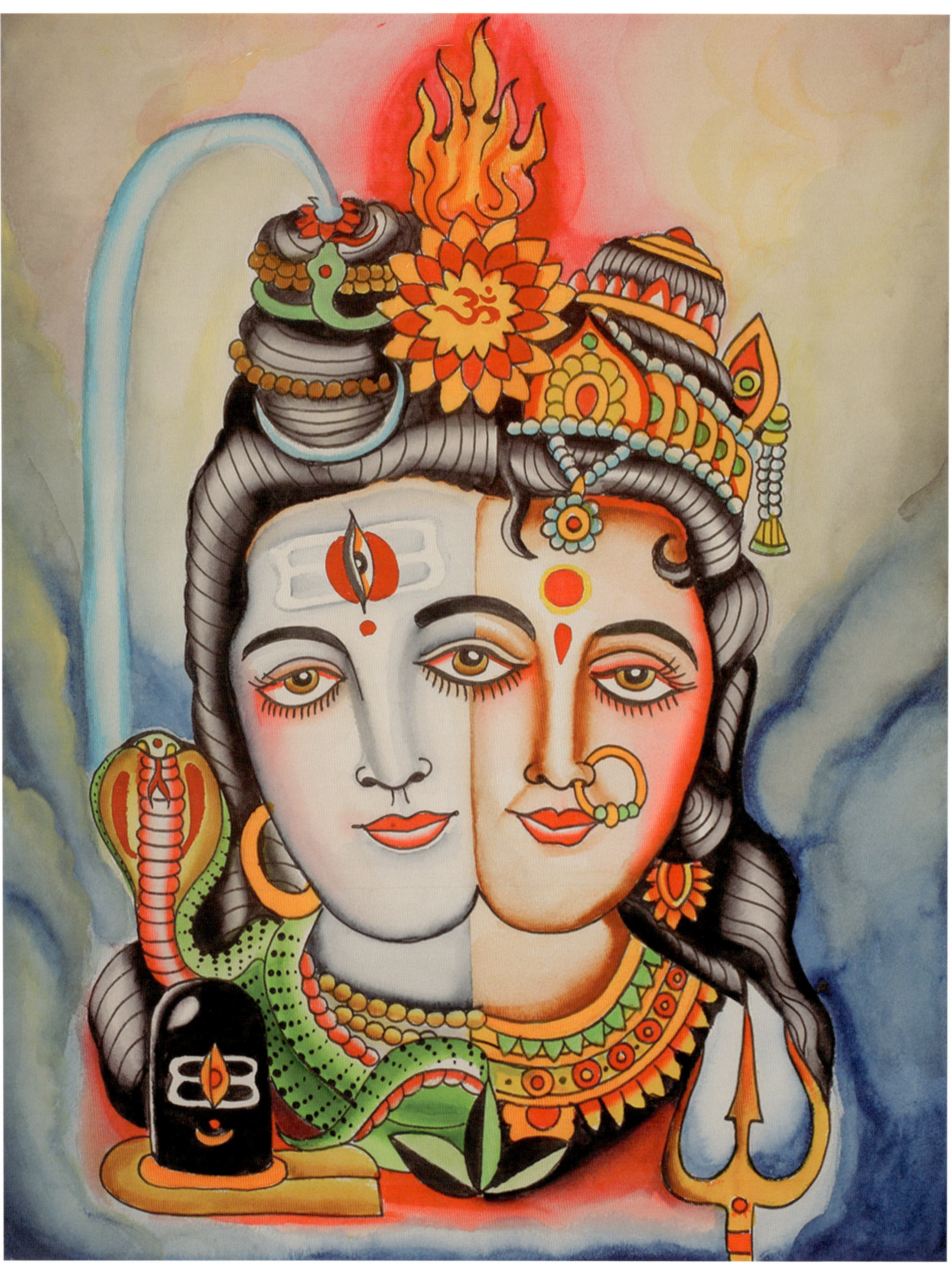

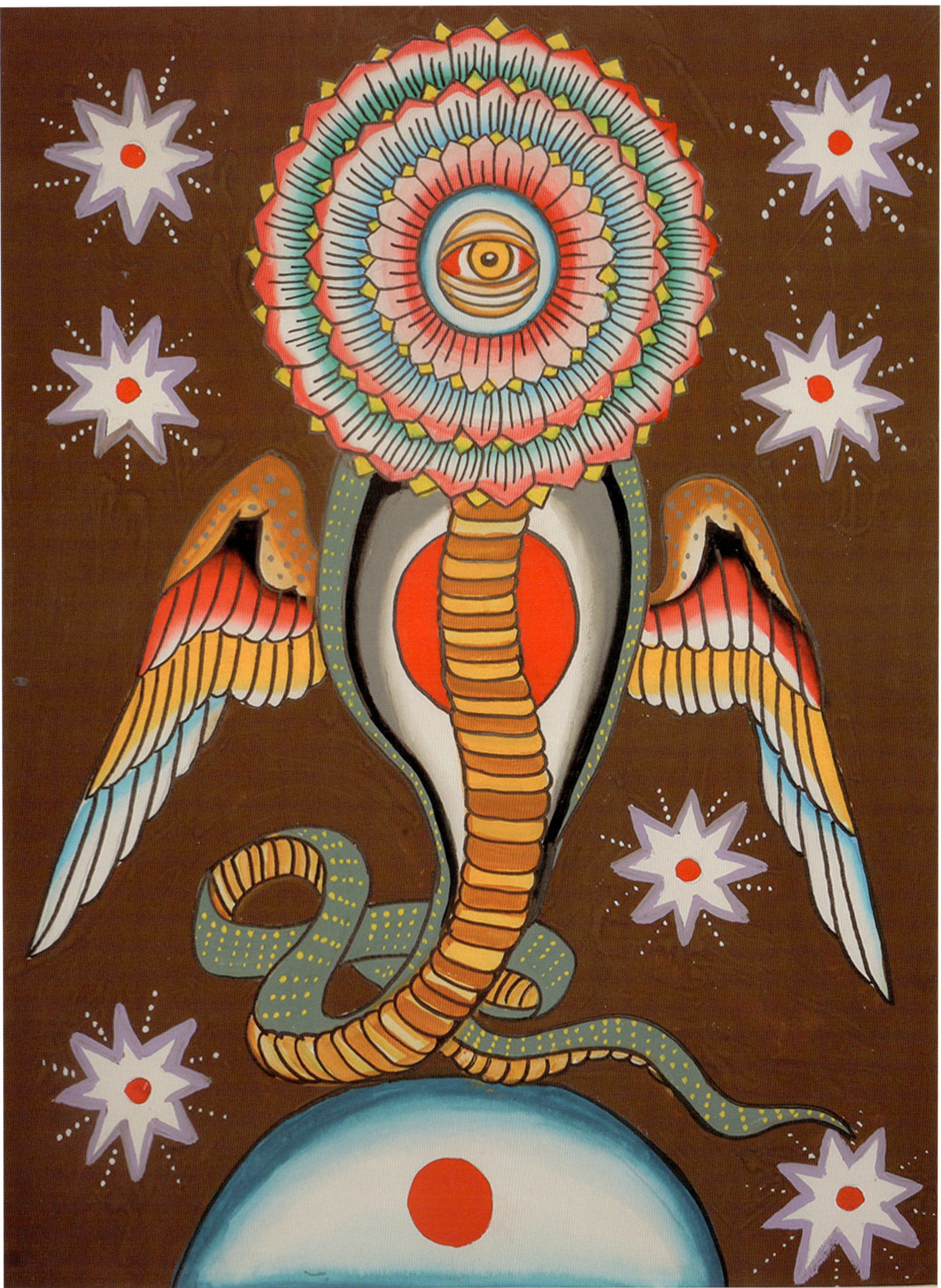

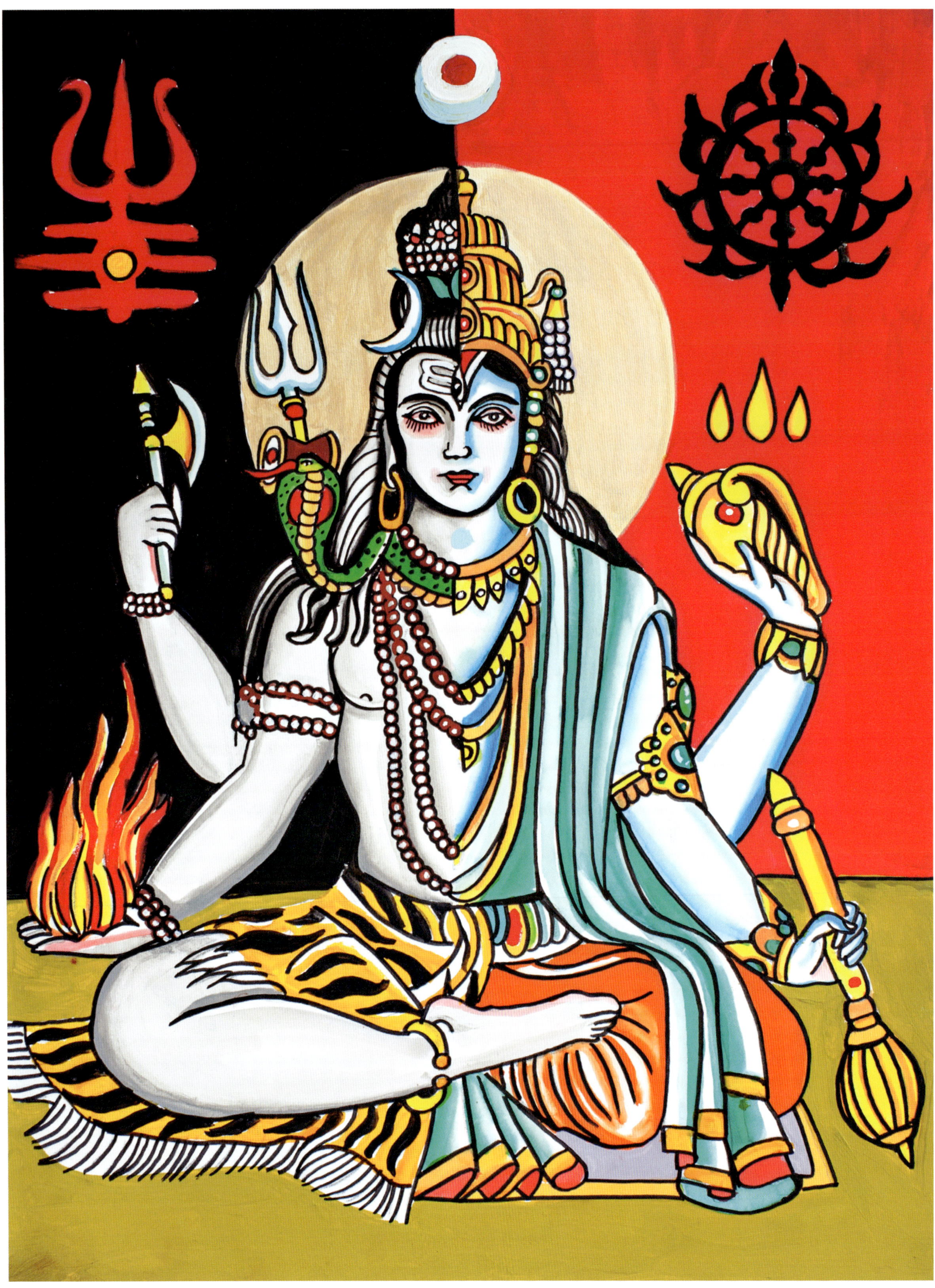

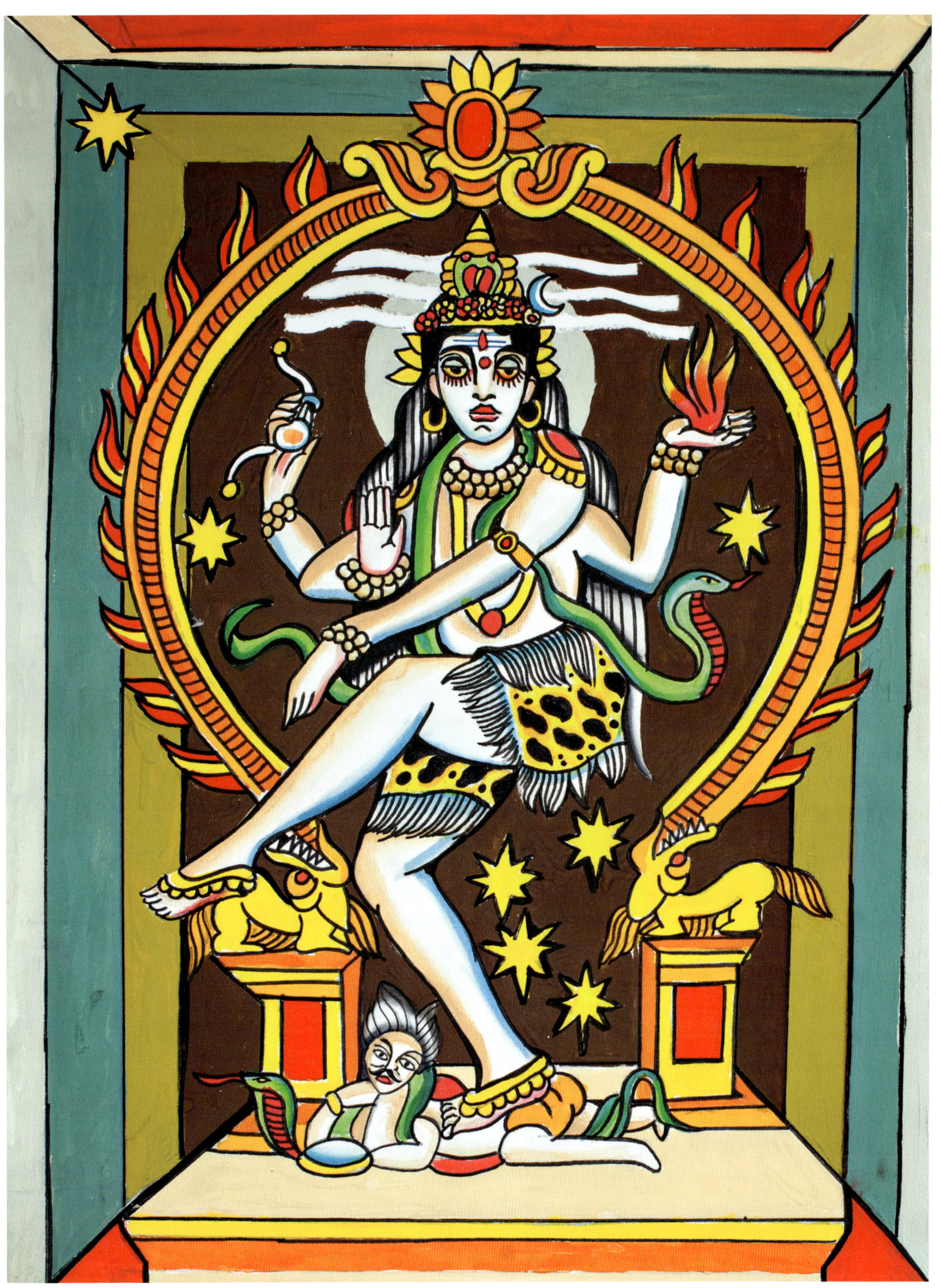

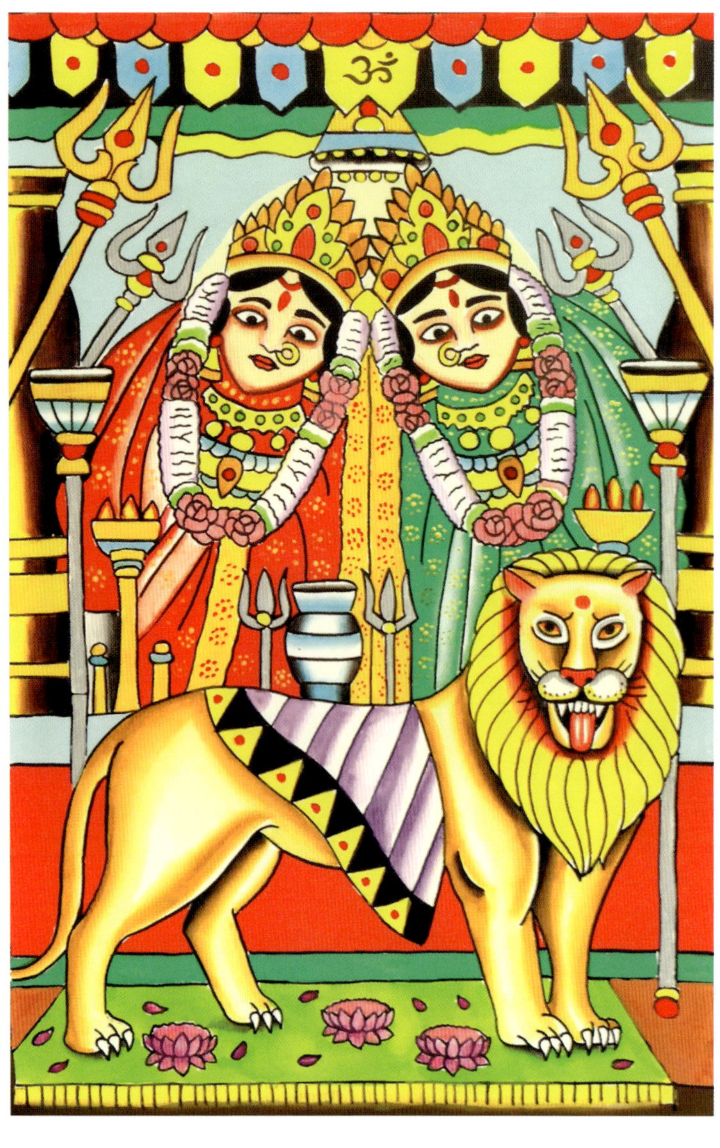

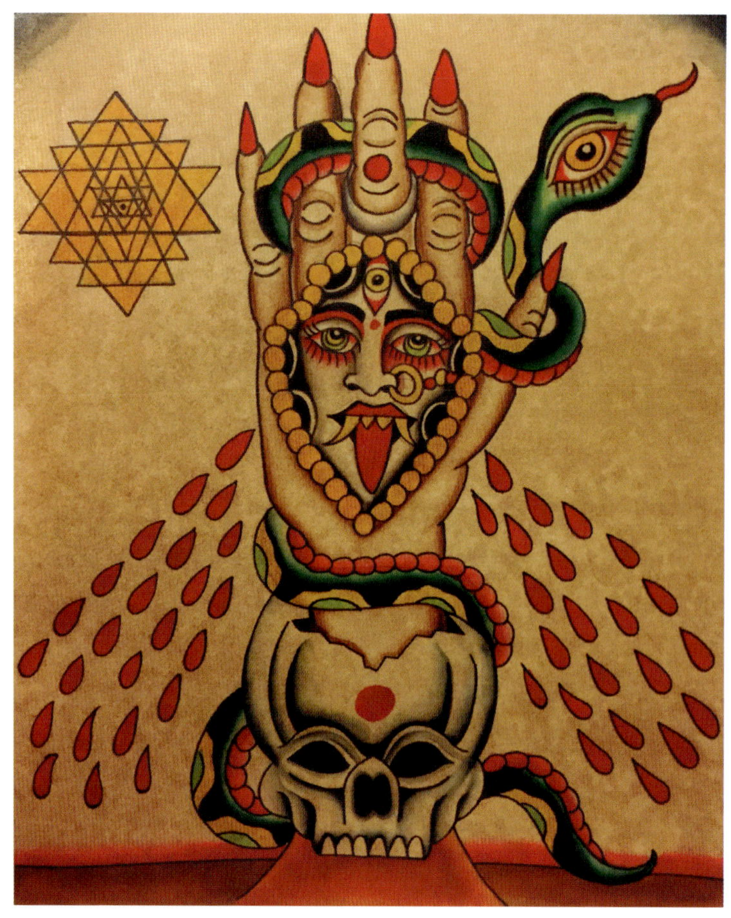

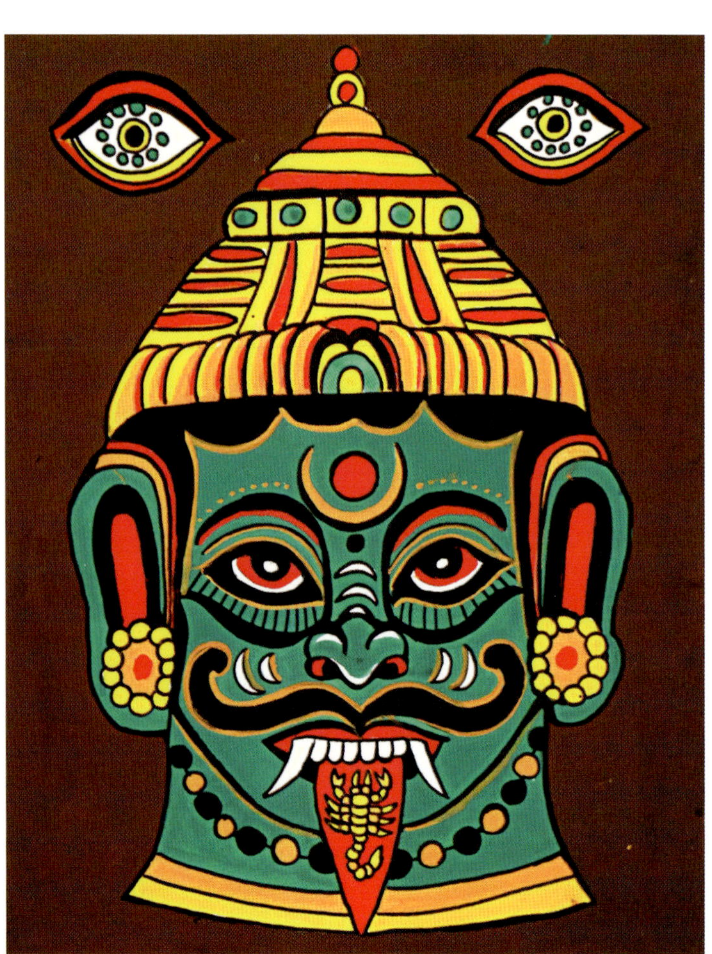

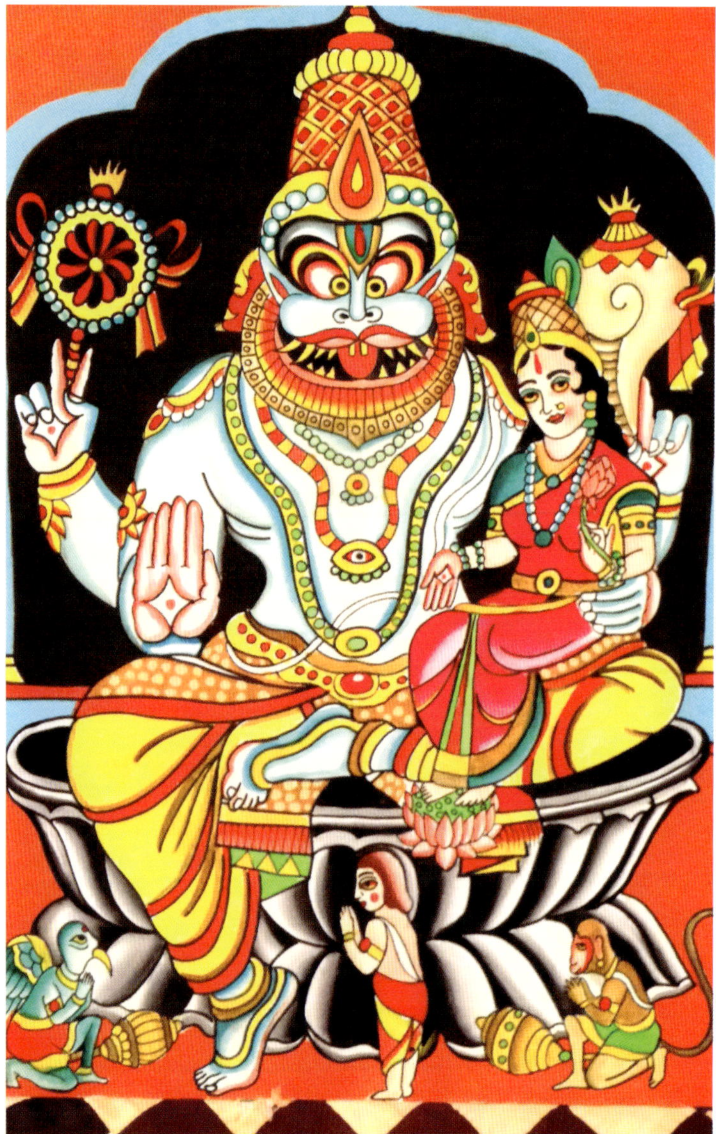

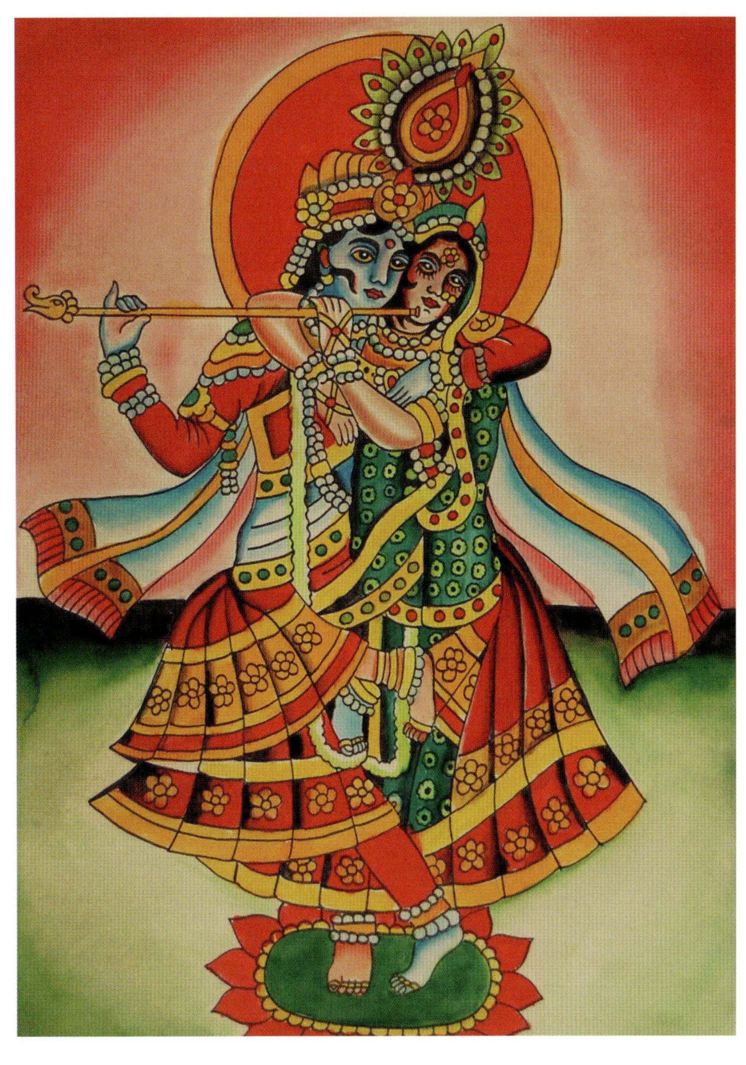
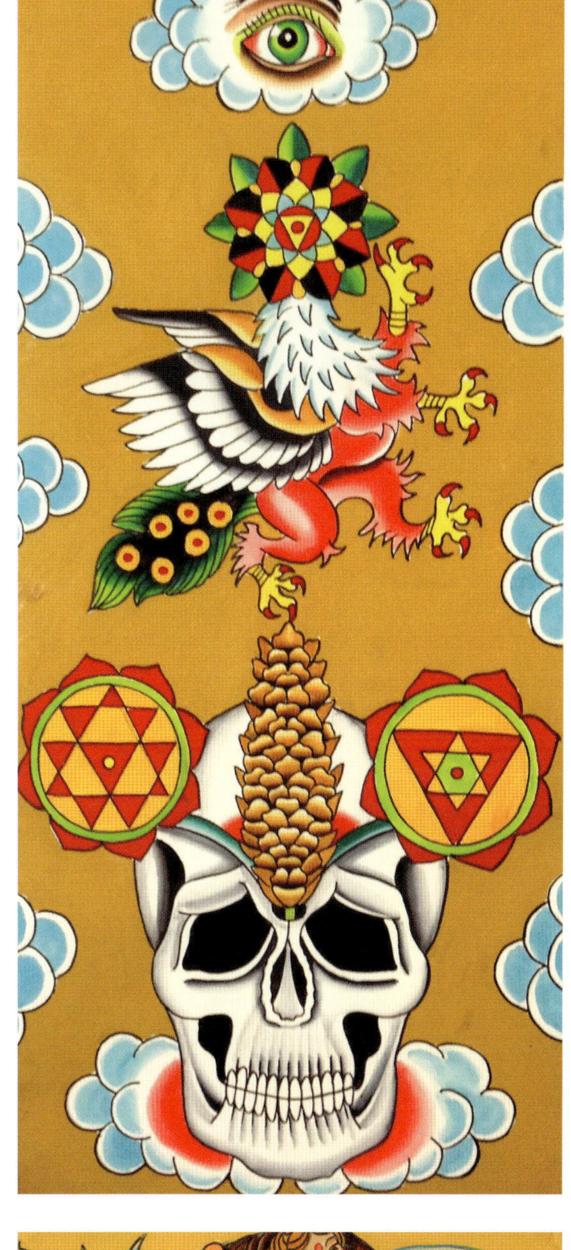
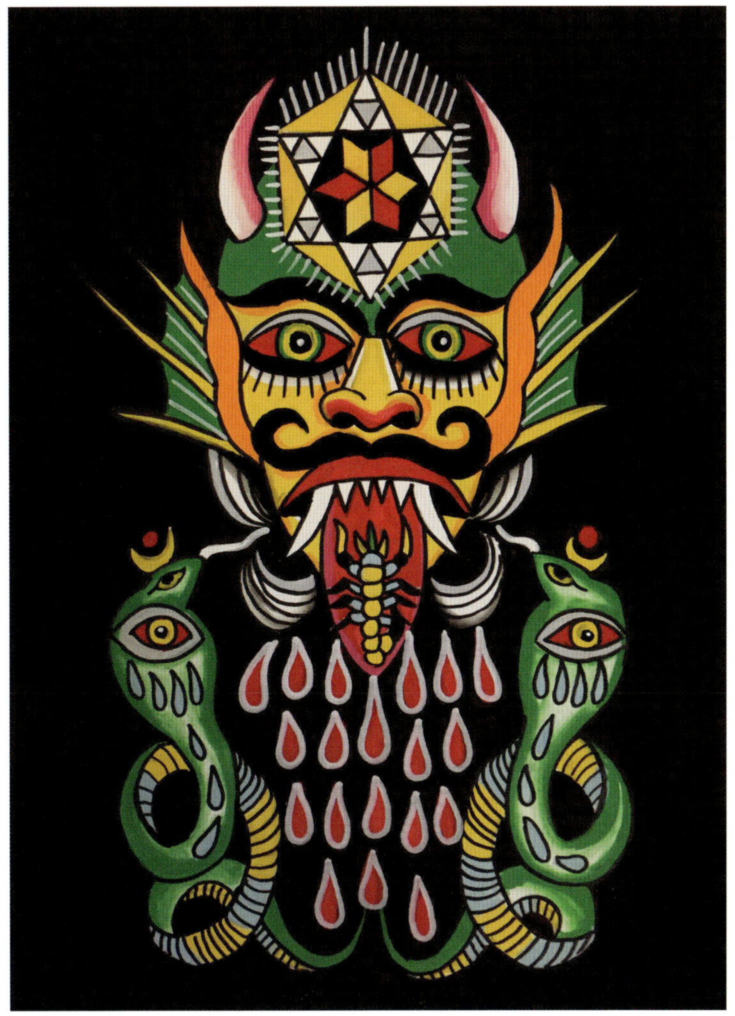
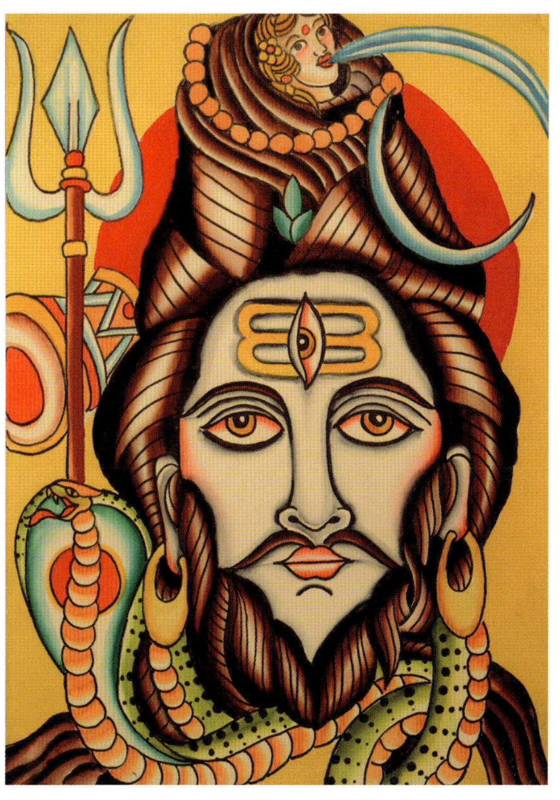

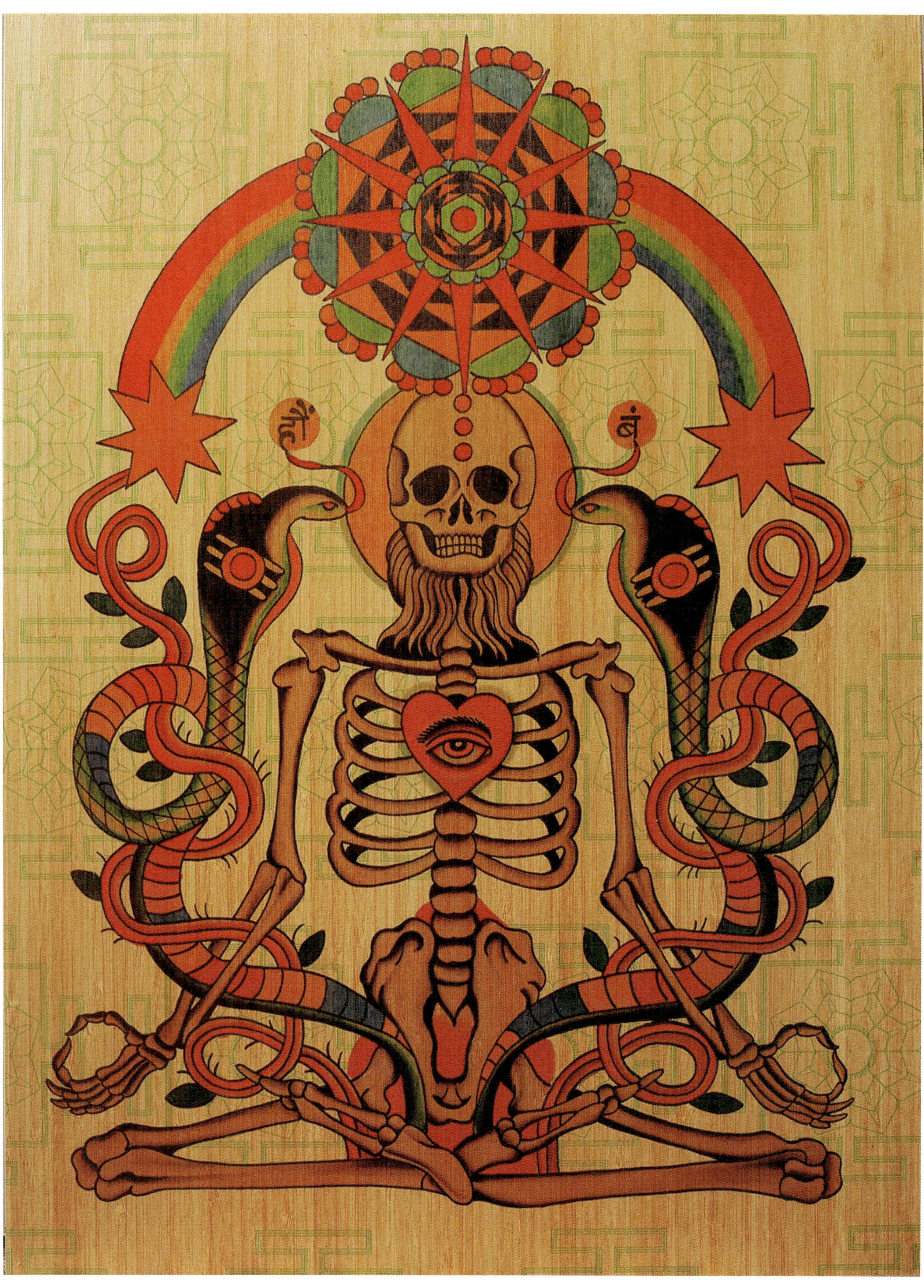

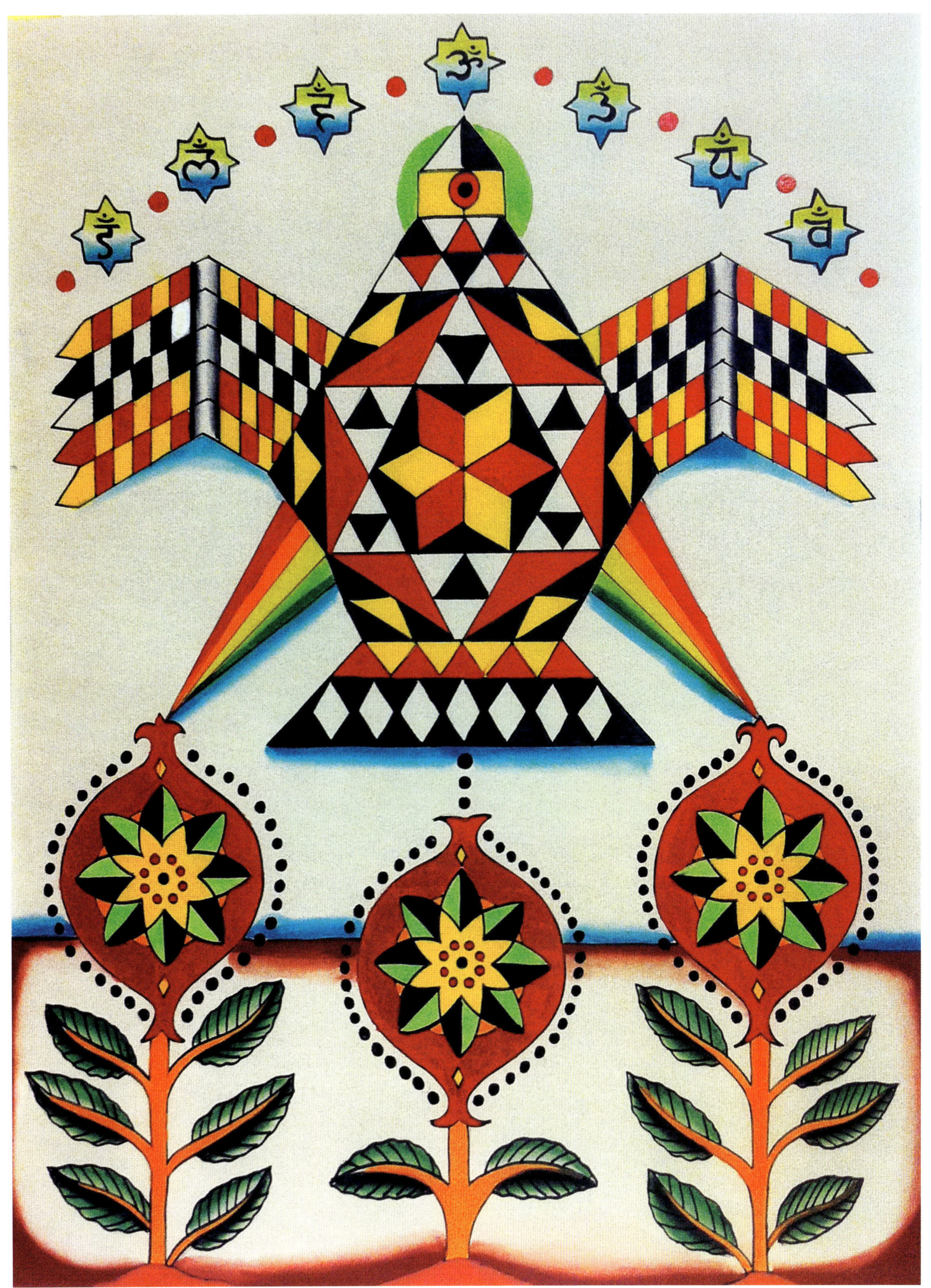

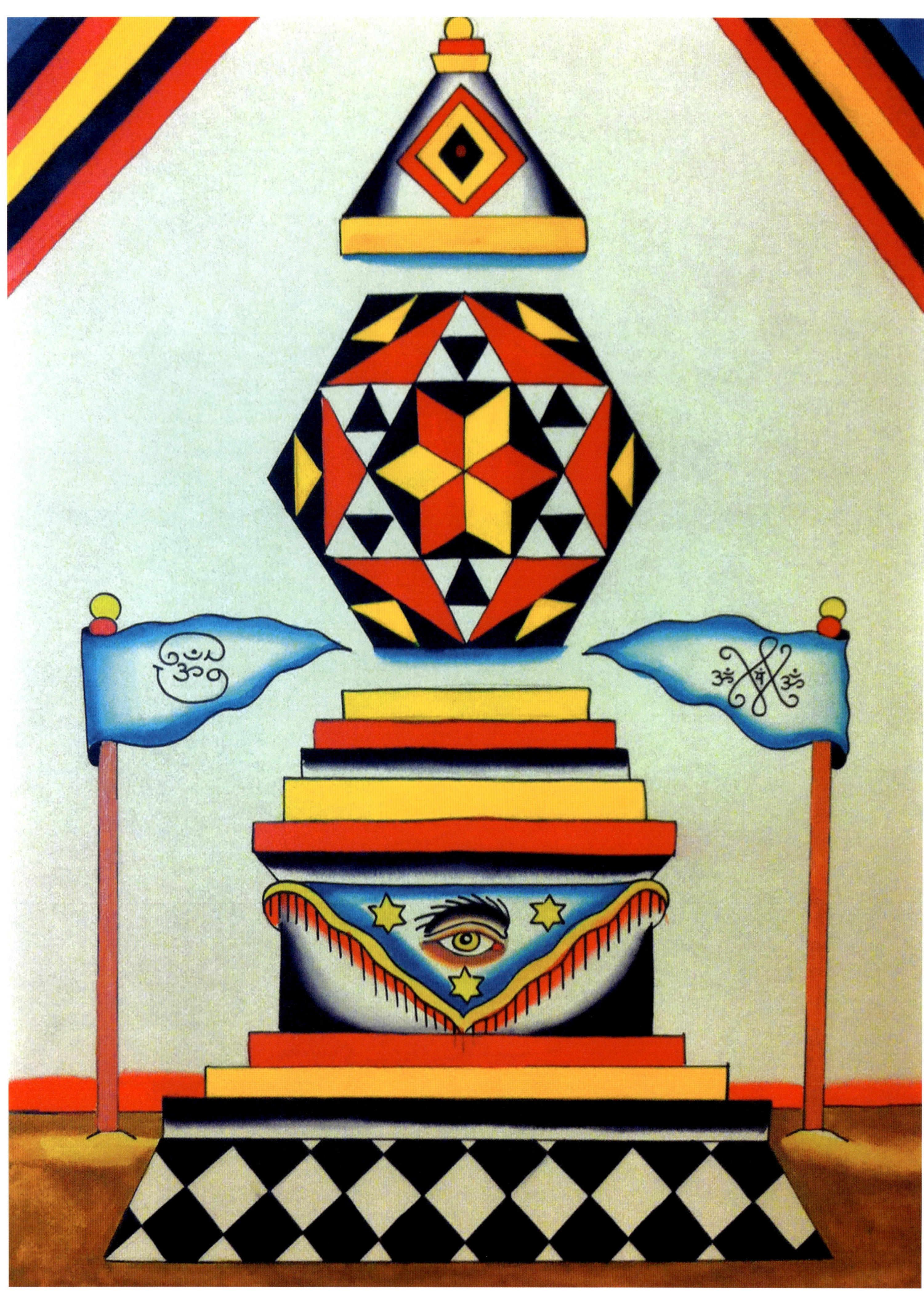

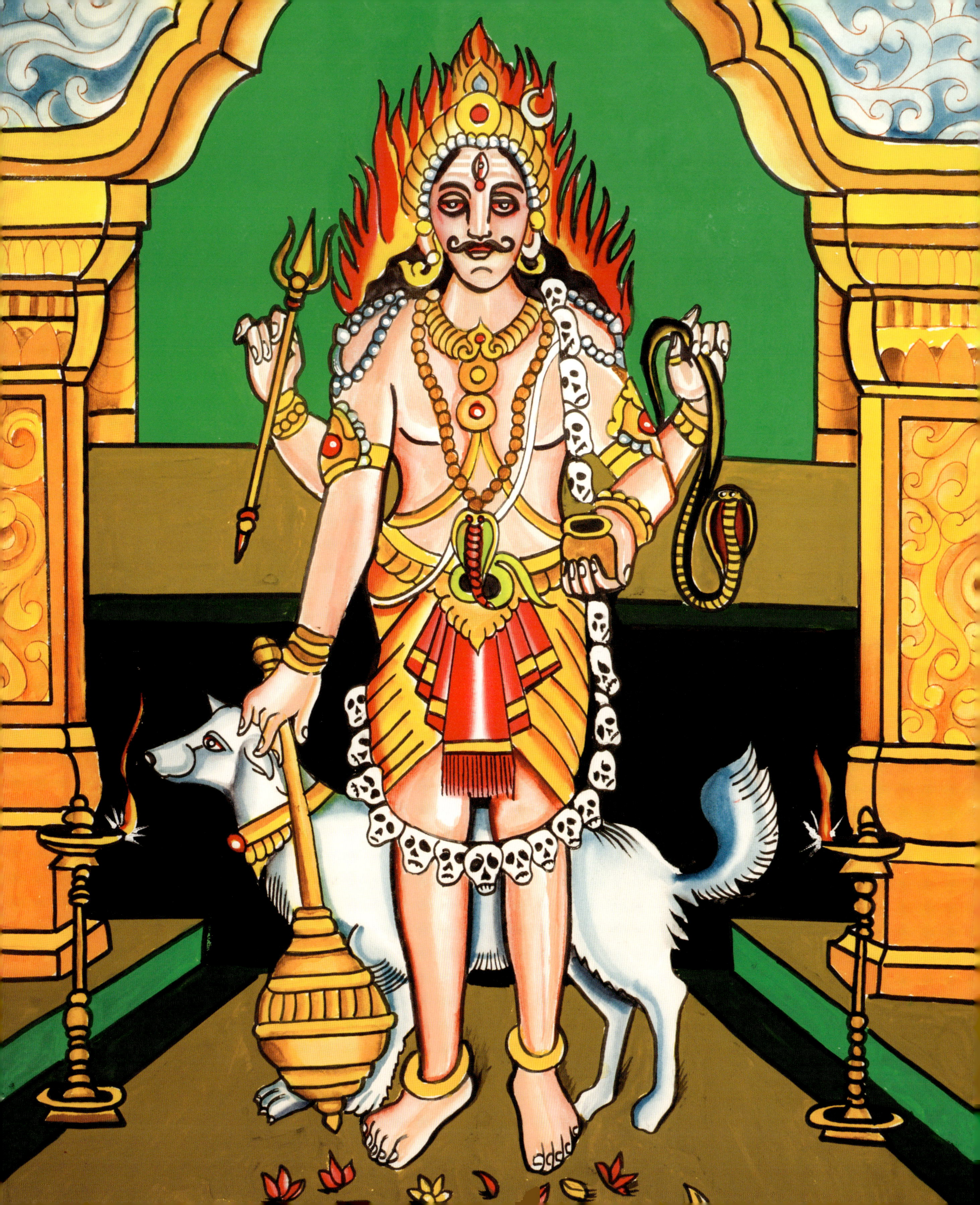

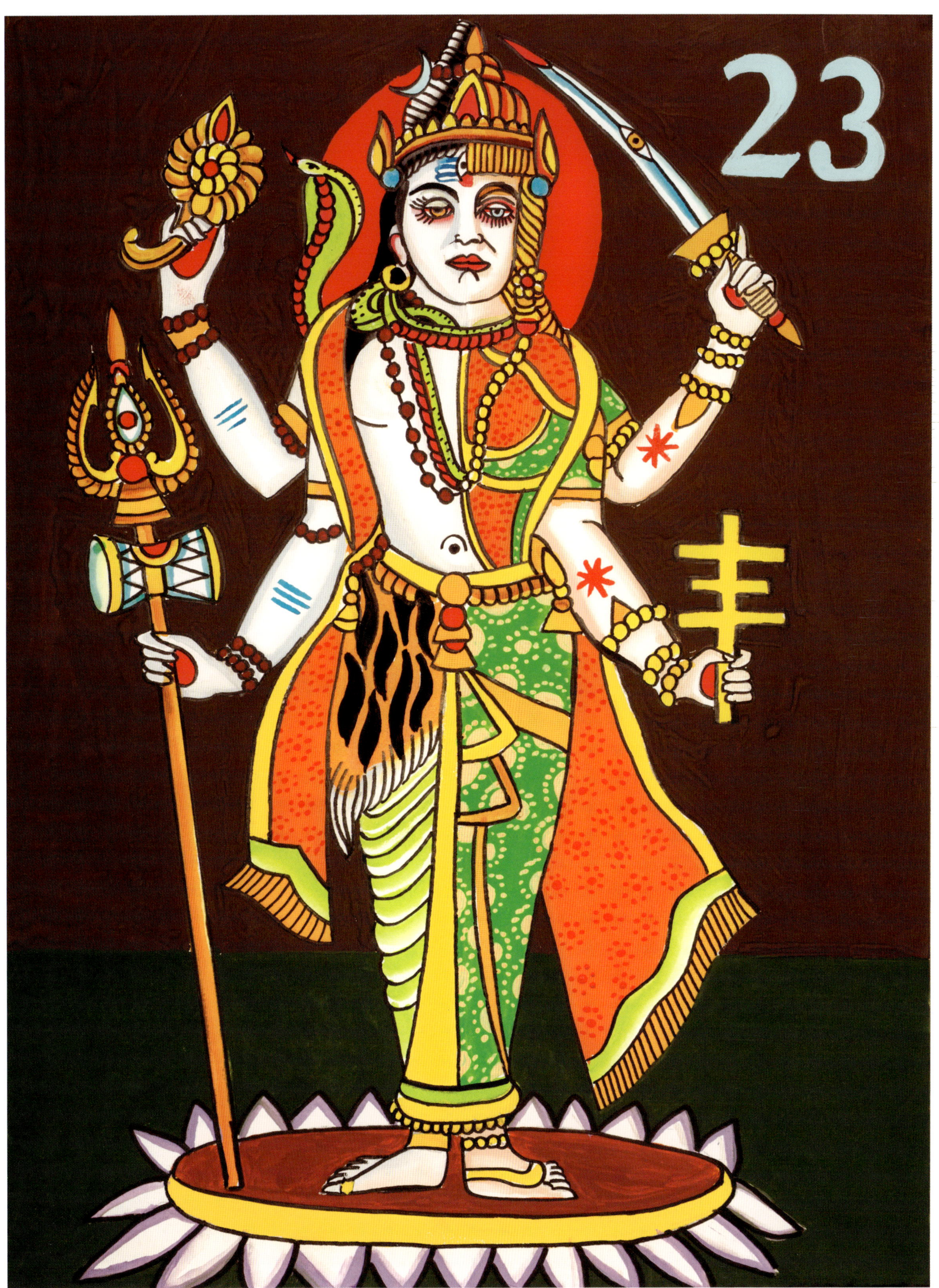

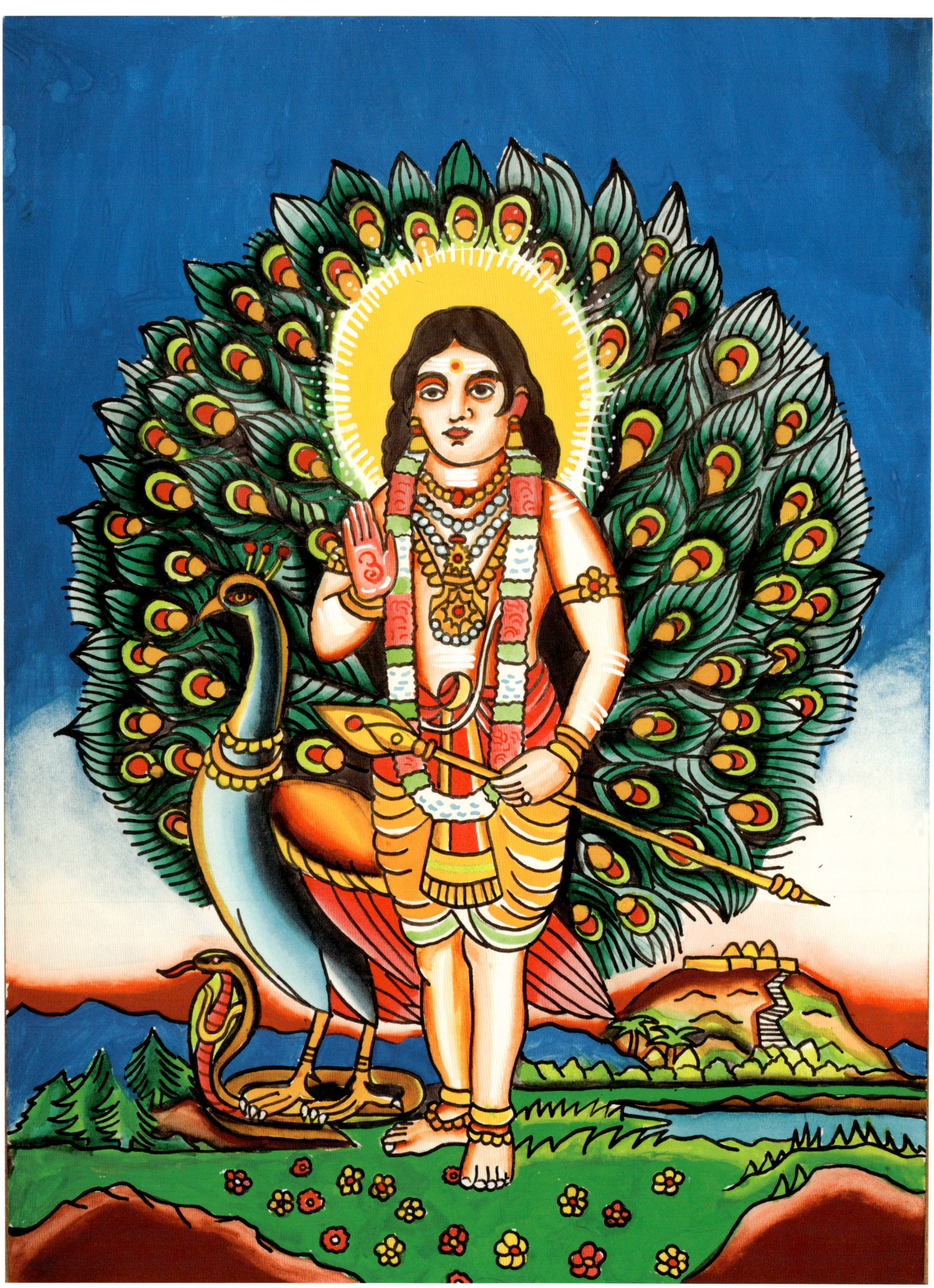

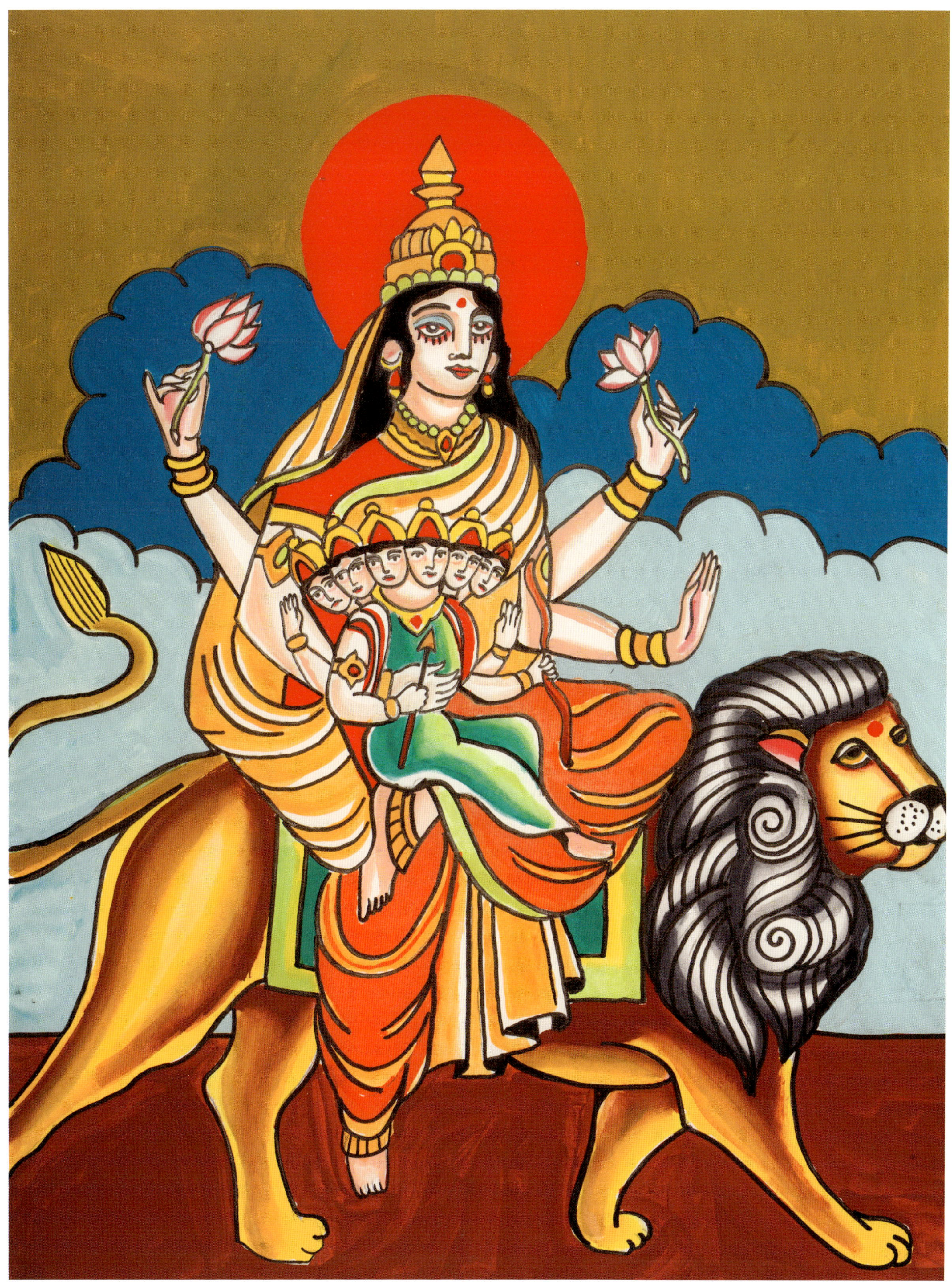

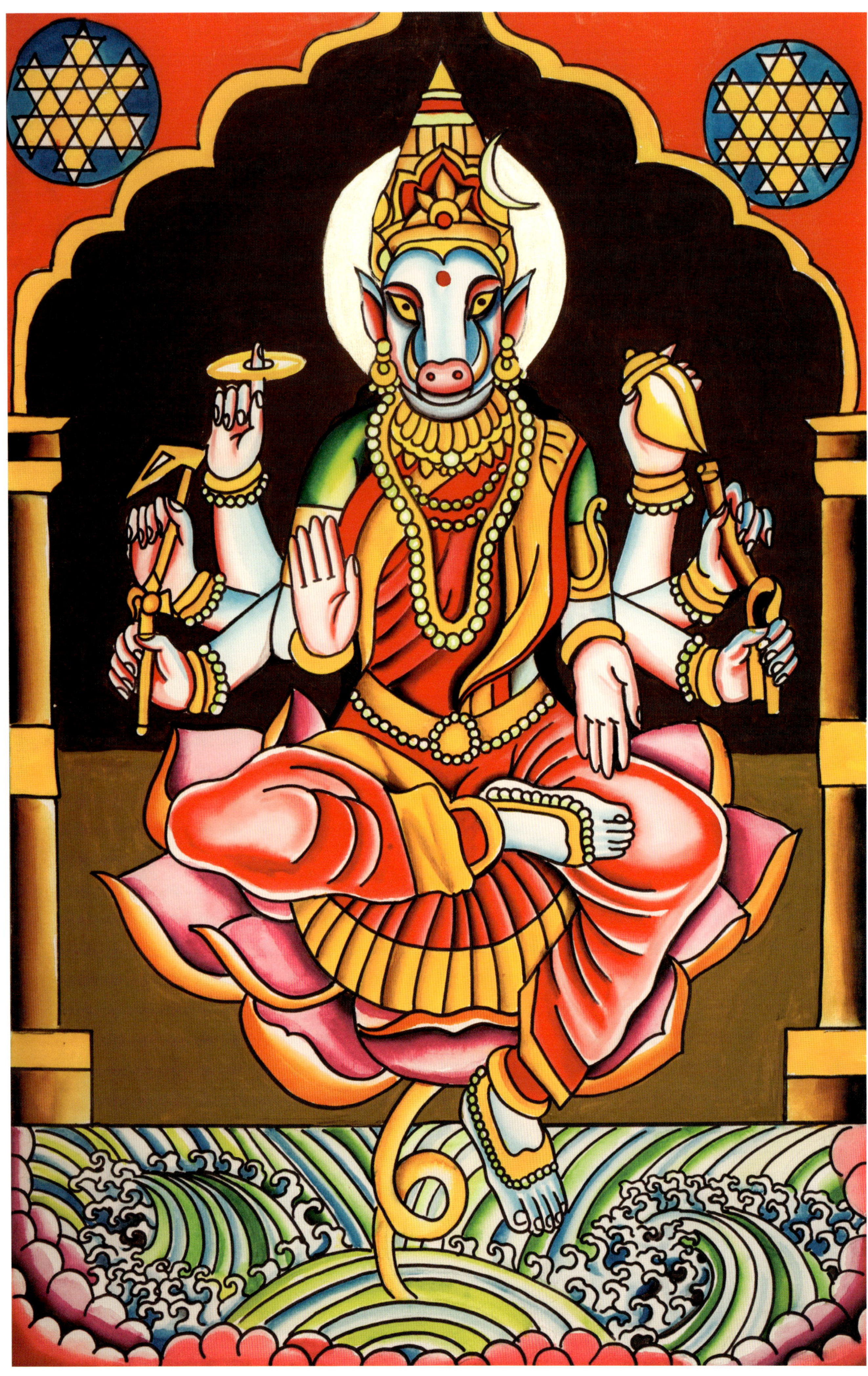

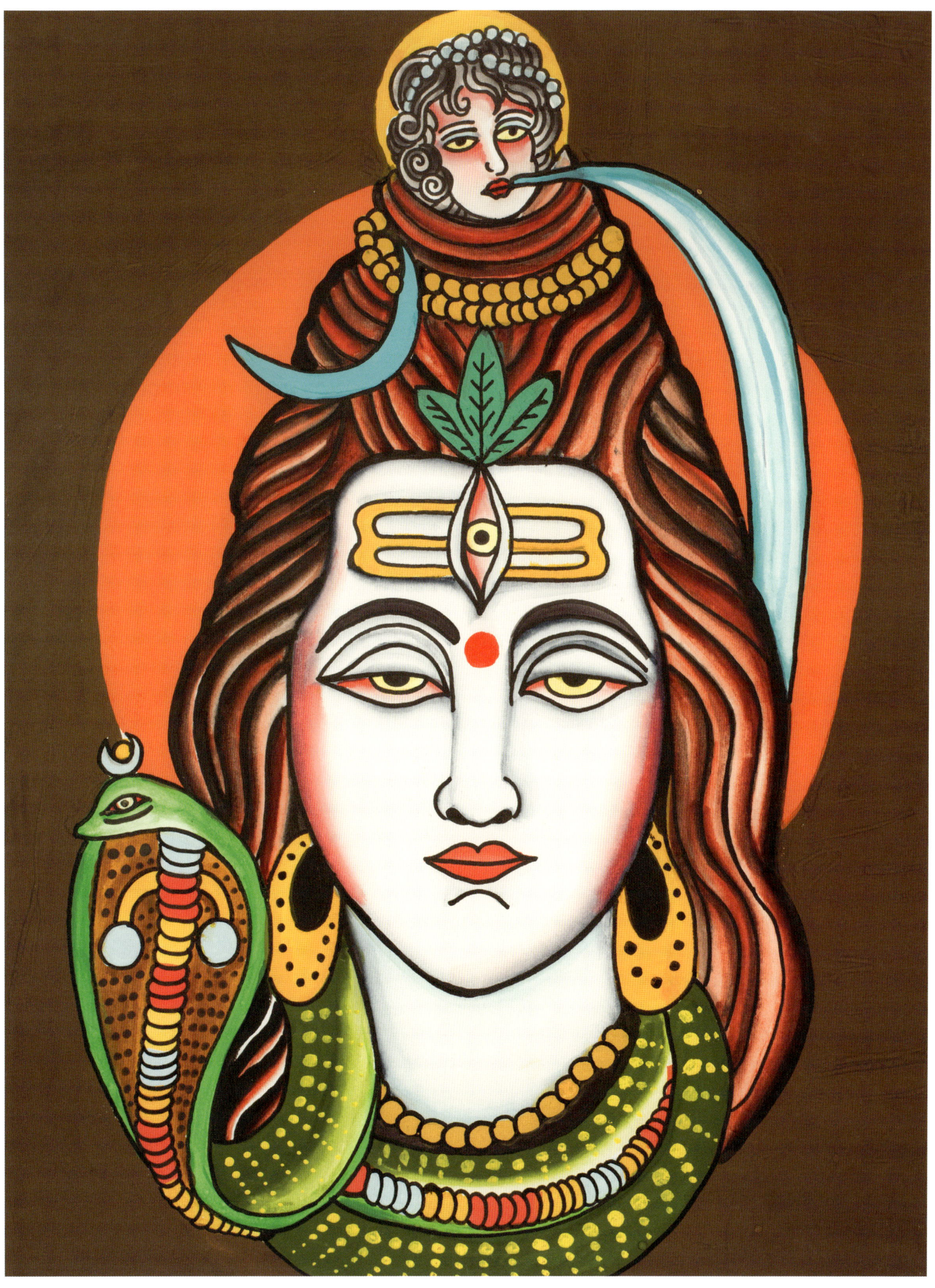

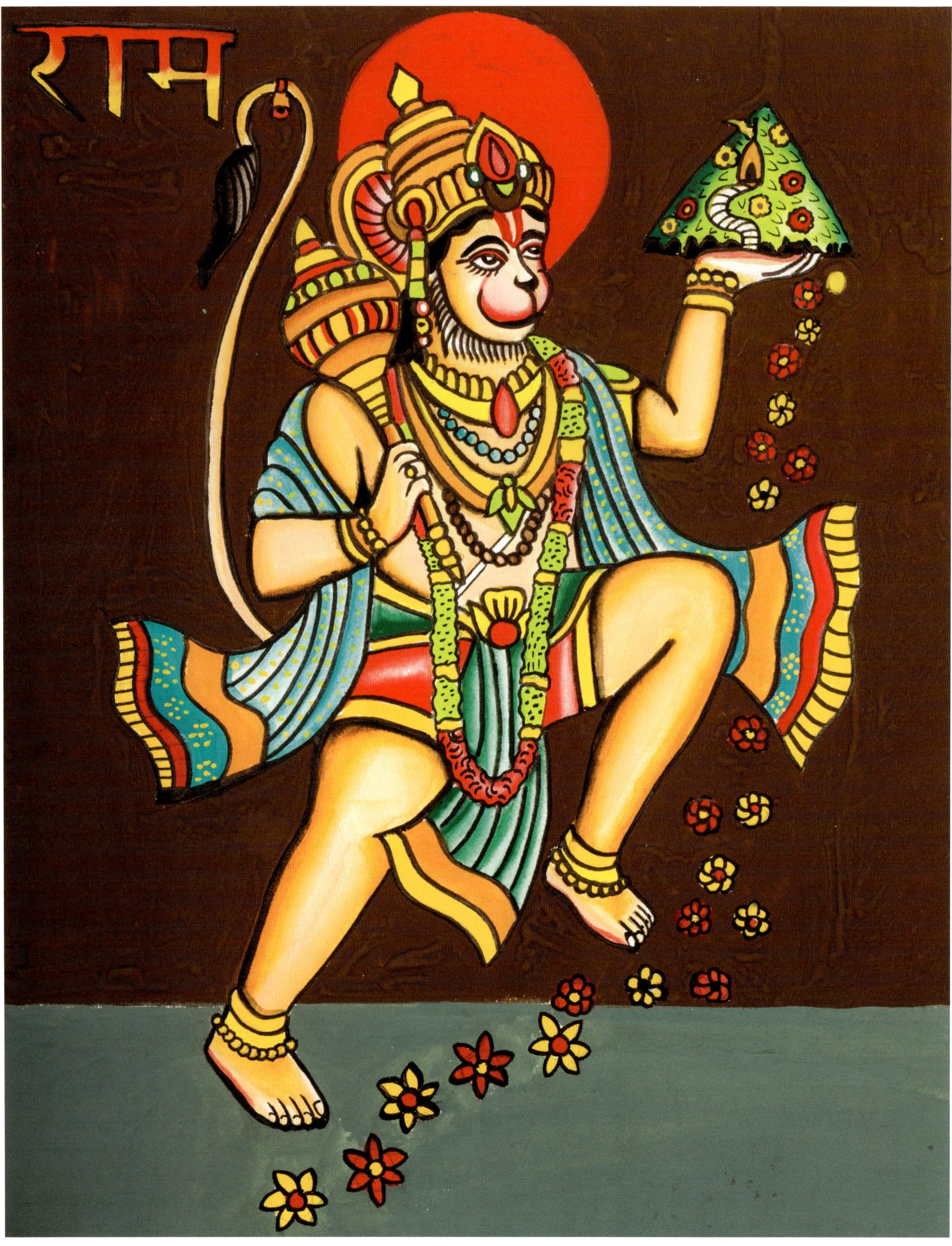
राम

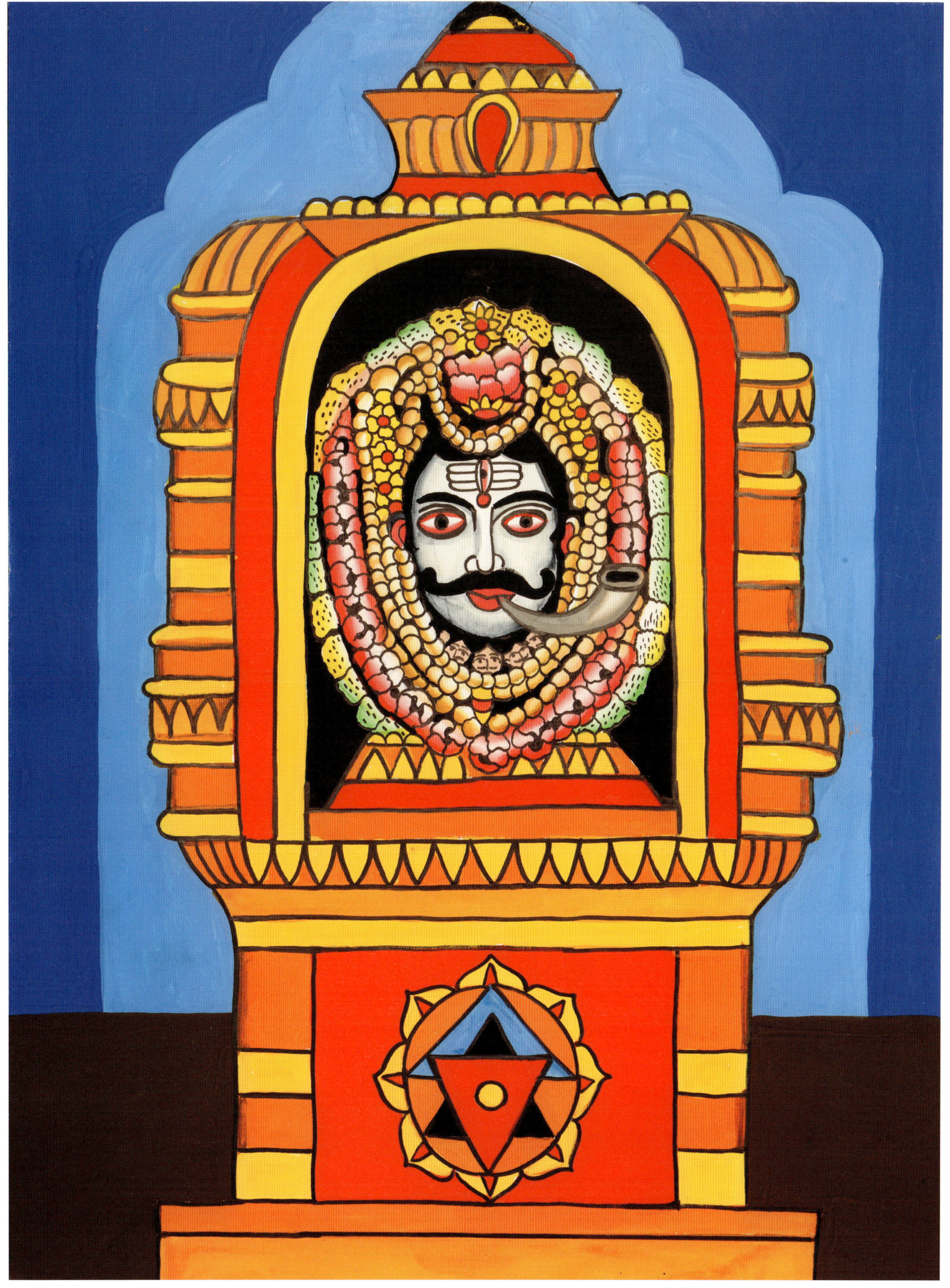

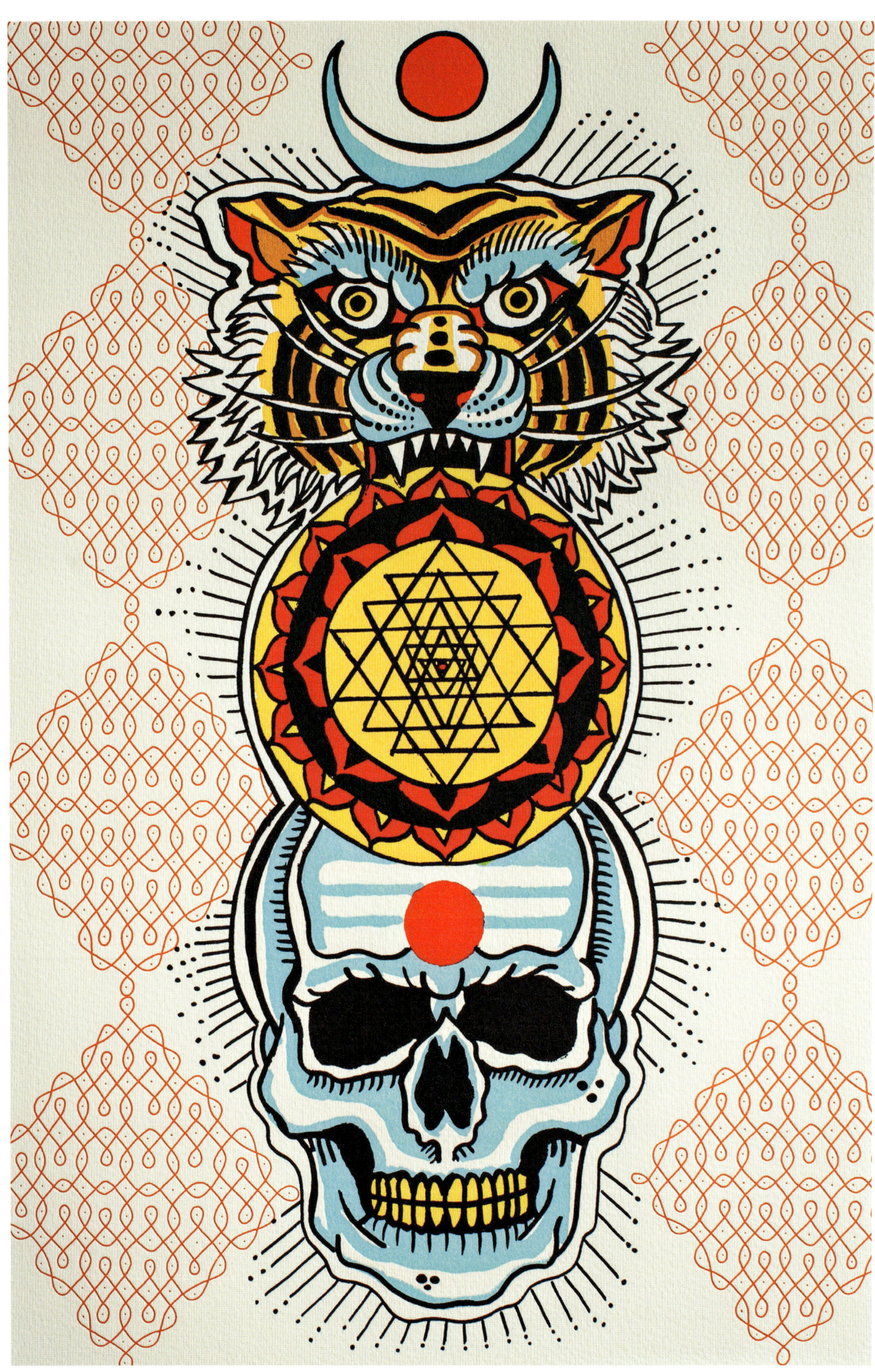

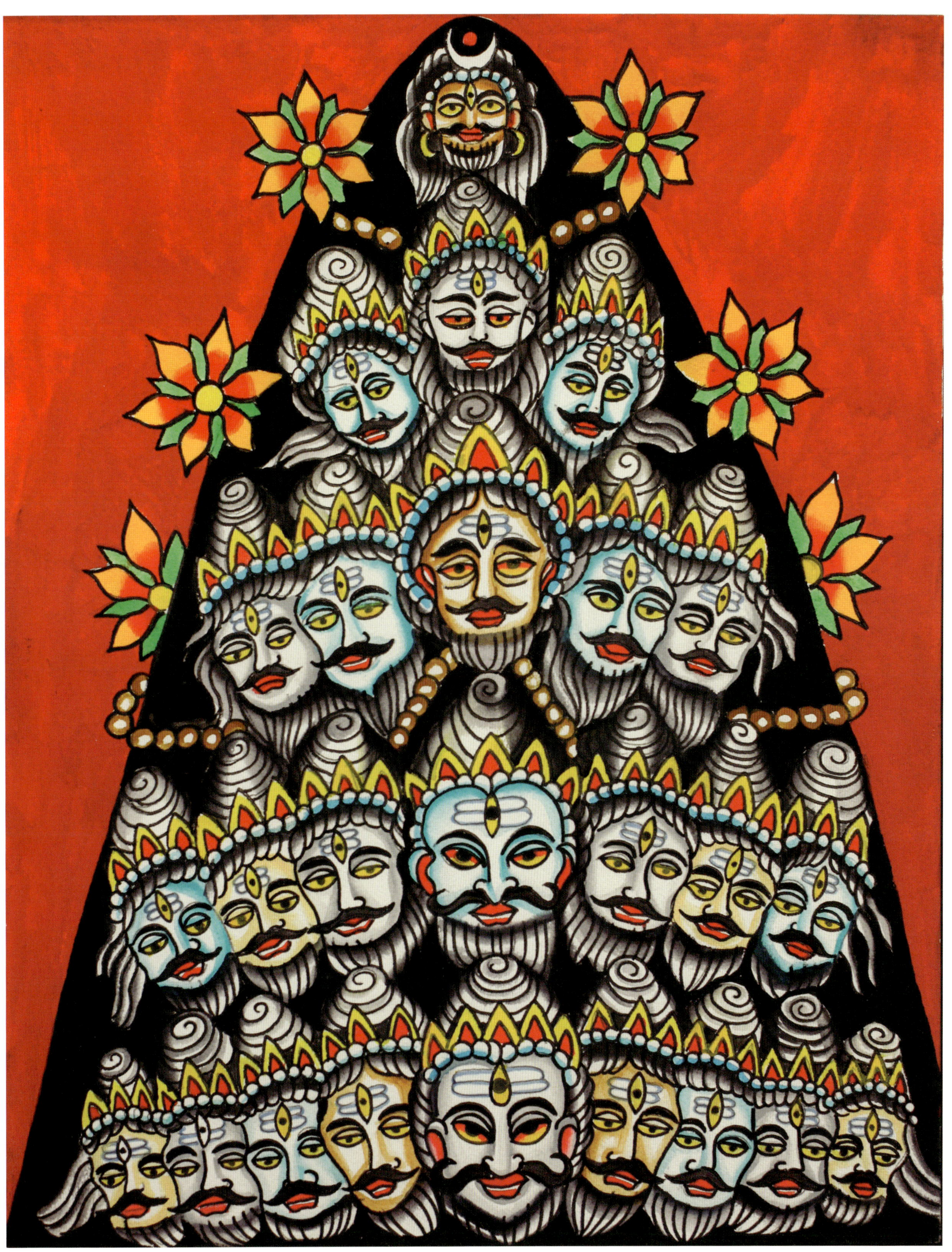

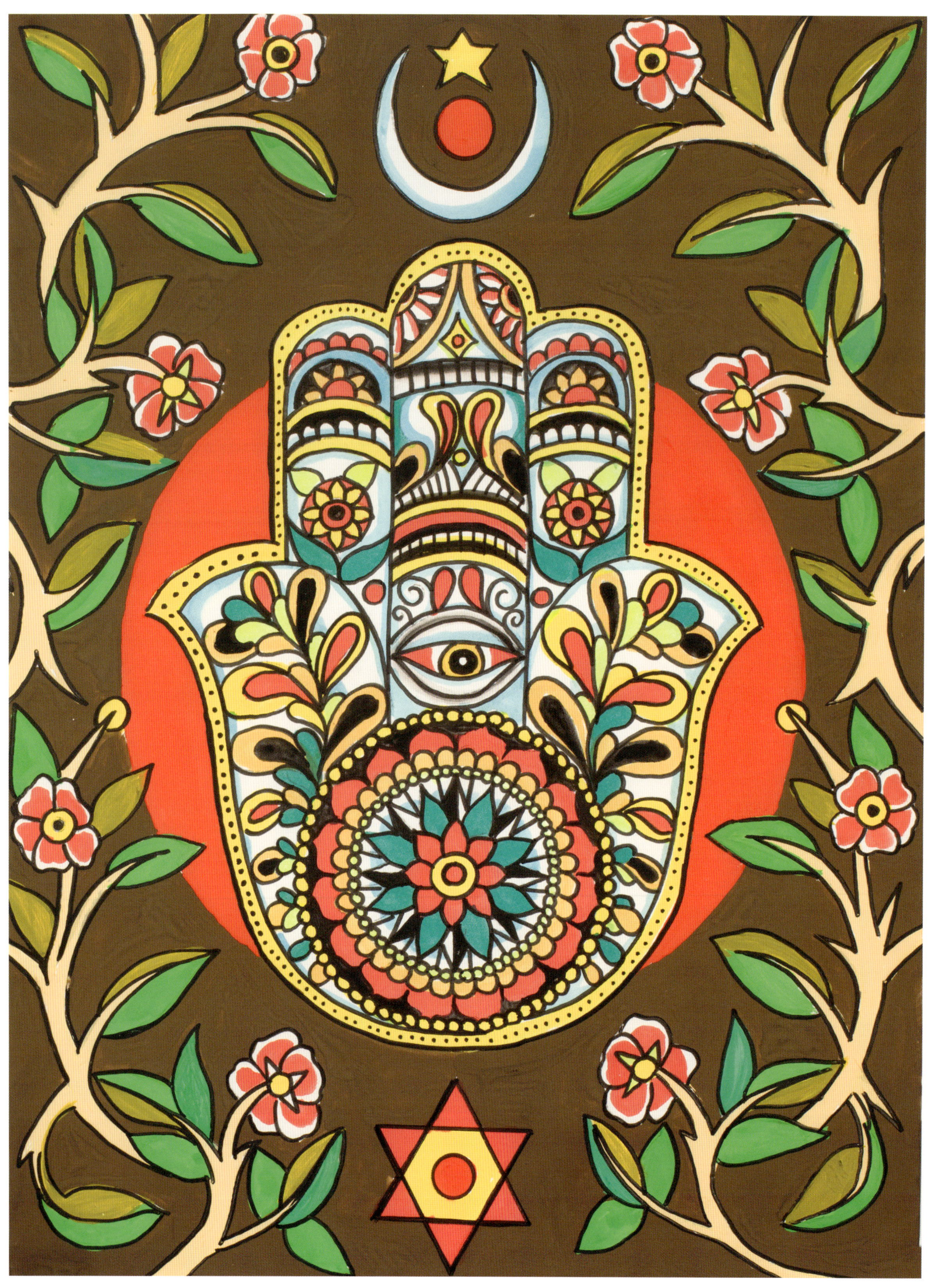

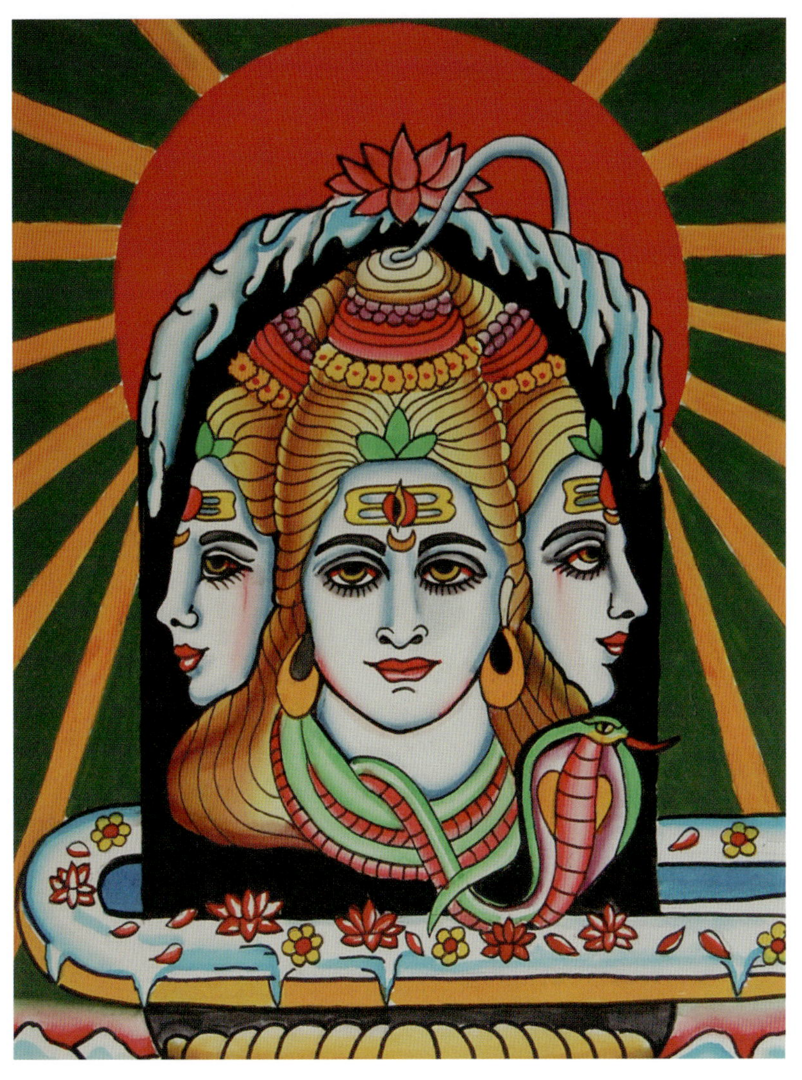
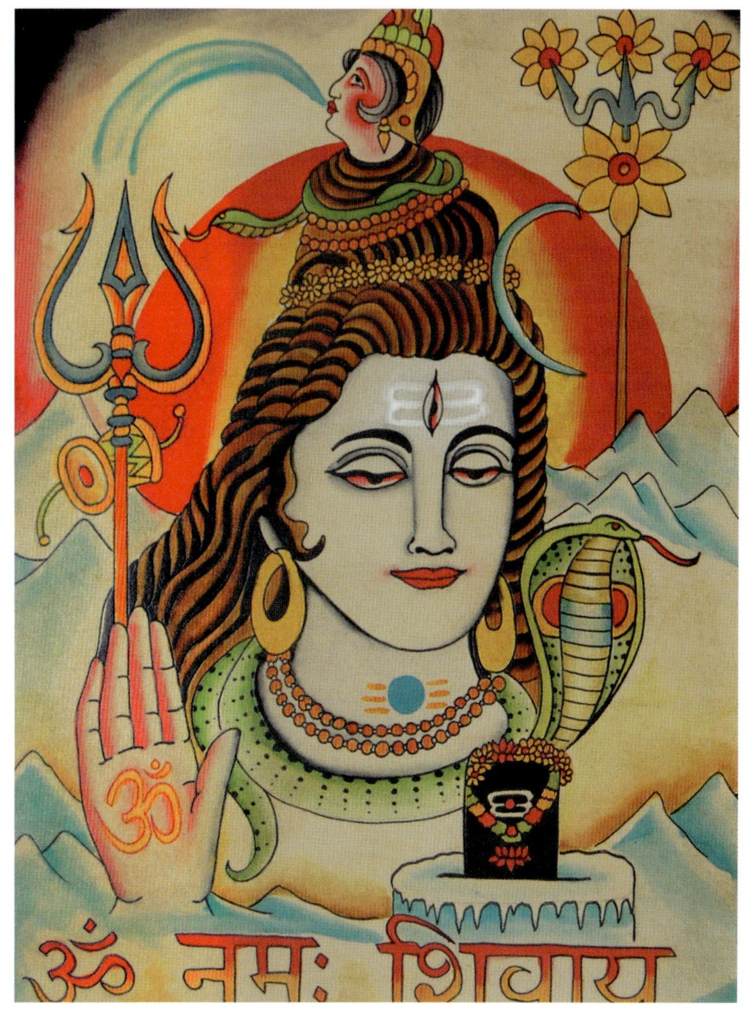
ॐ नमः शिवाय
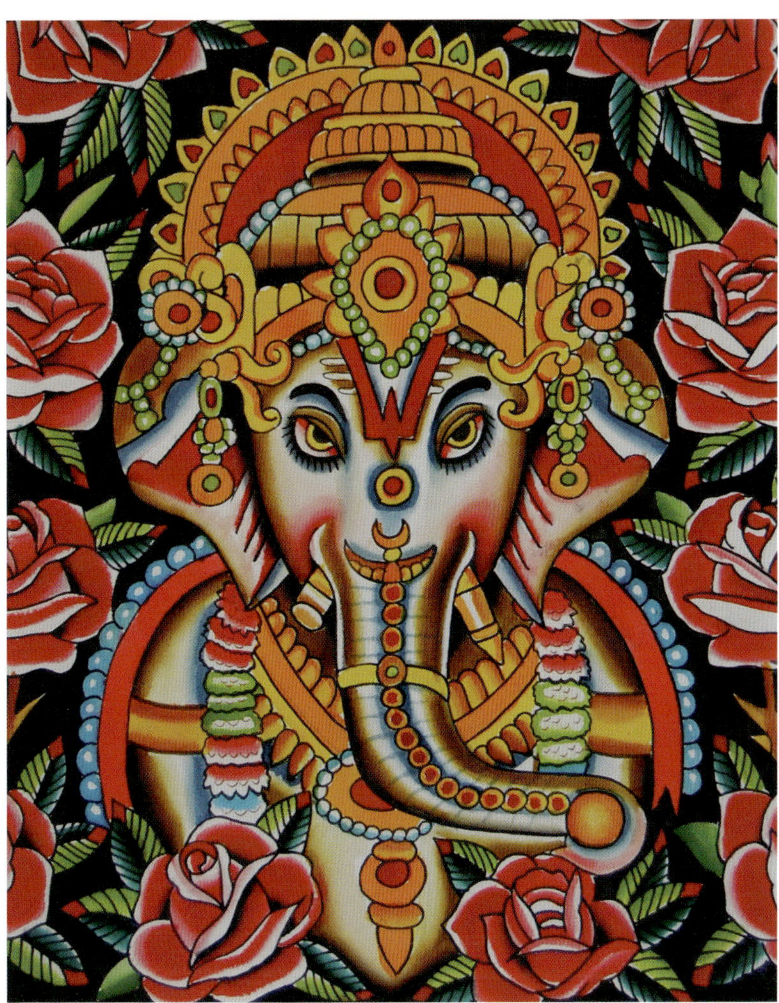
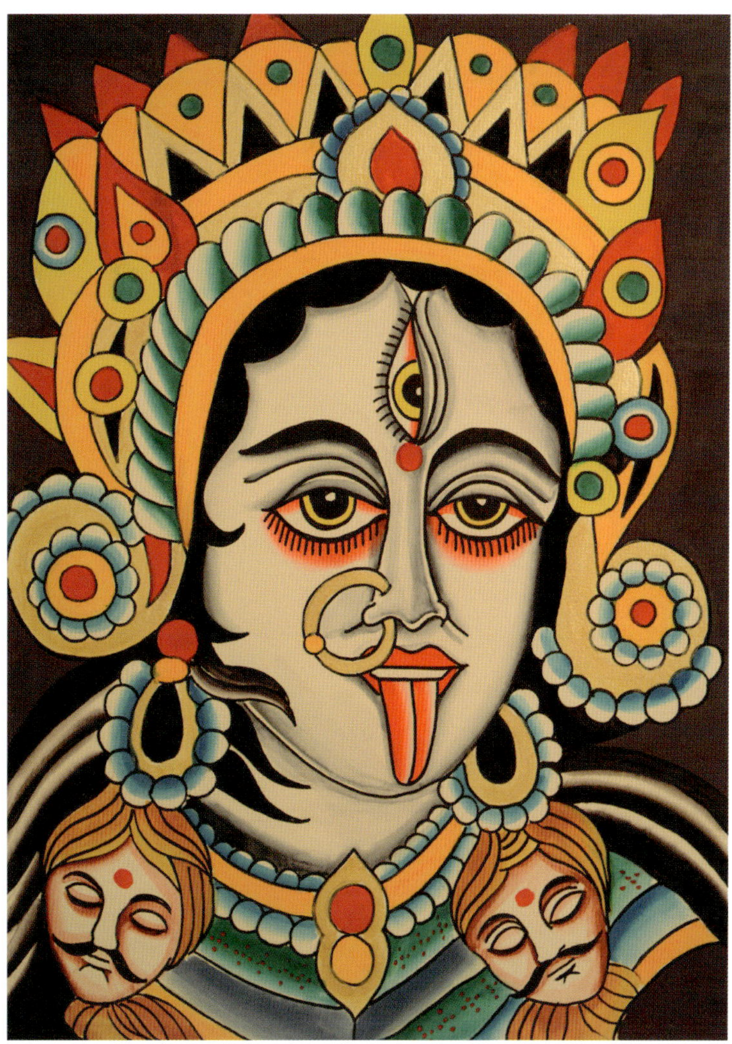

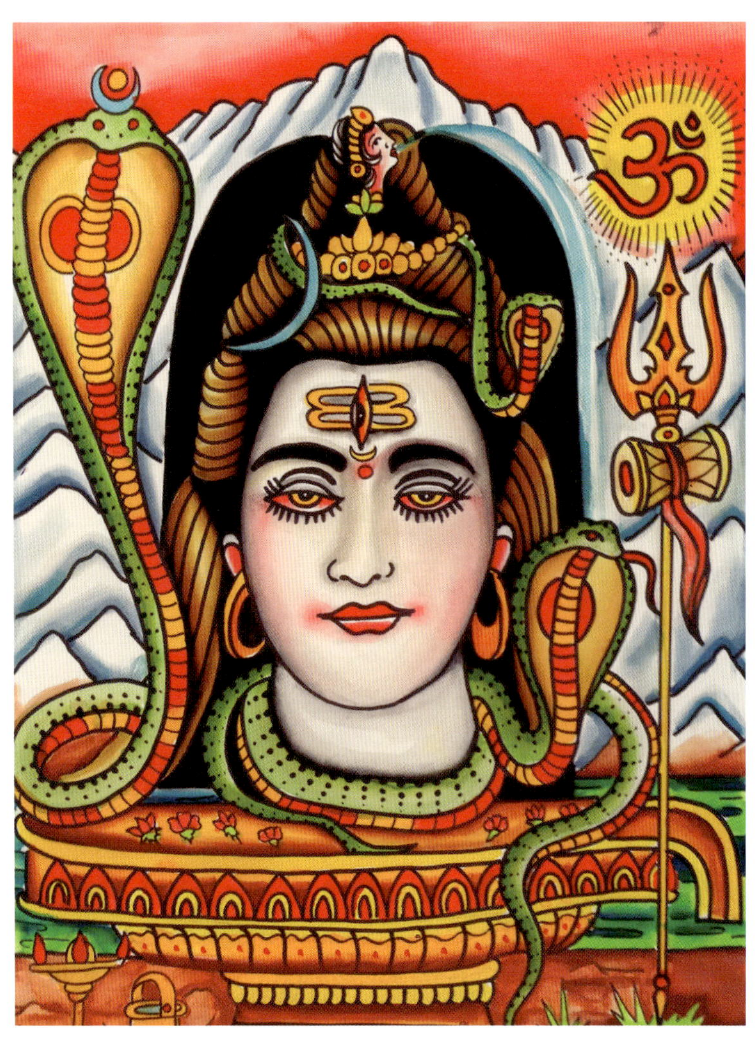
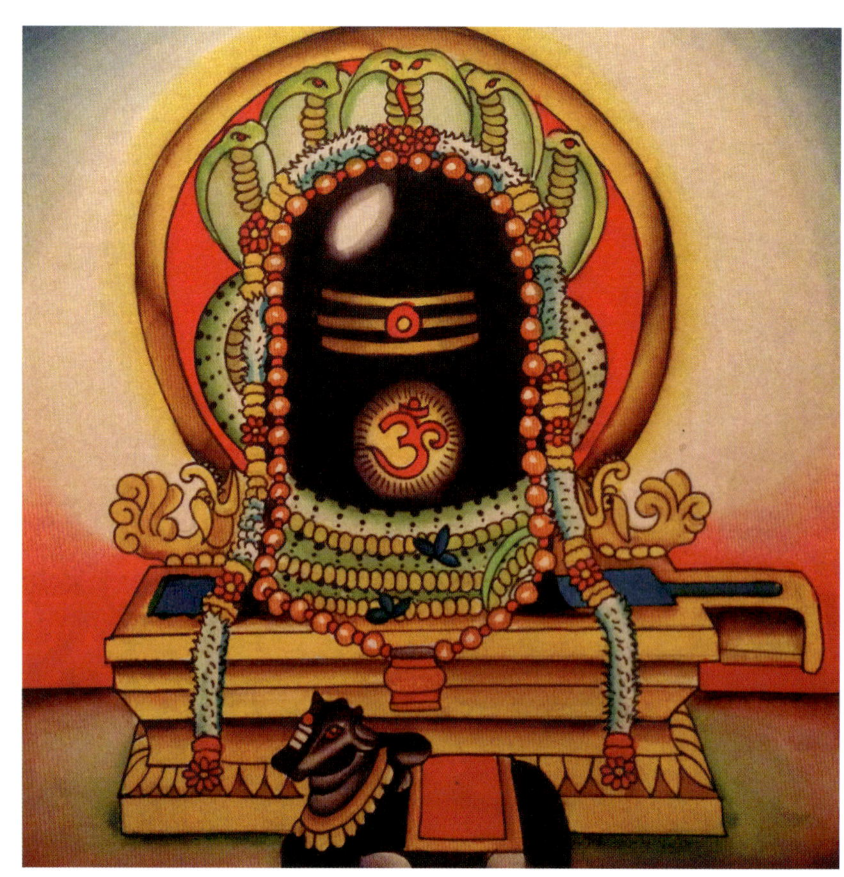
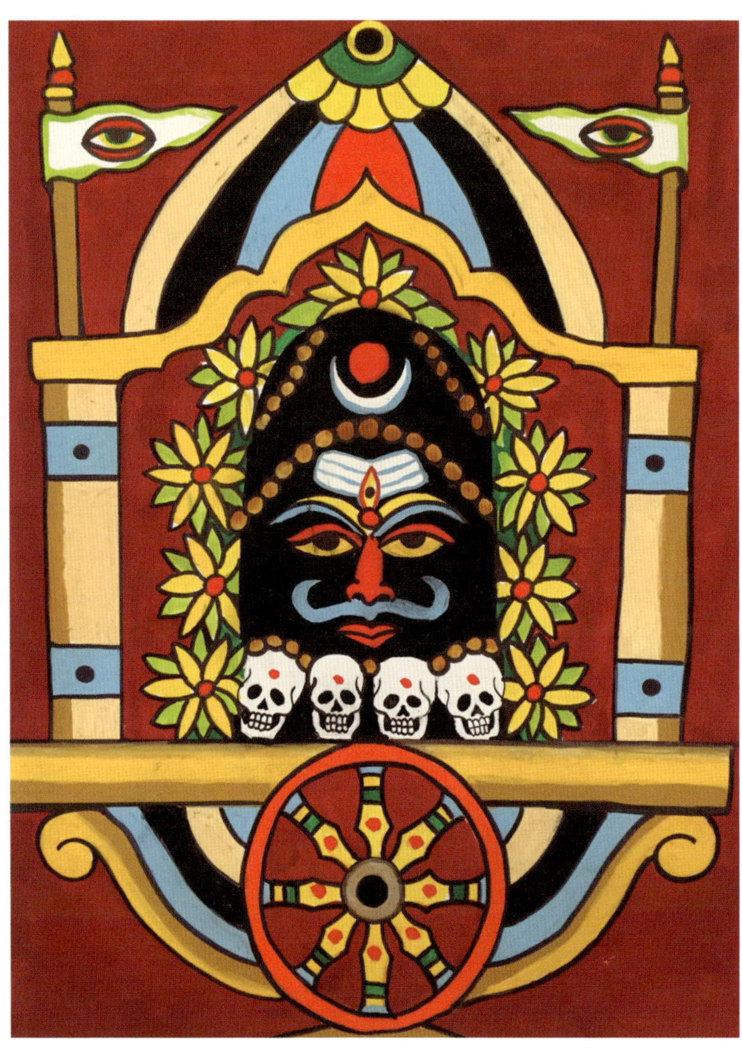
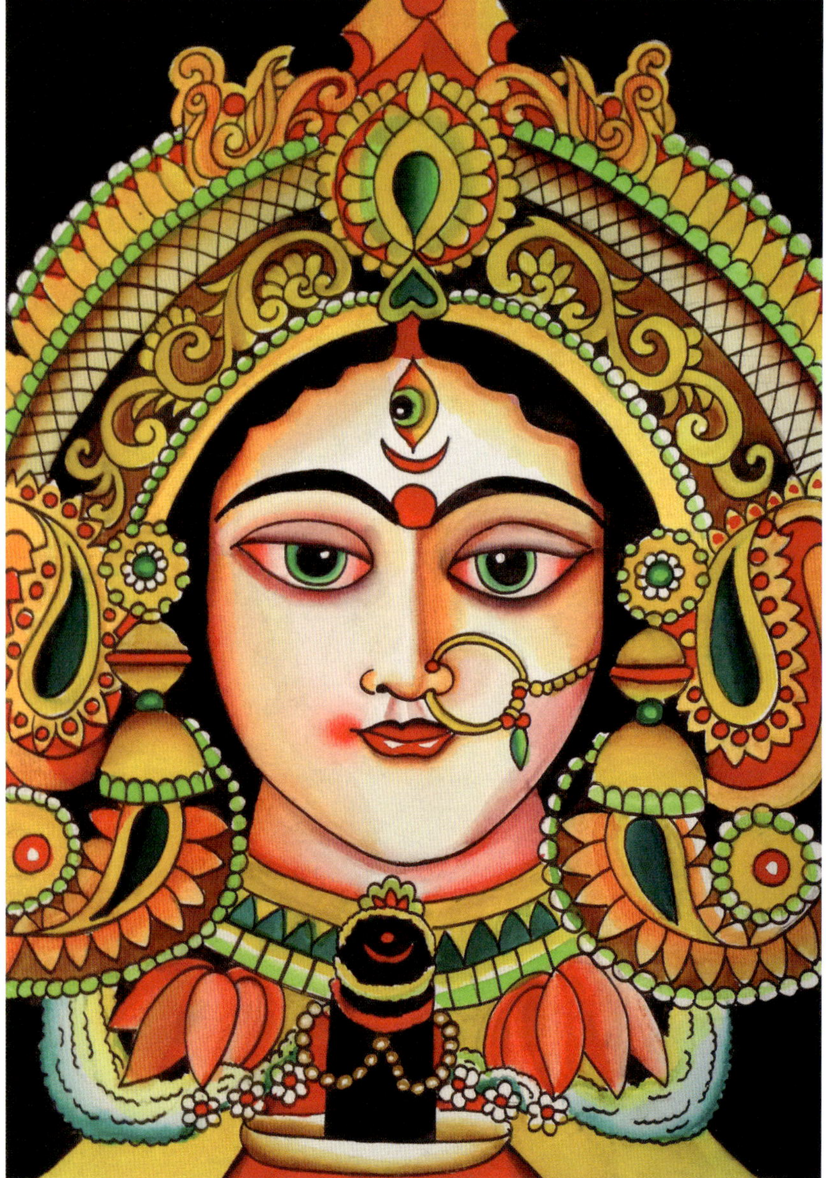

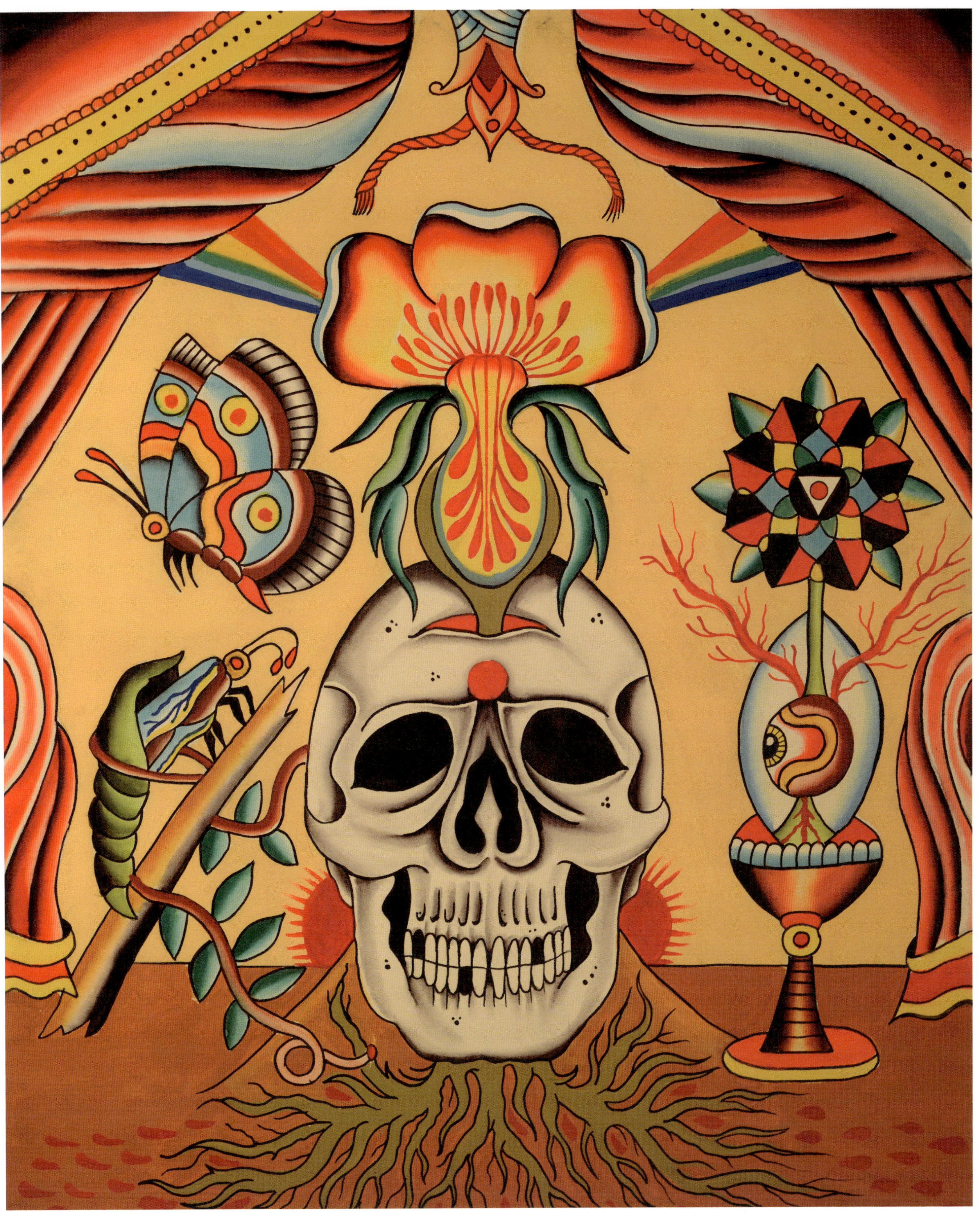

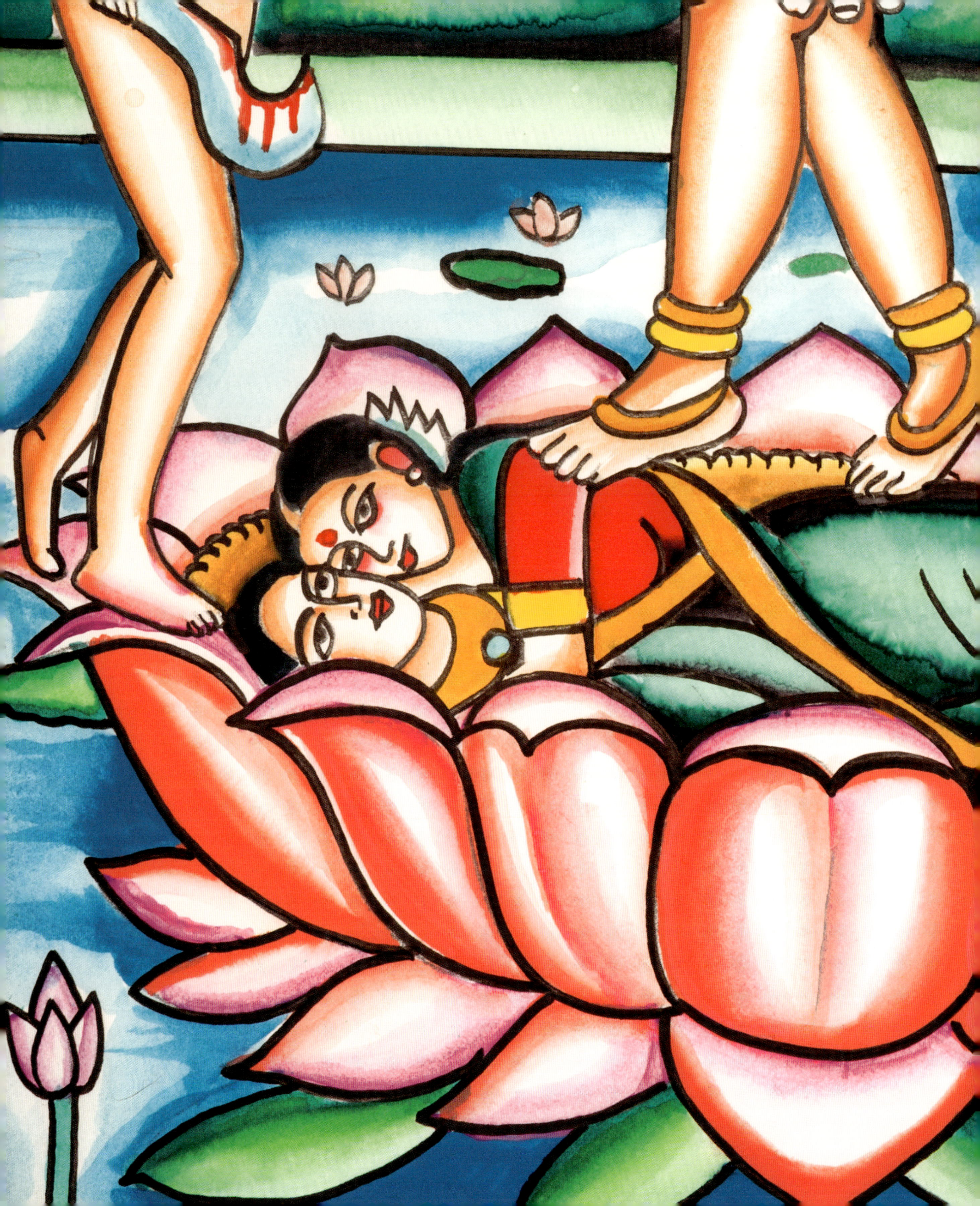

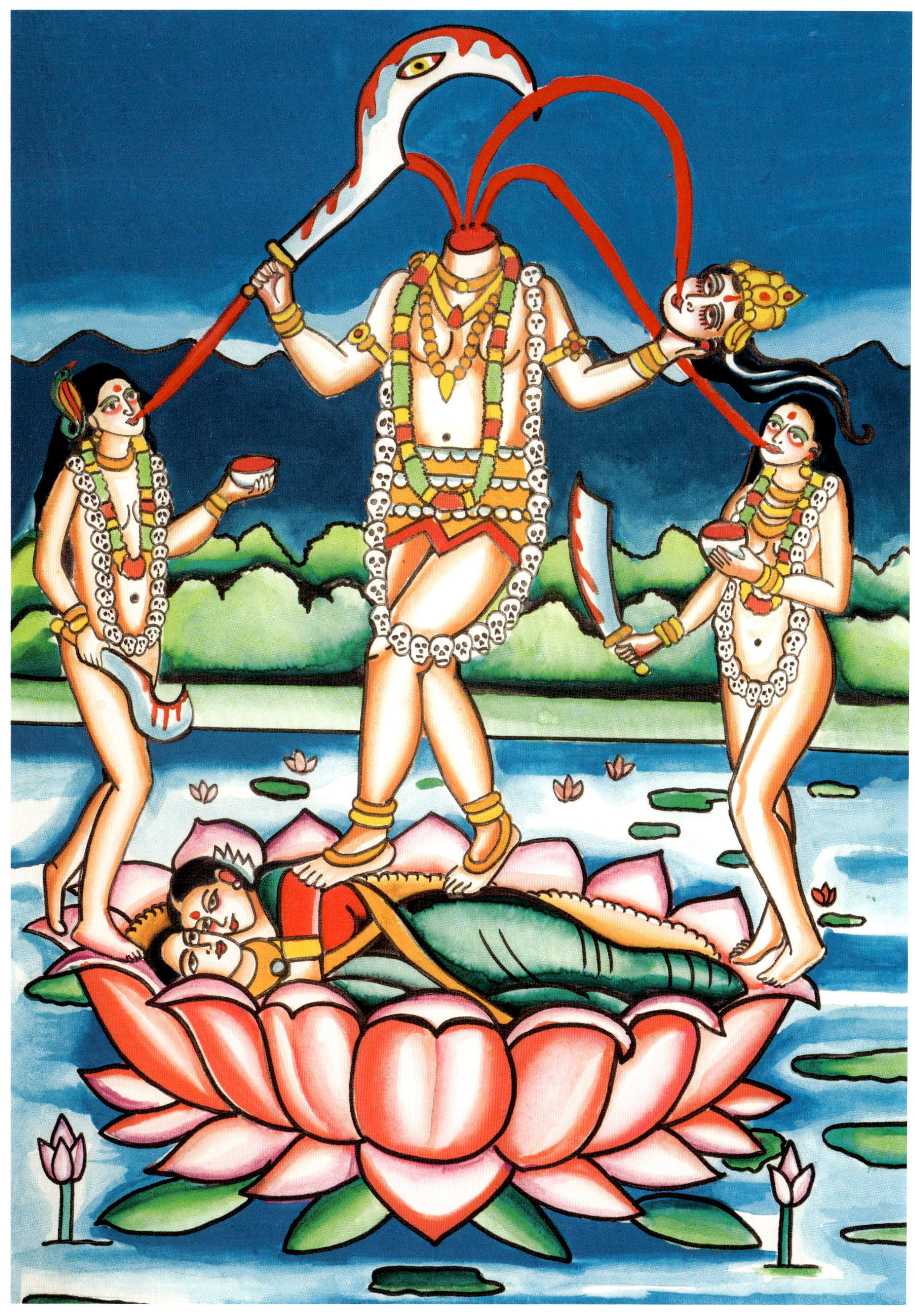

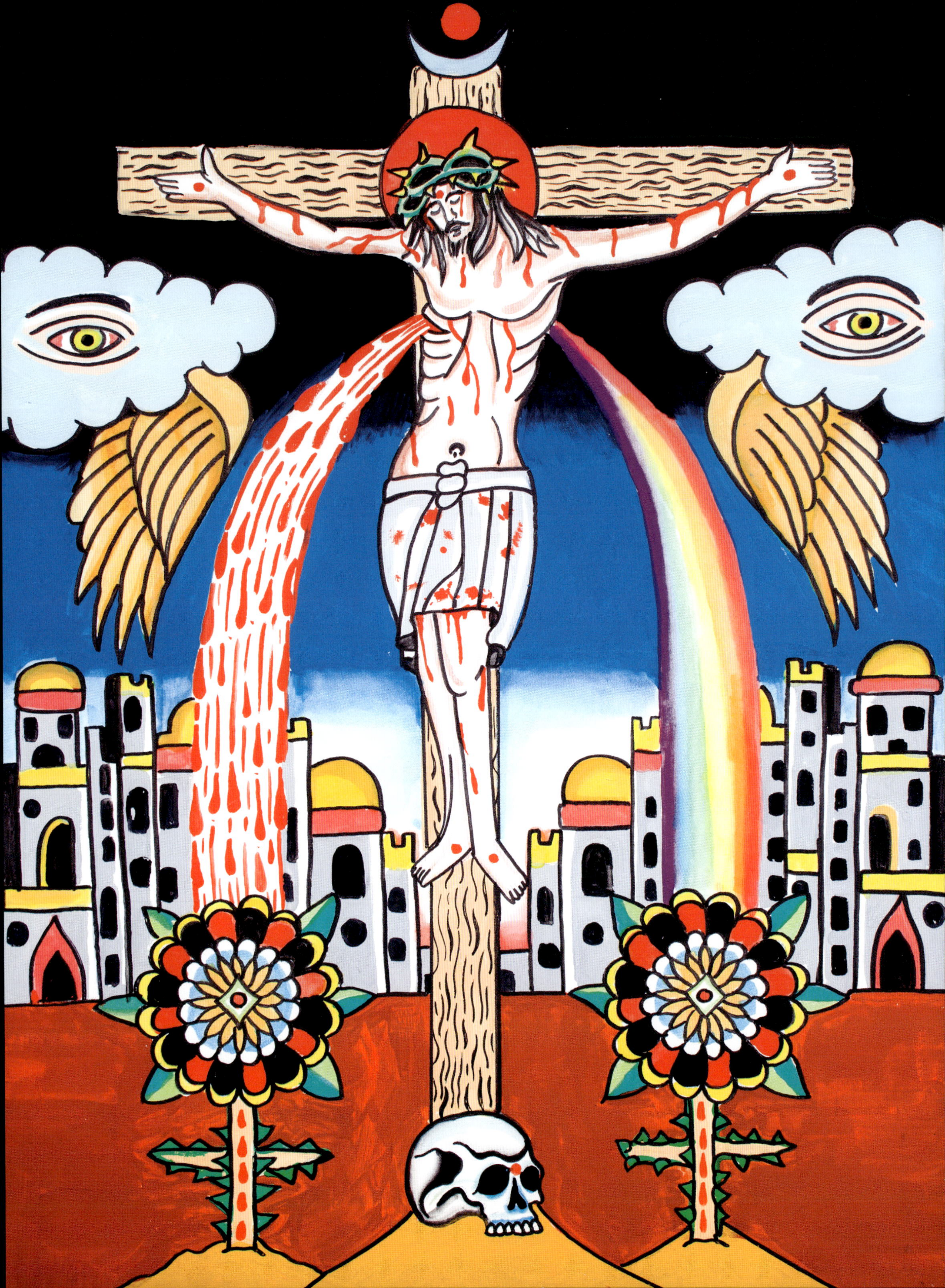

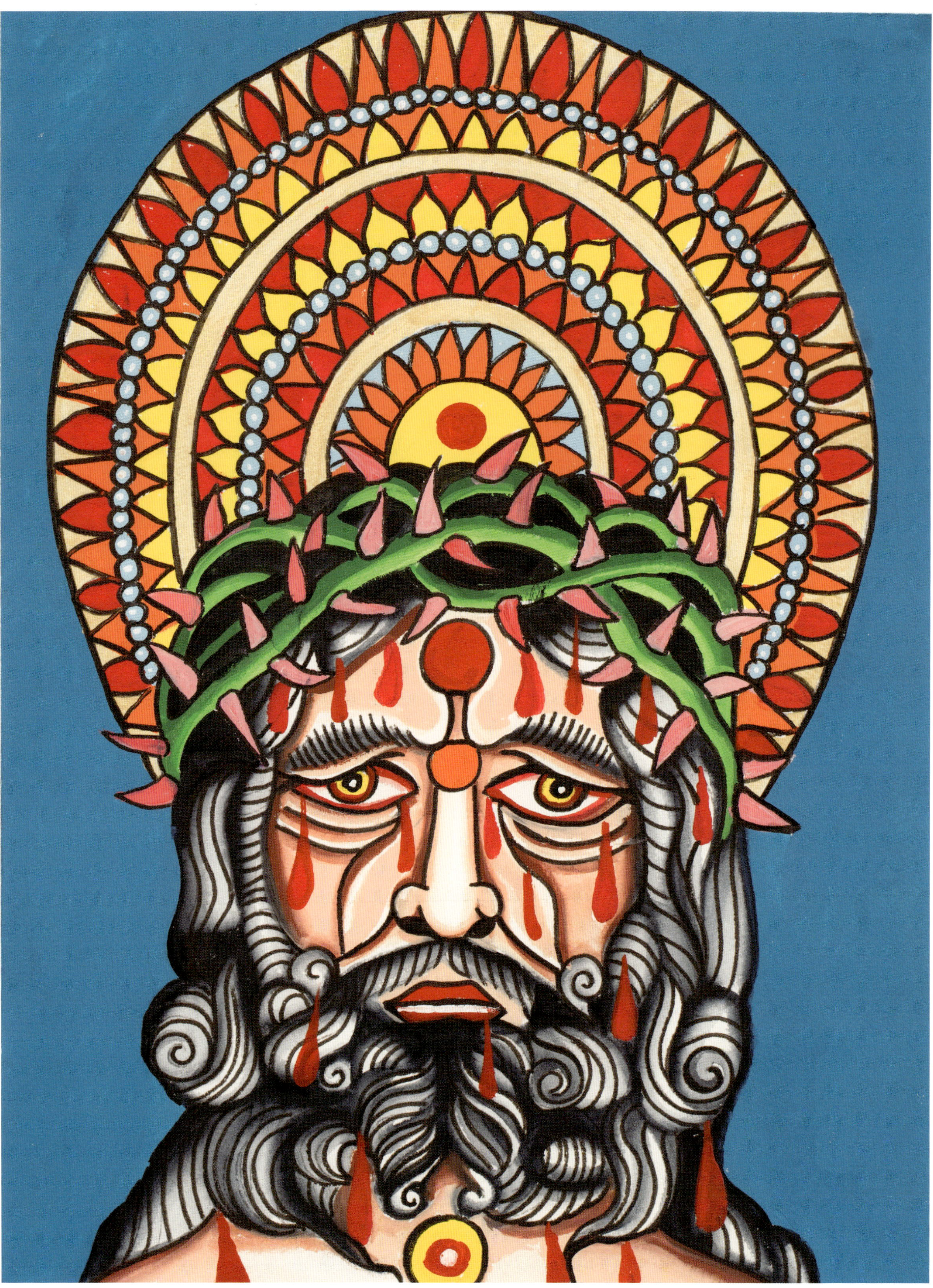

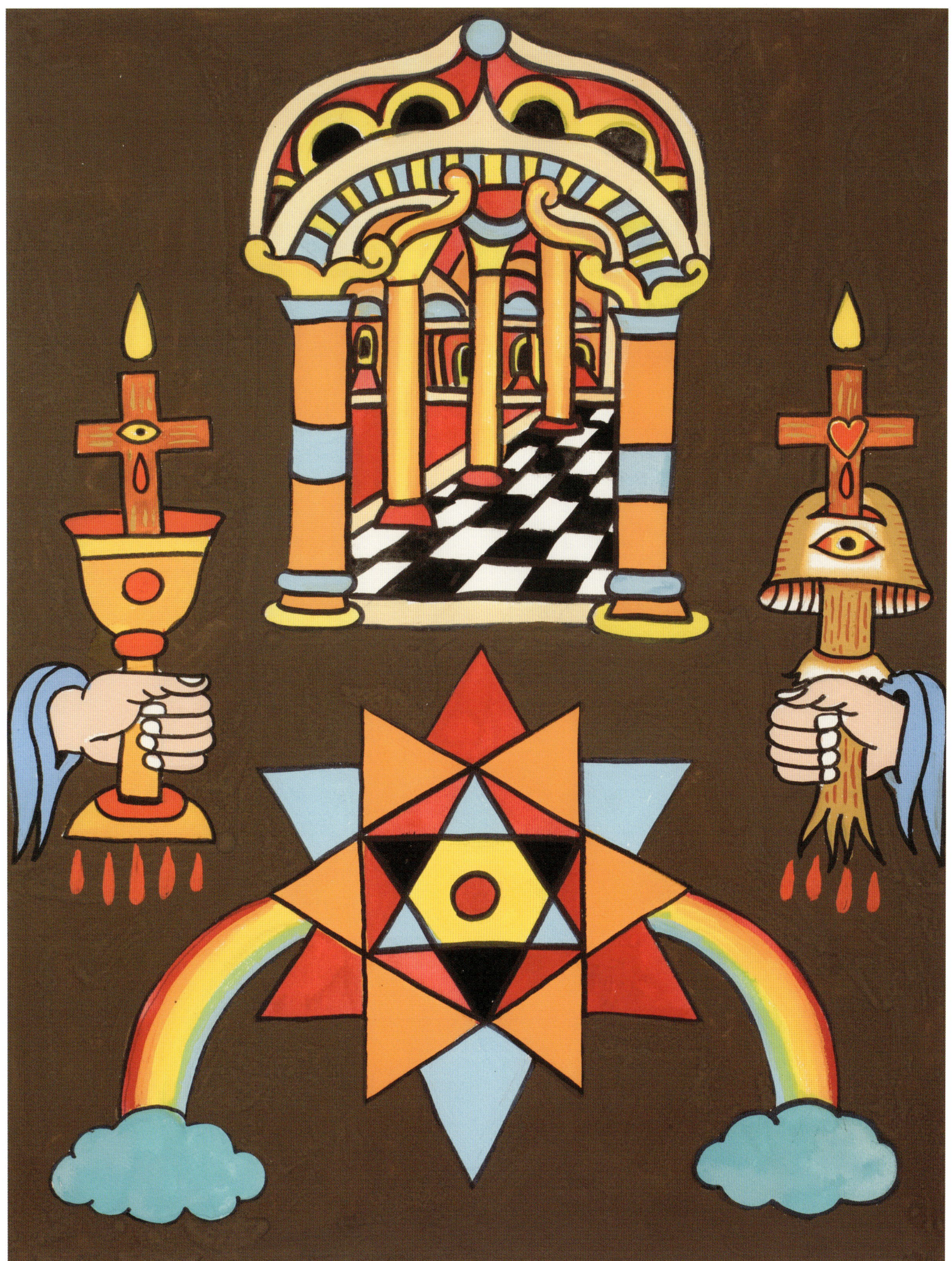

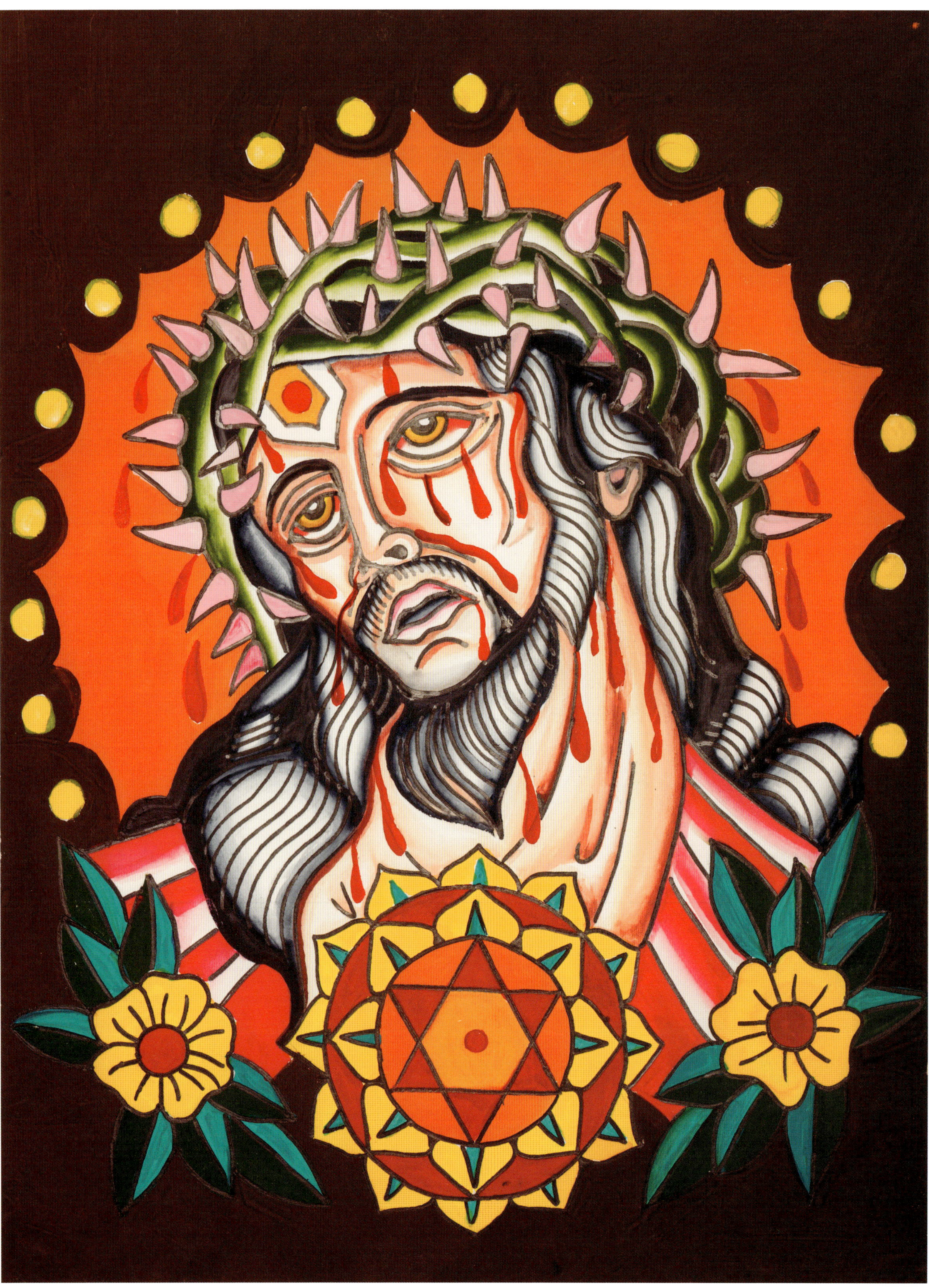

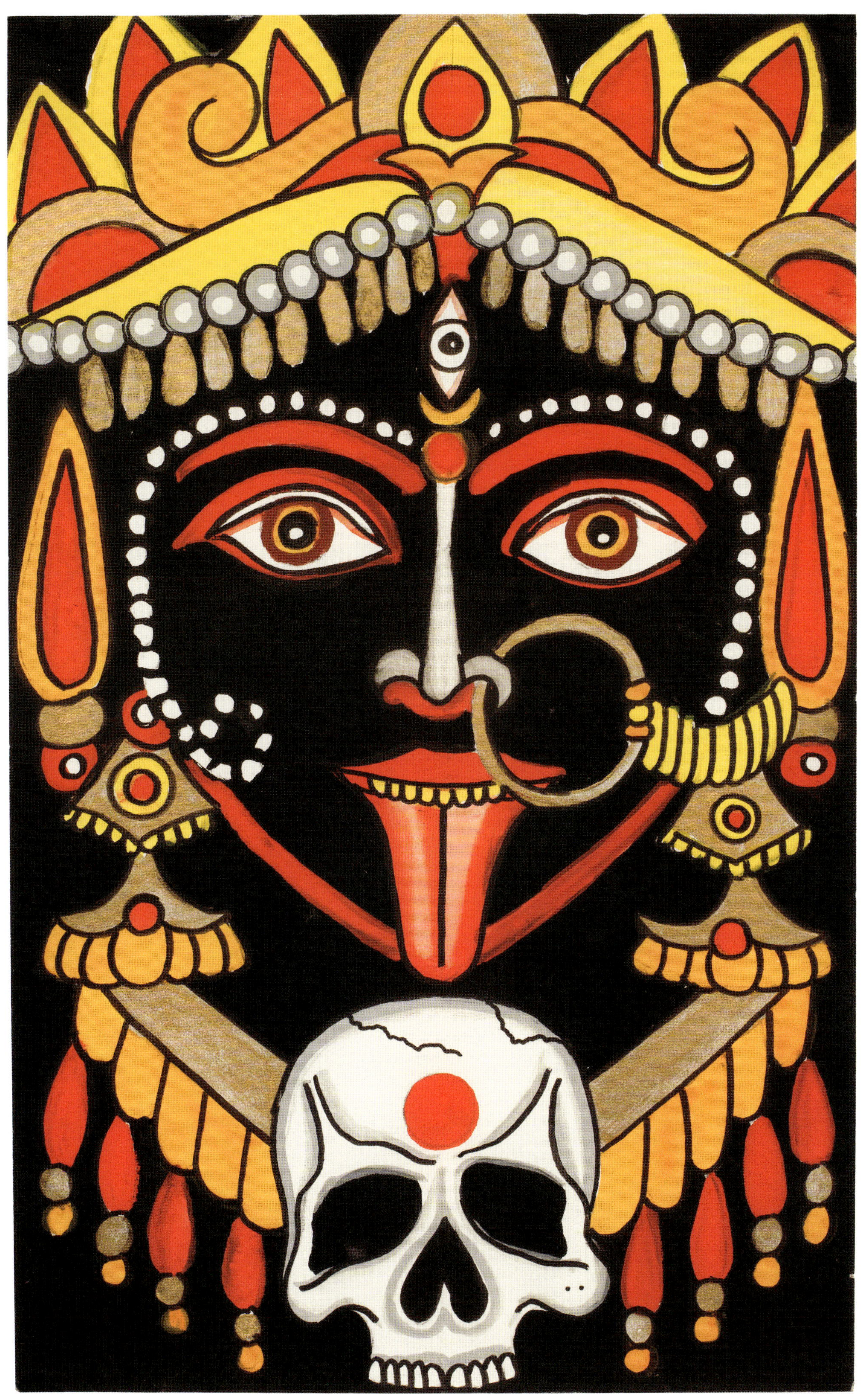

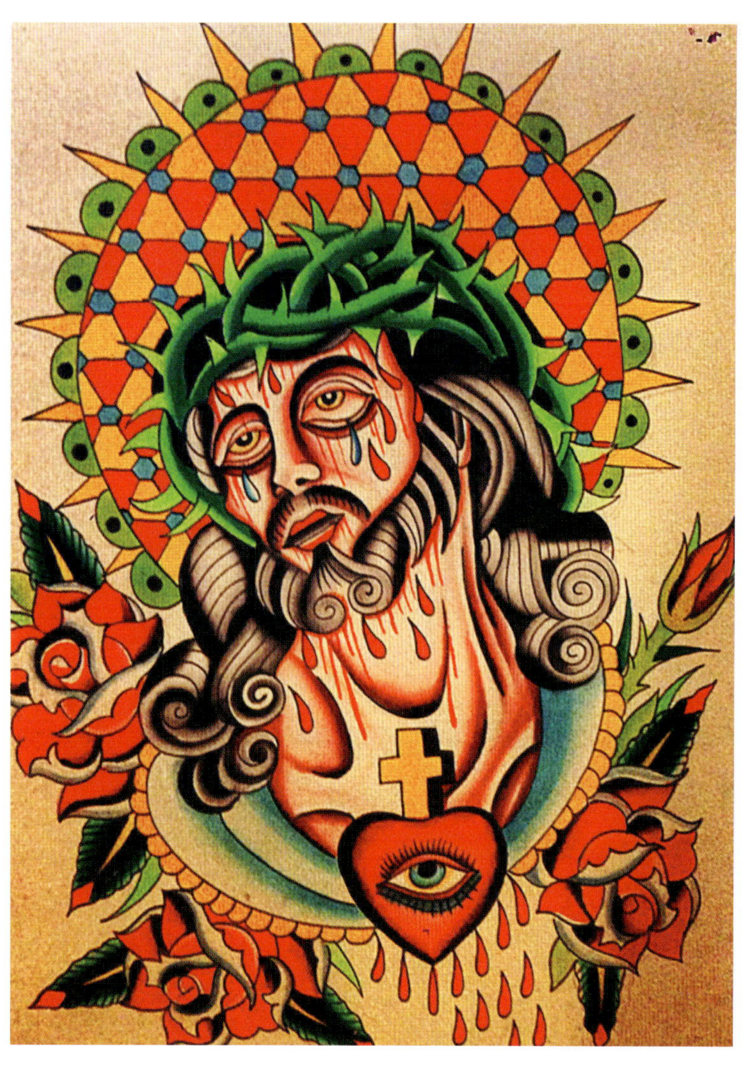

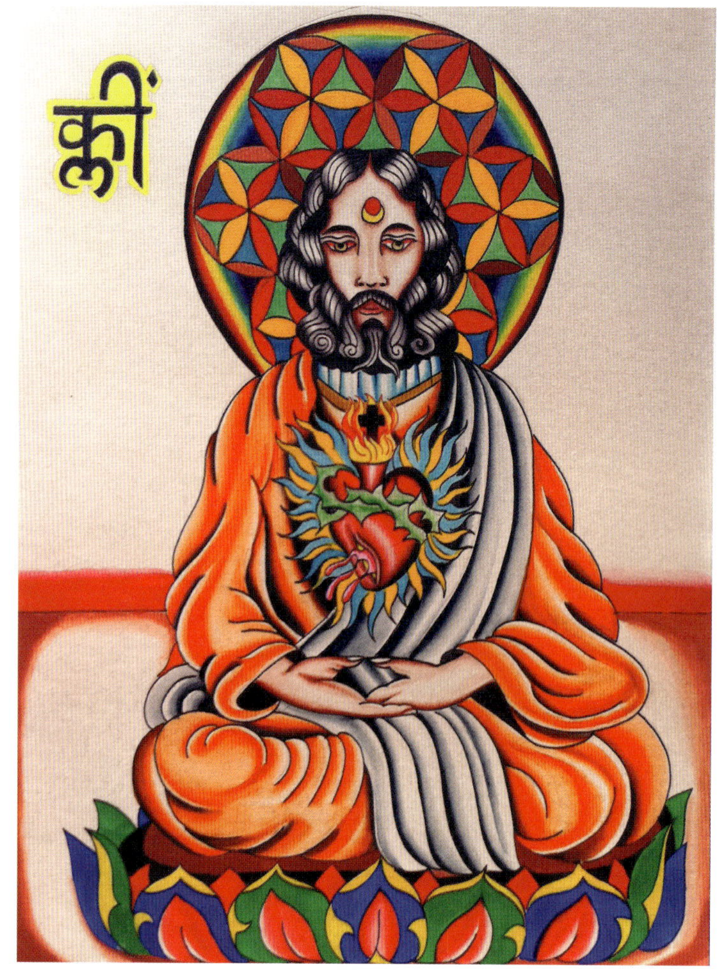
क्रीं

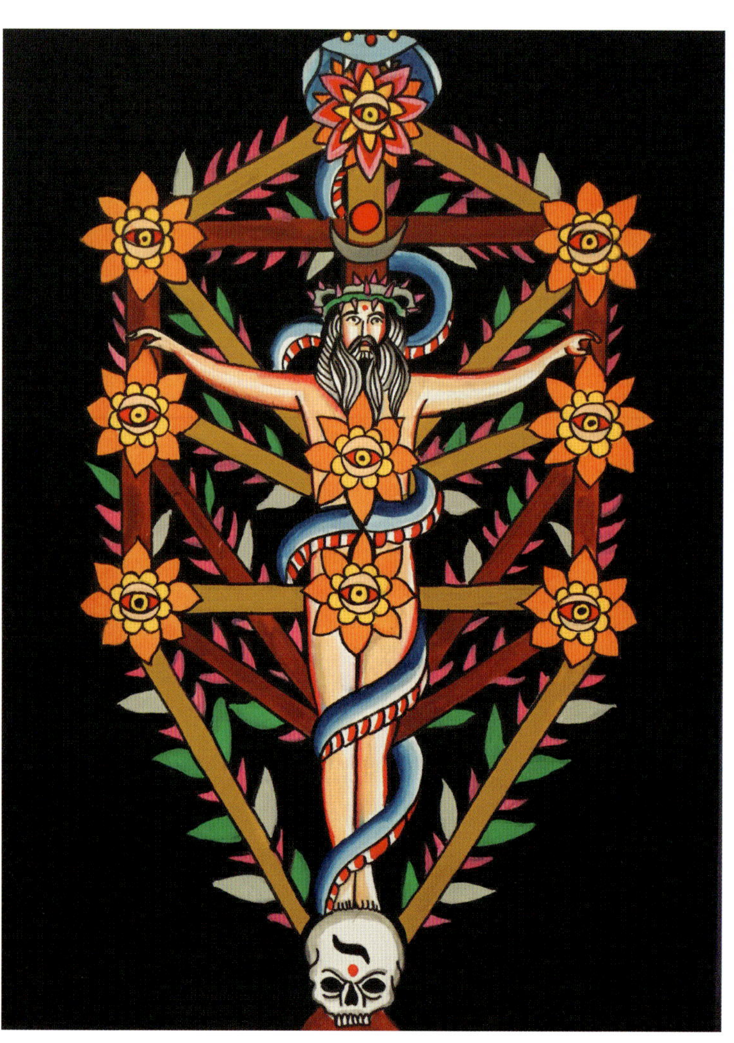

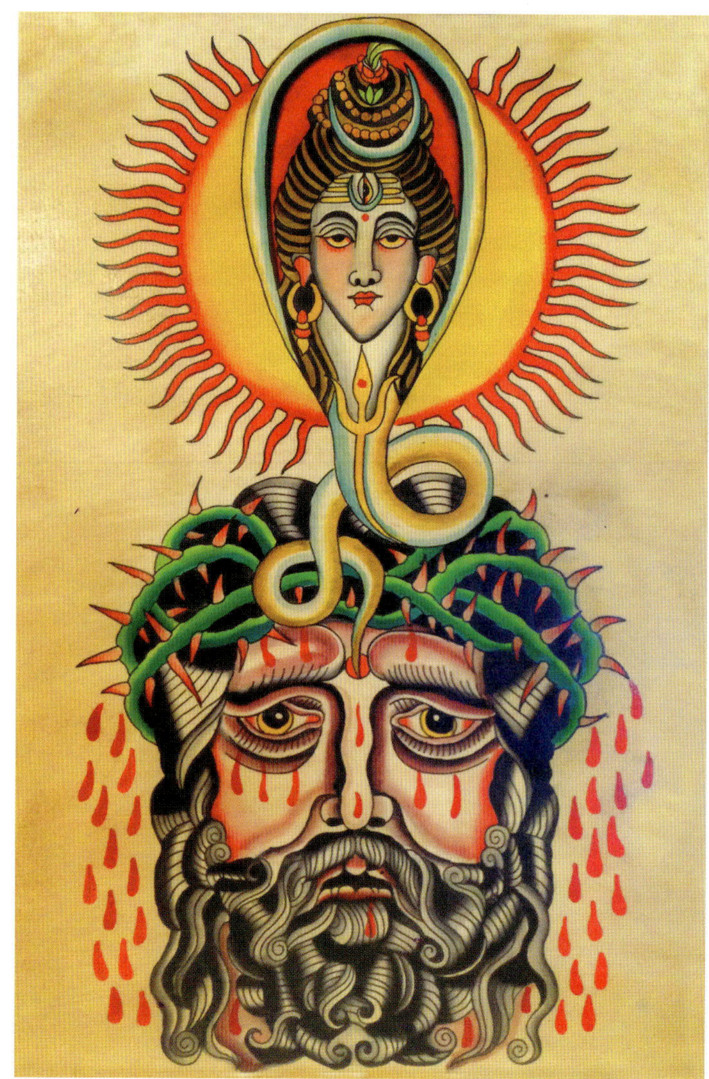

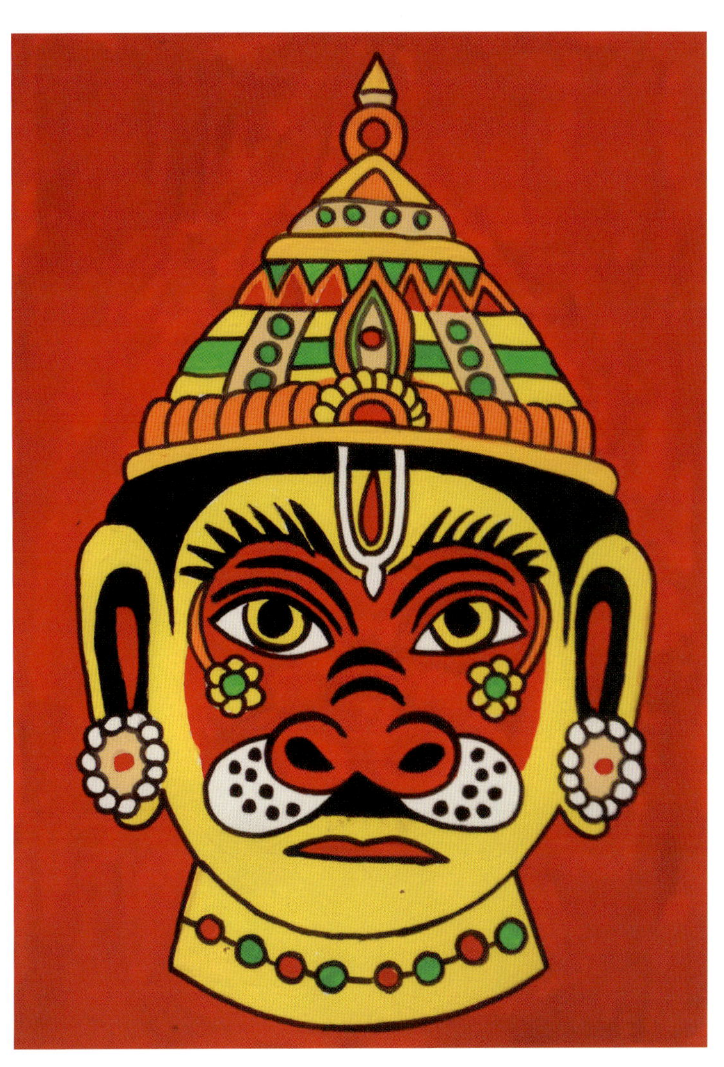

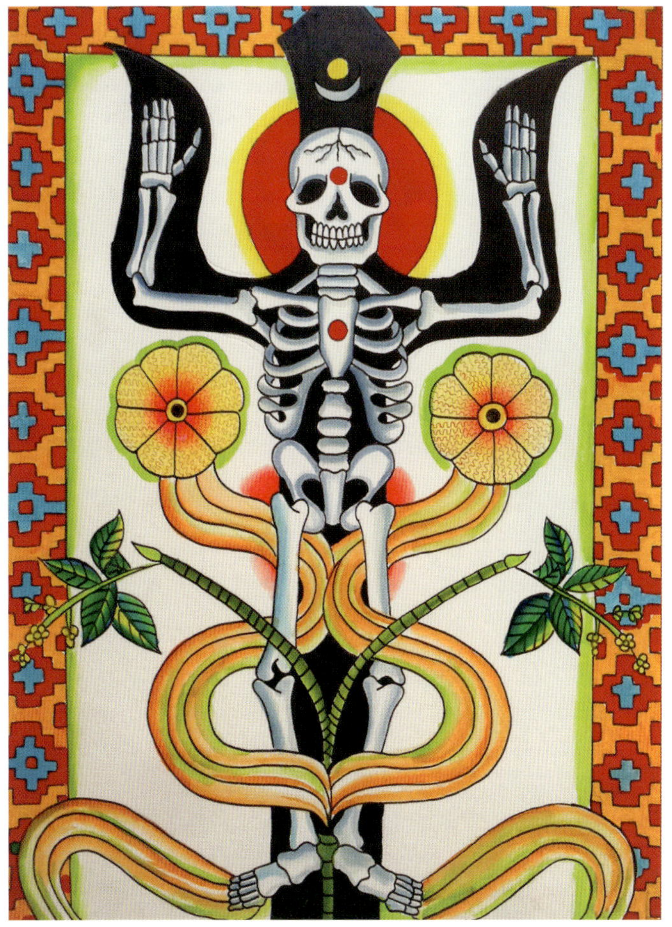

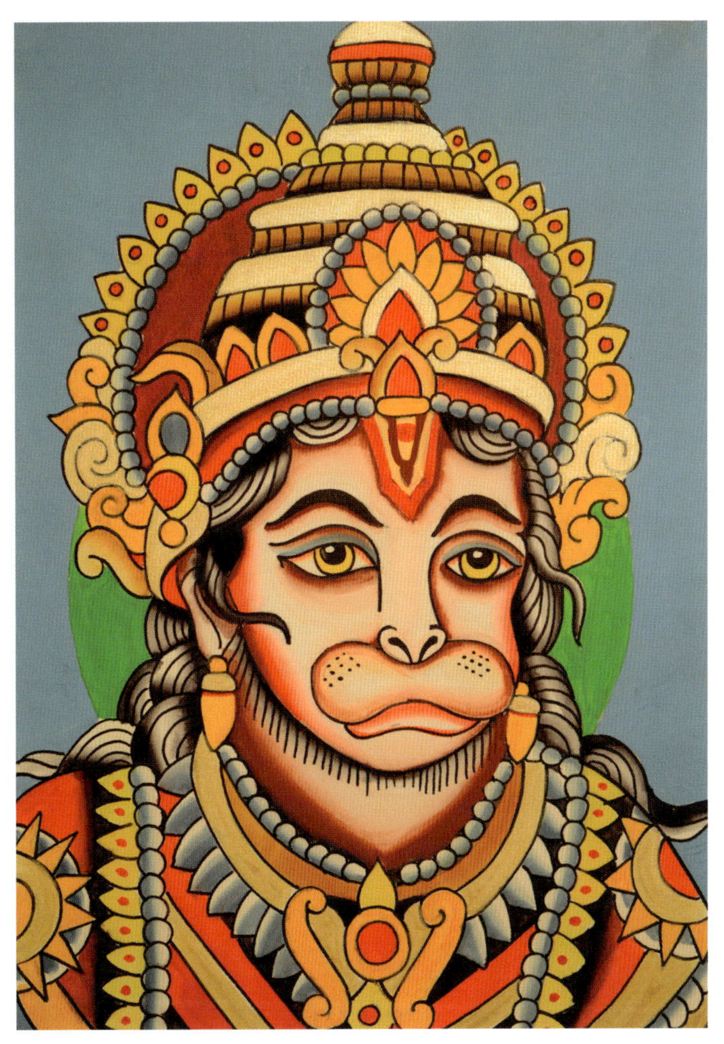

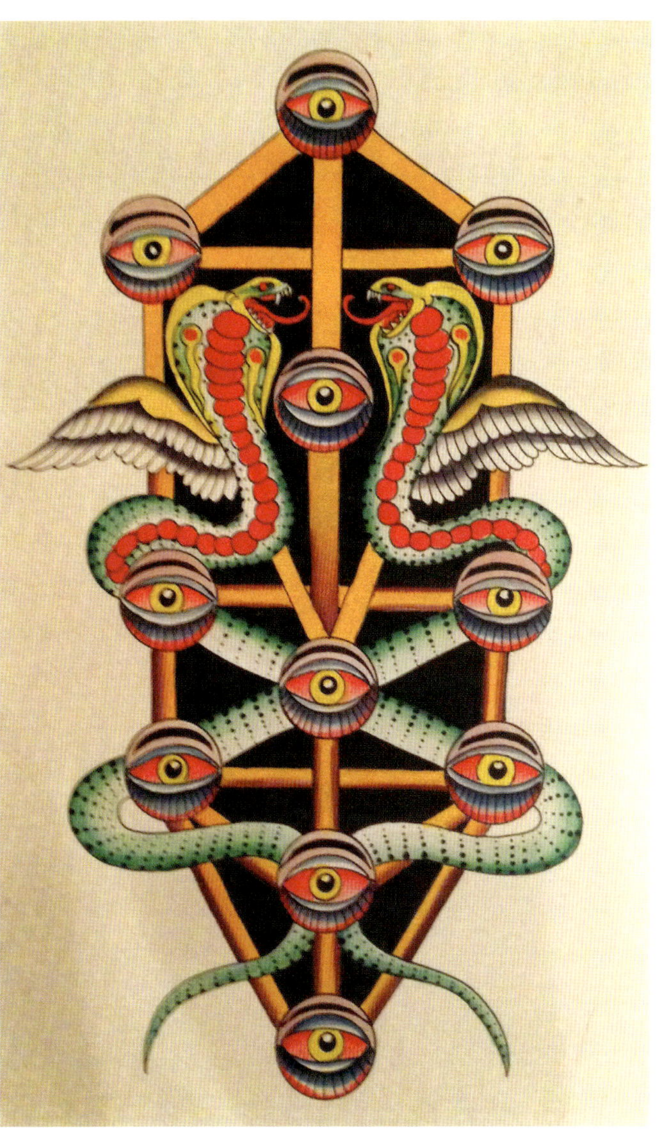

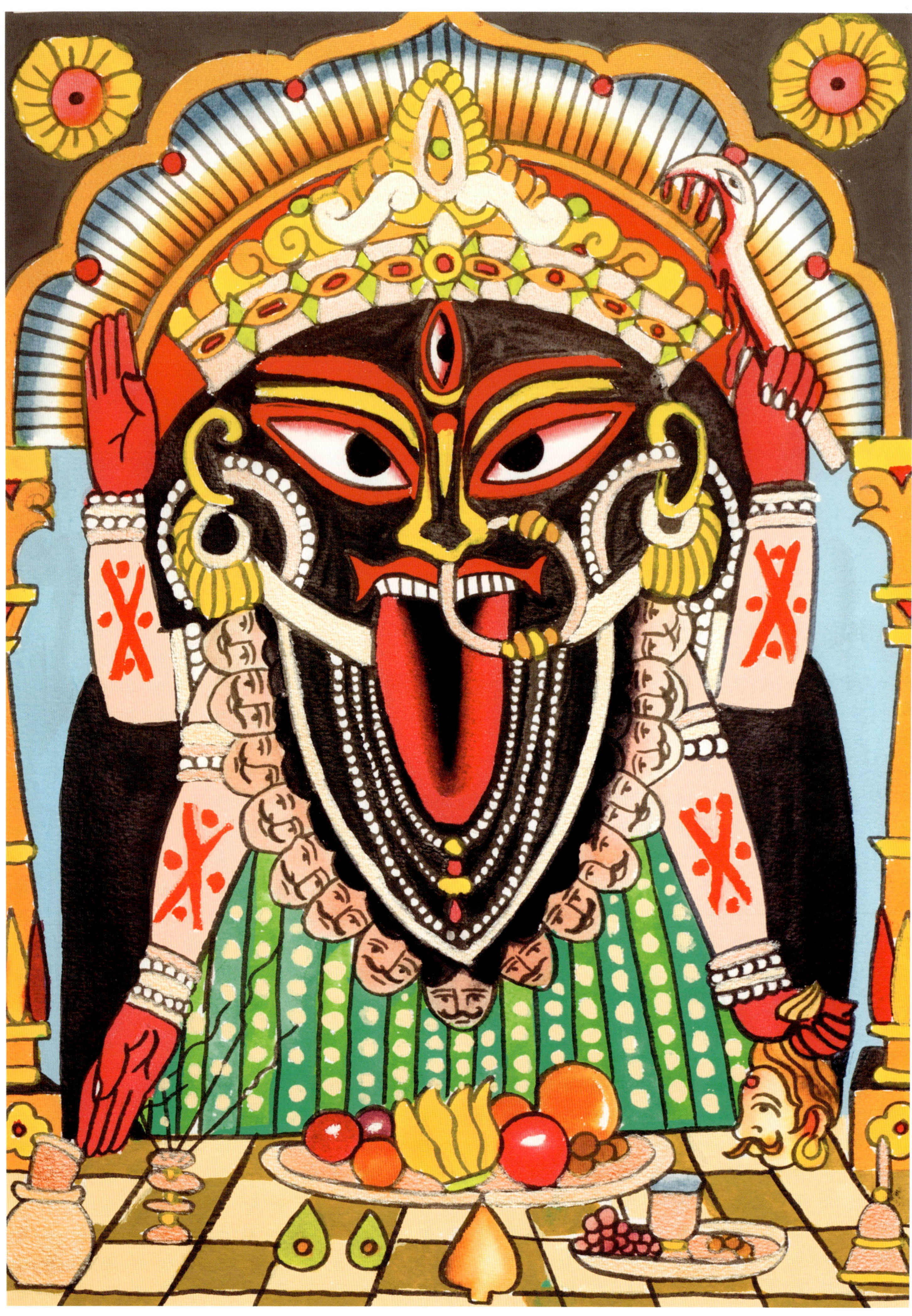

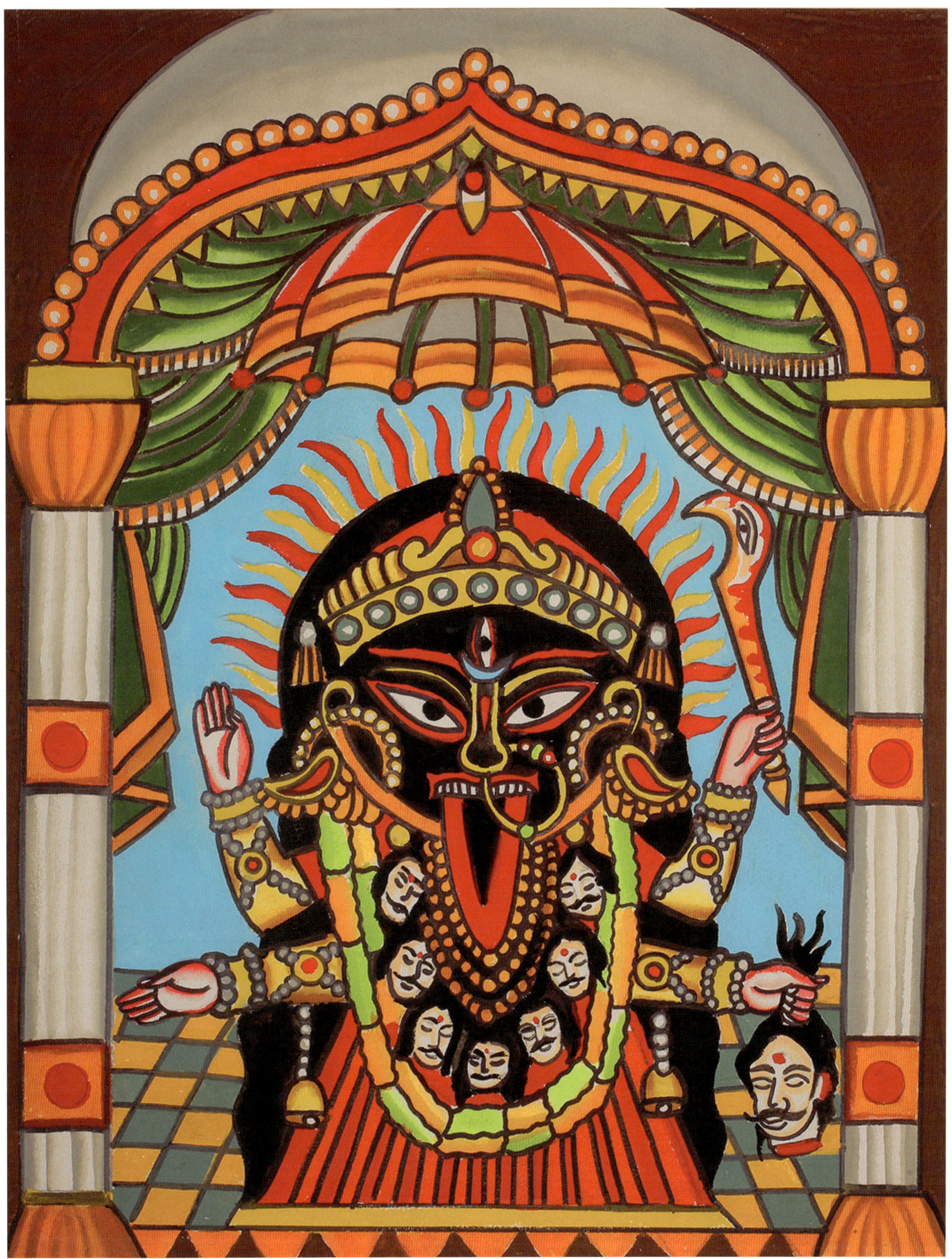

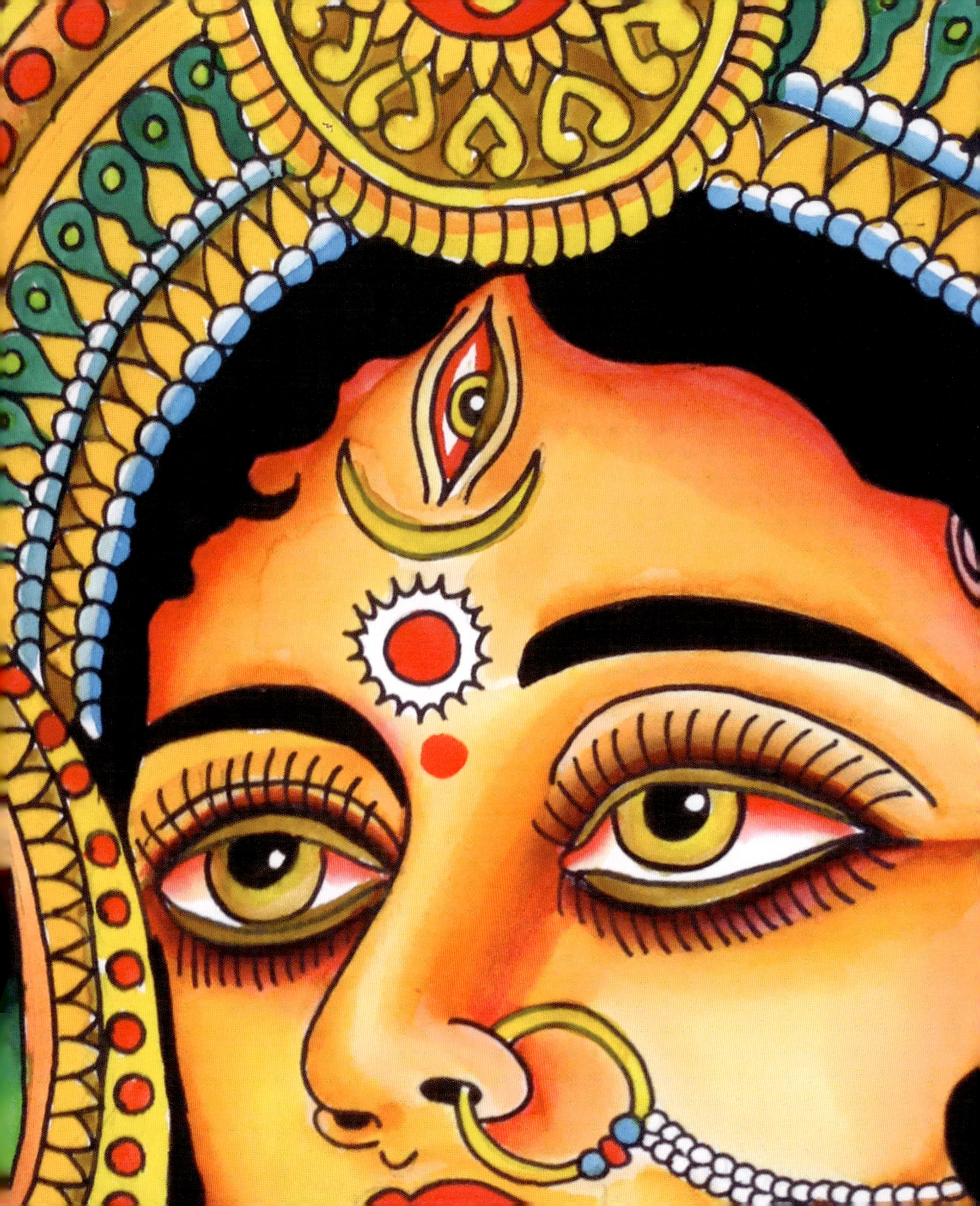

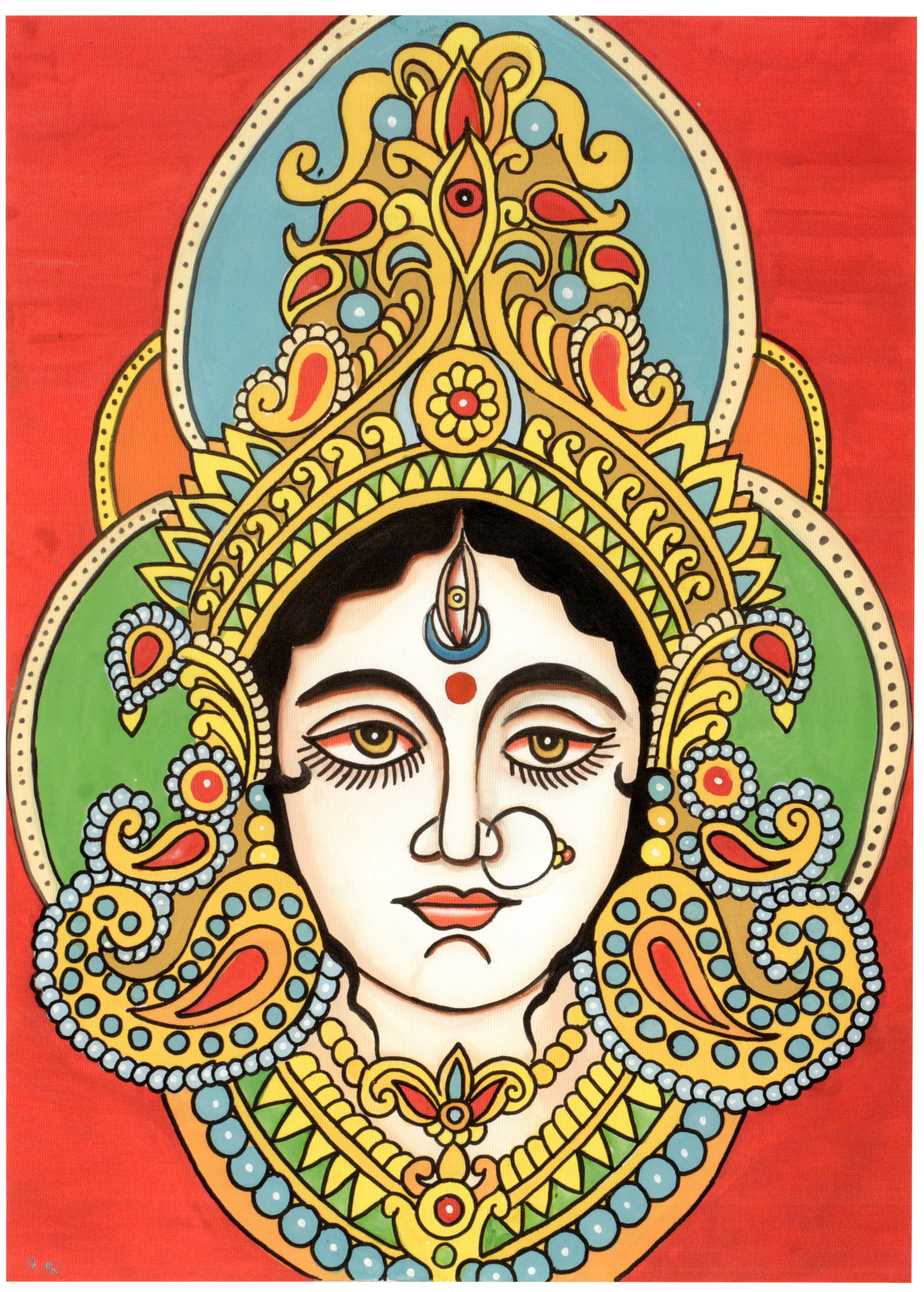

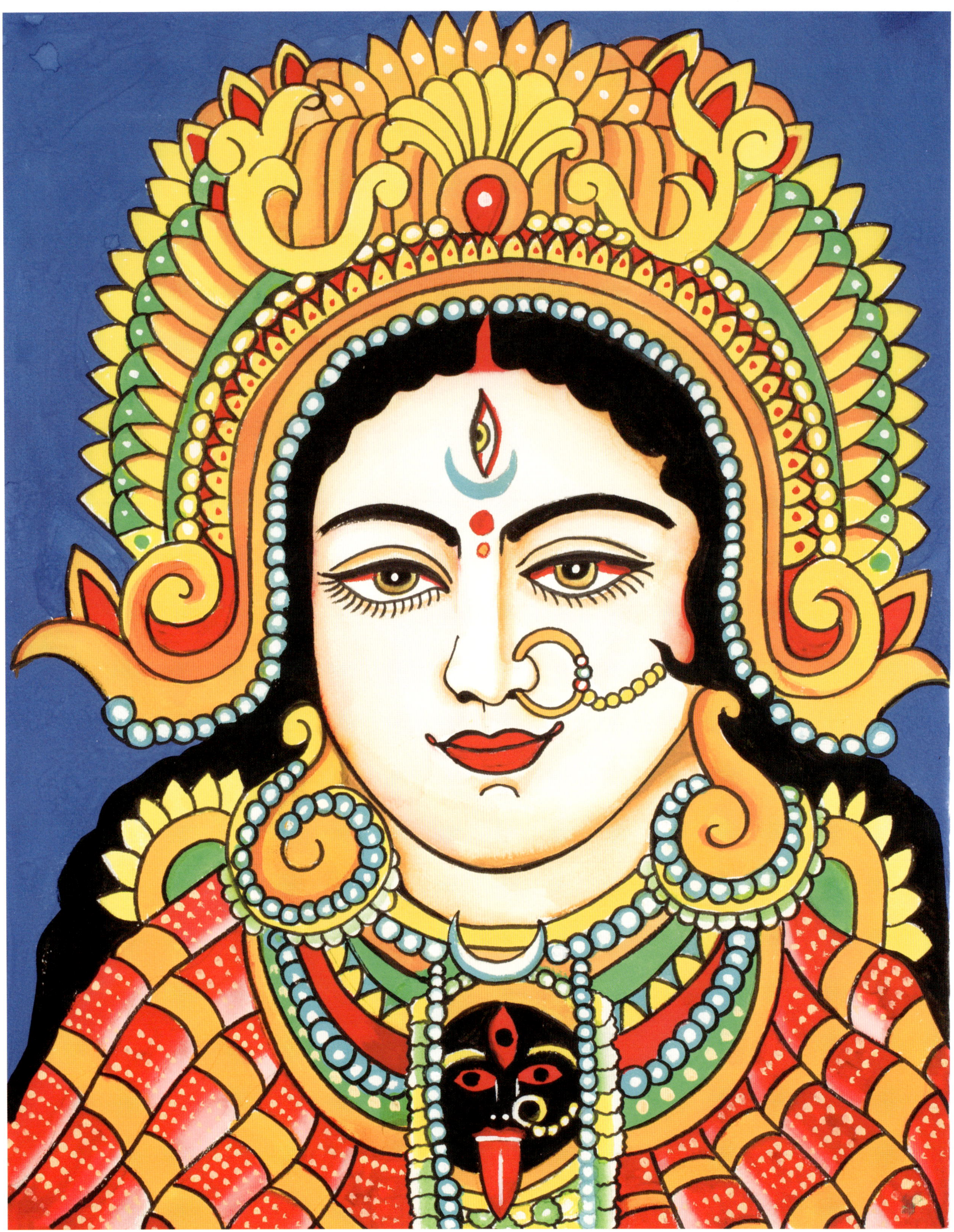

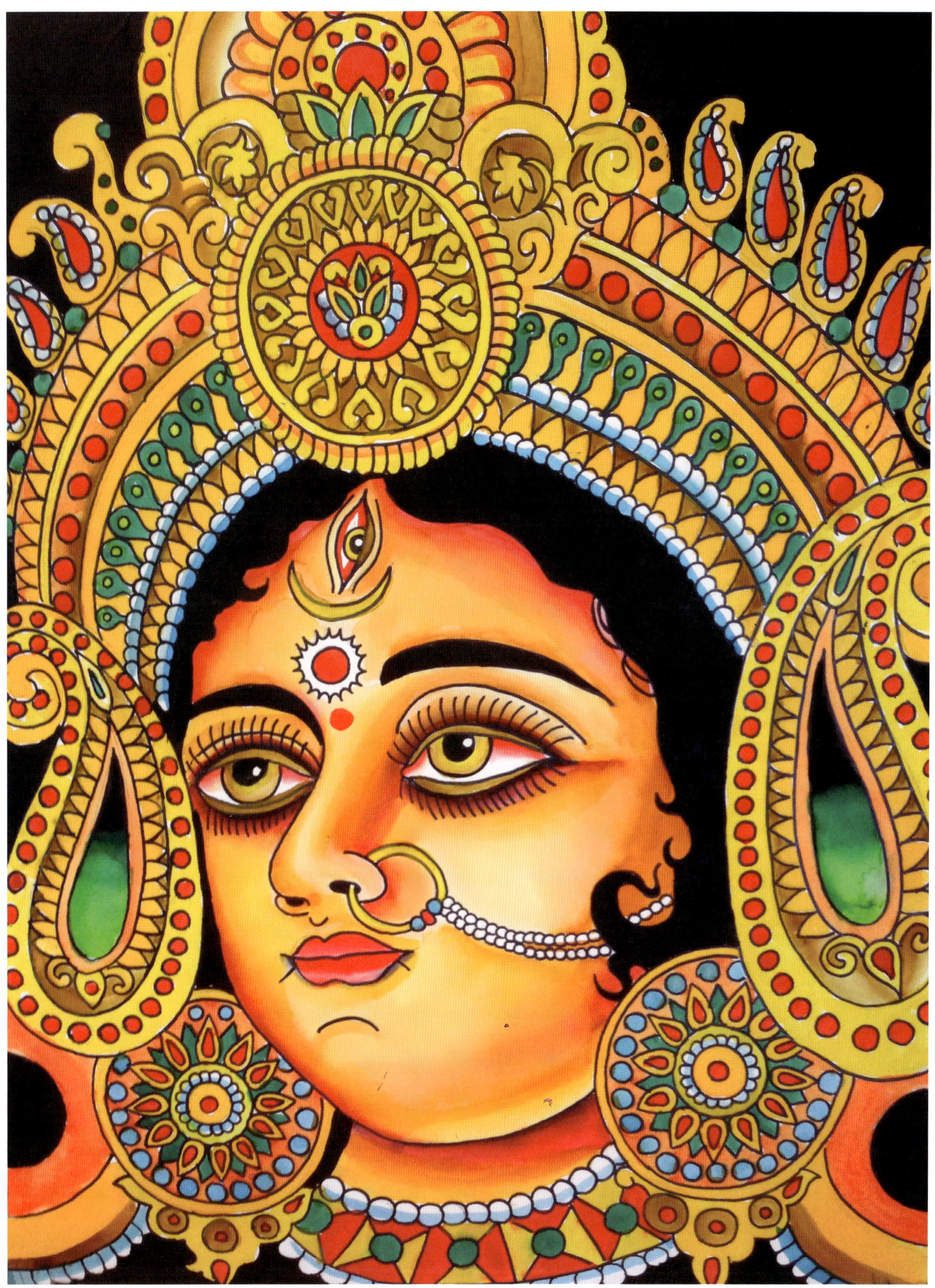

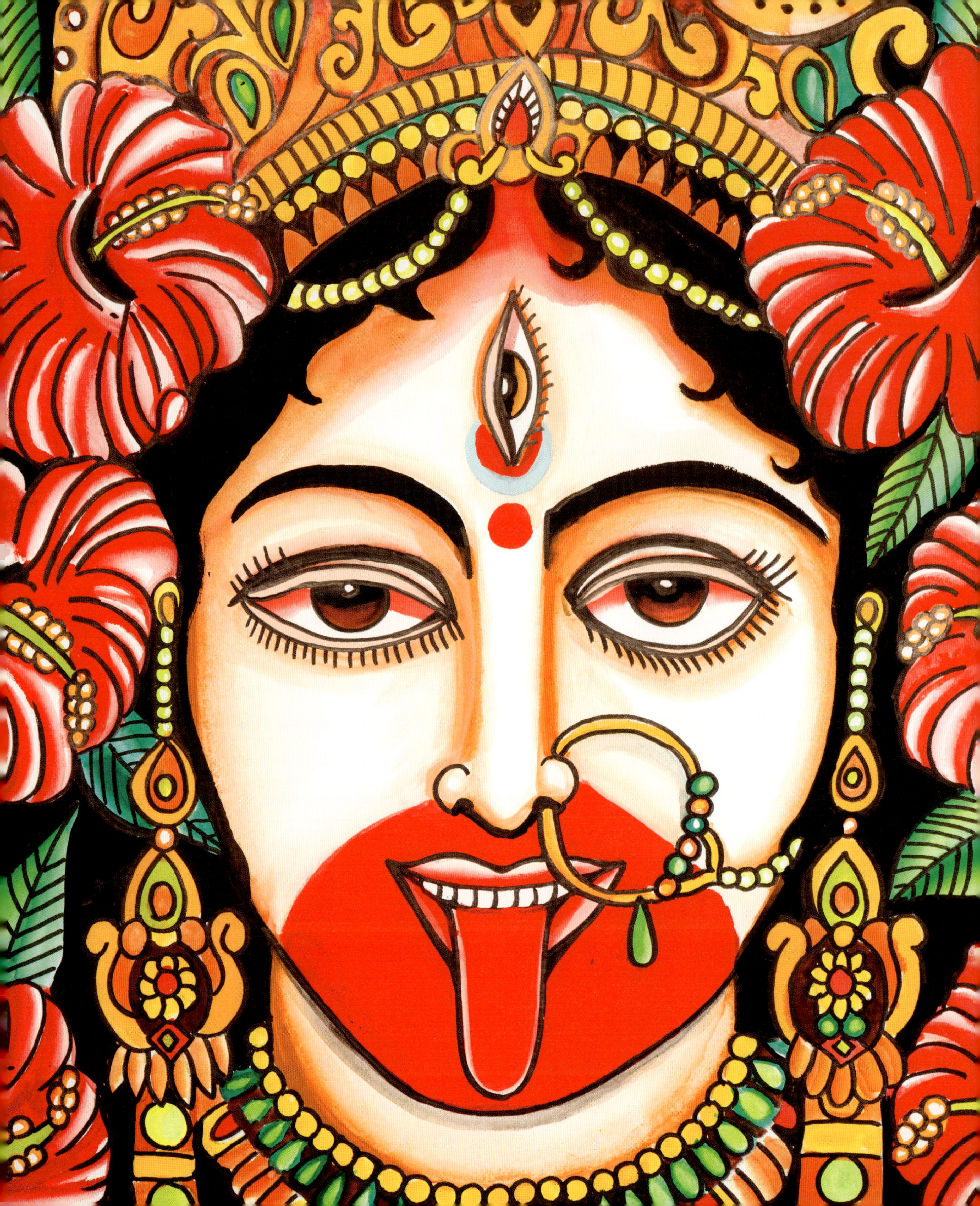

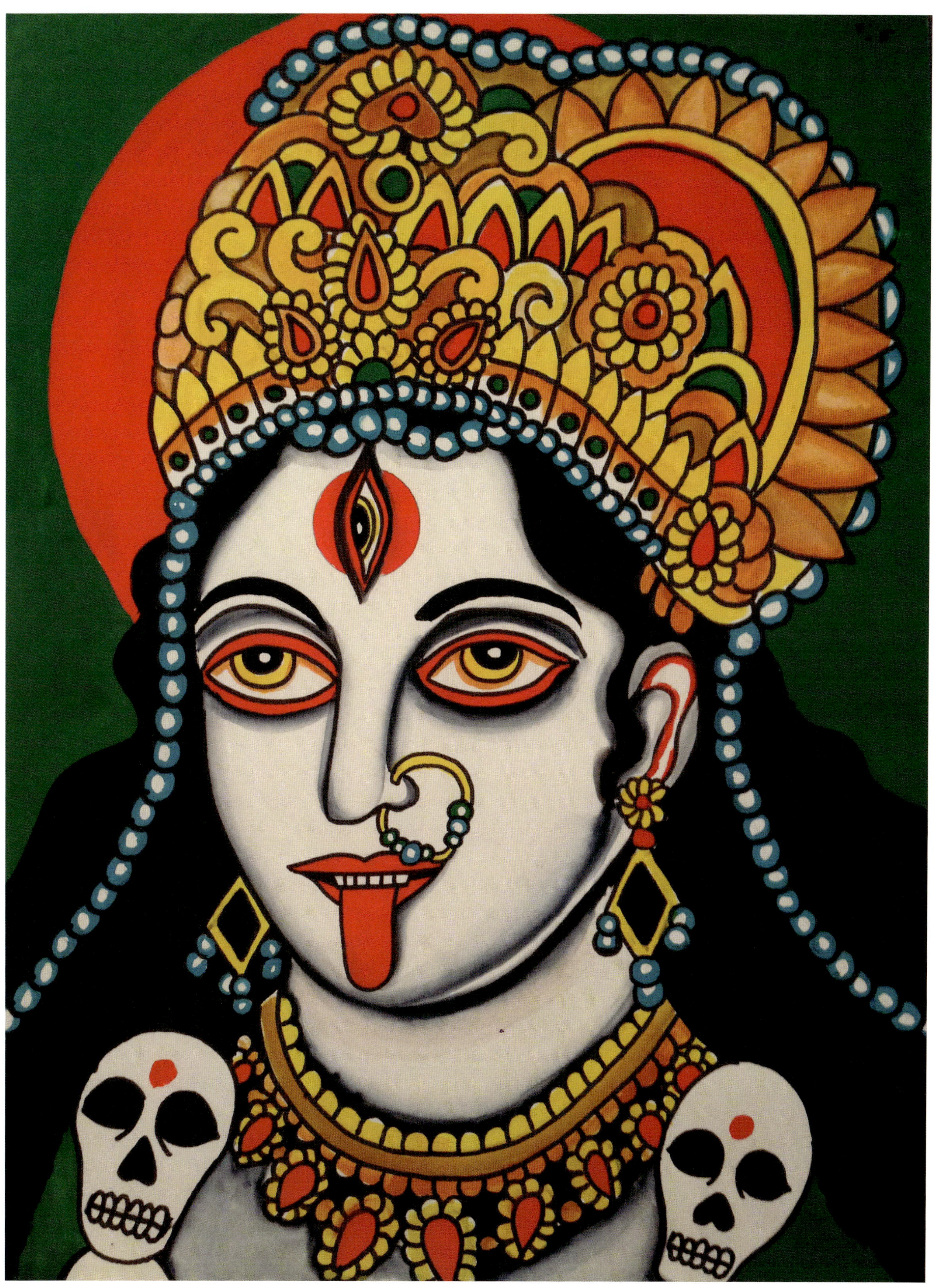

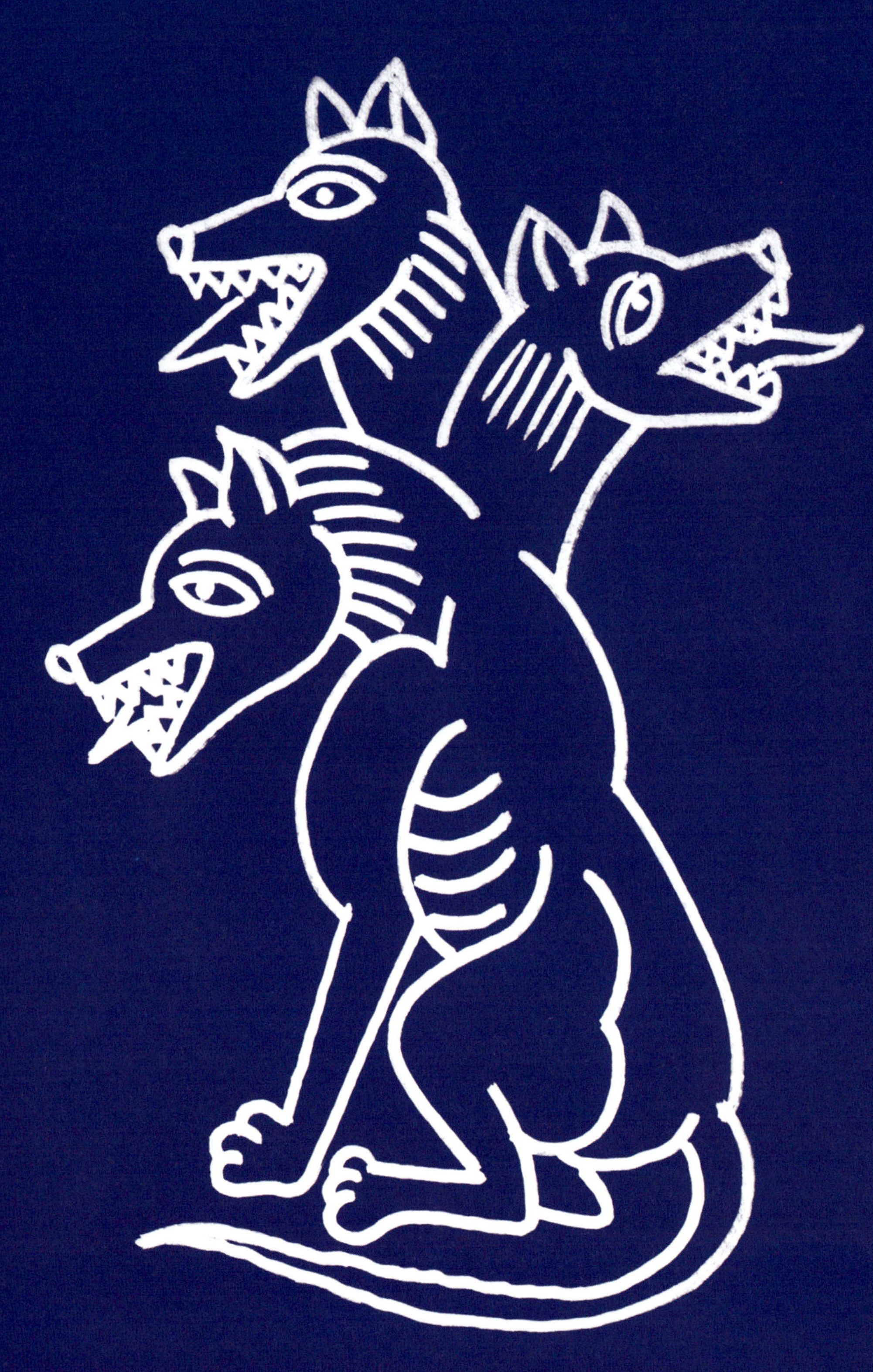

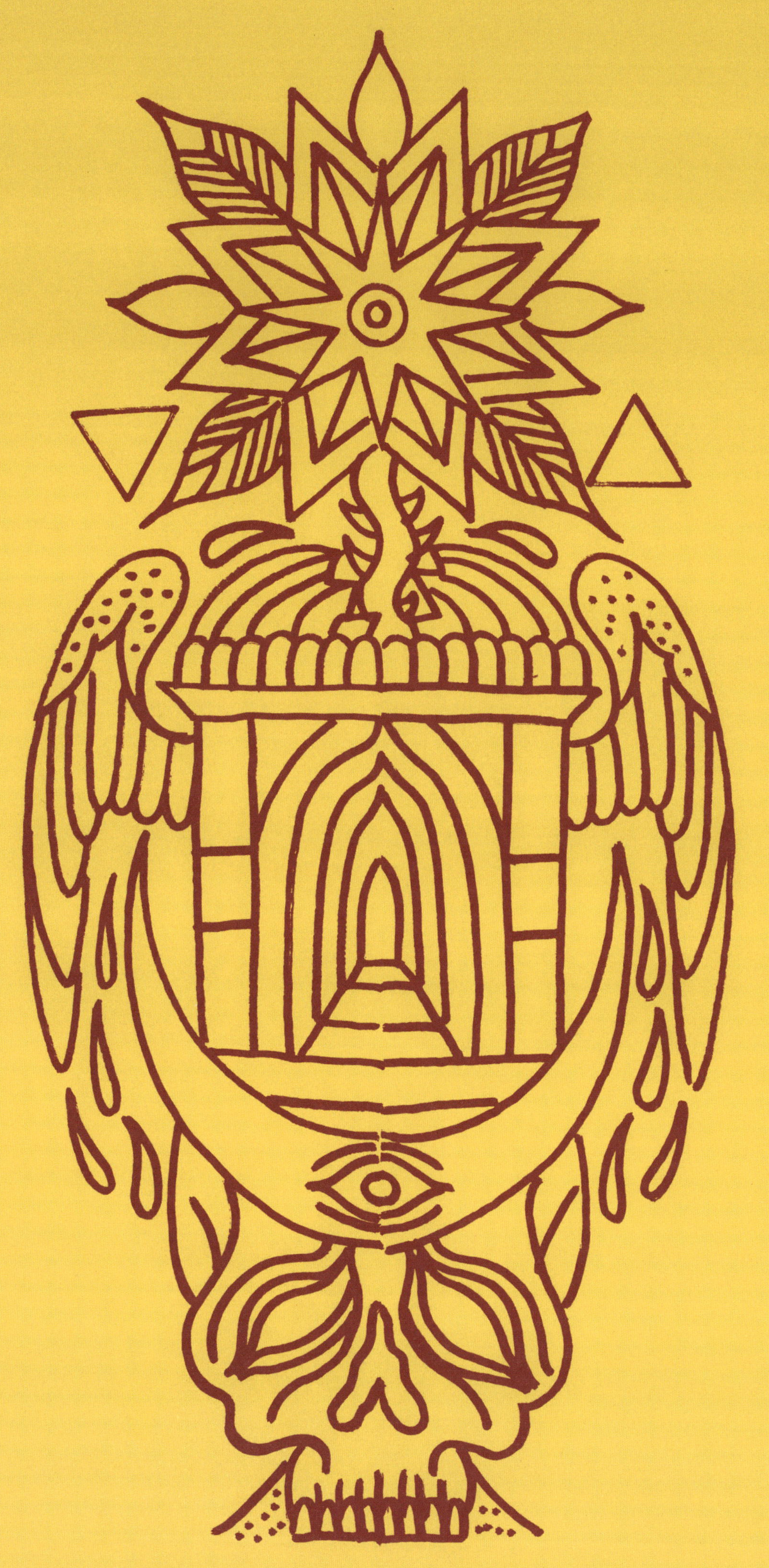

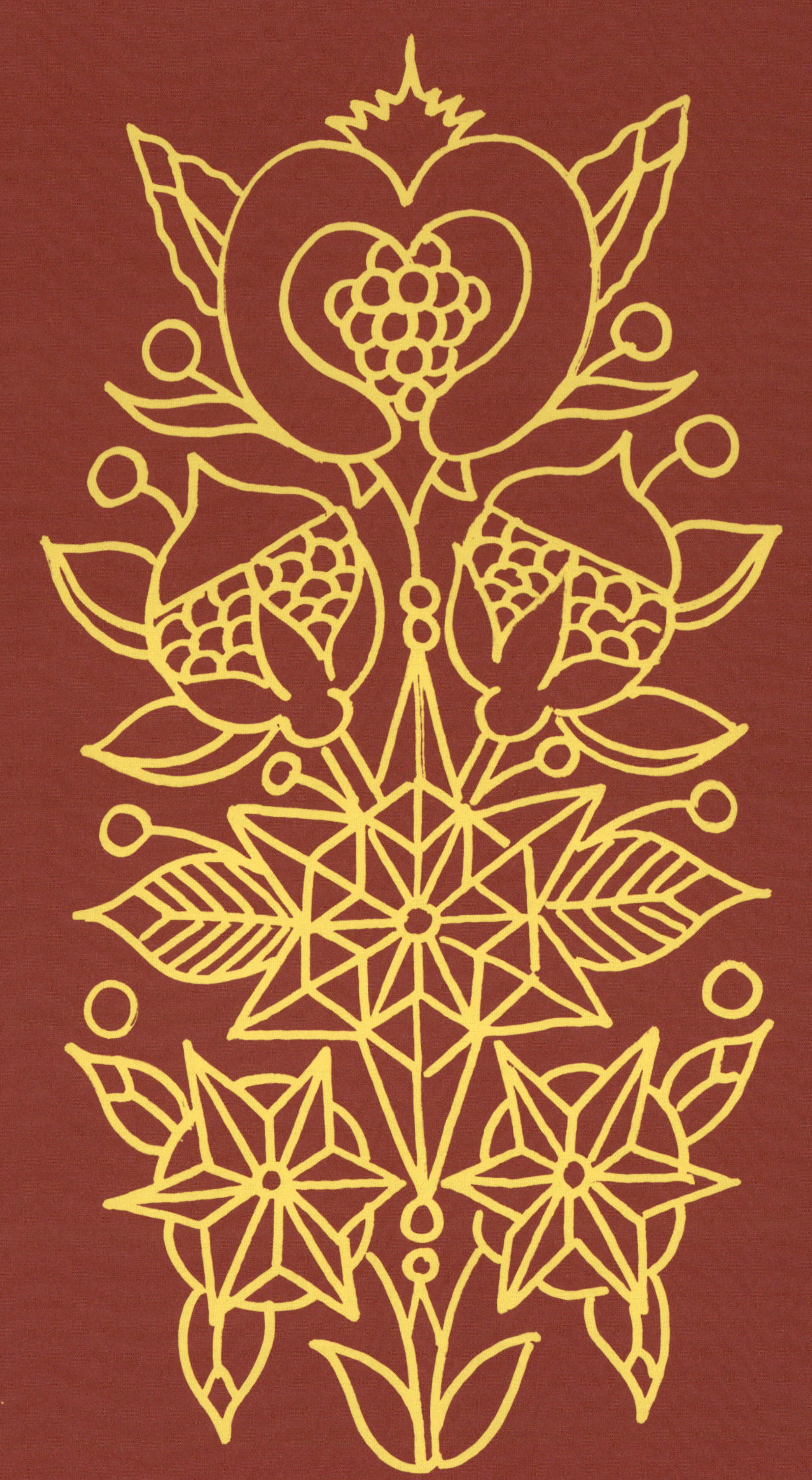

ROBERT RYAN
SKETCH BOOK

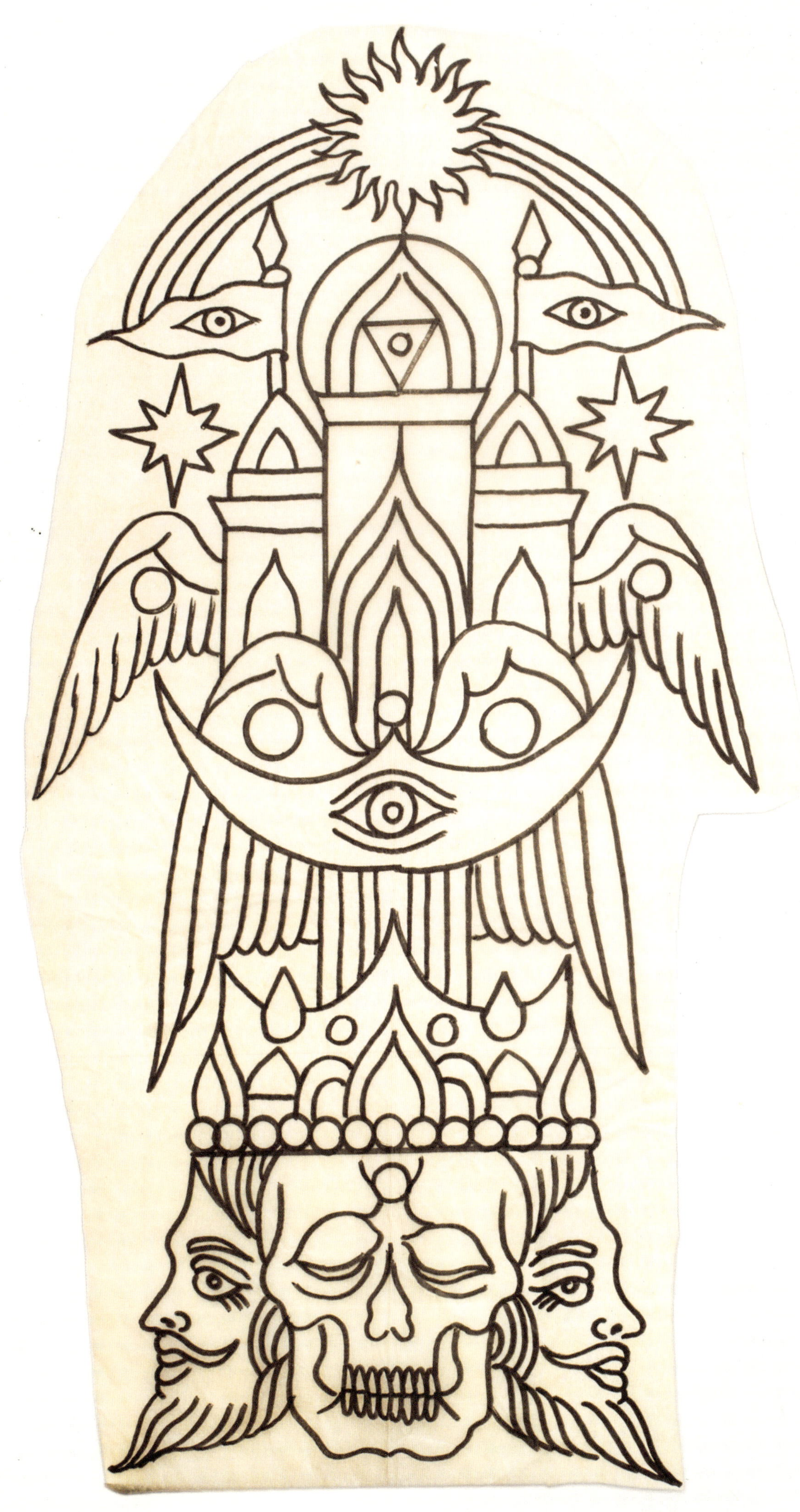

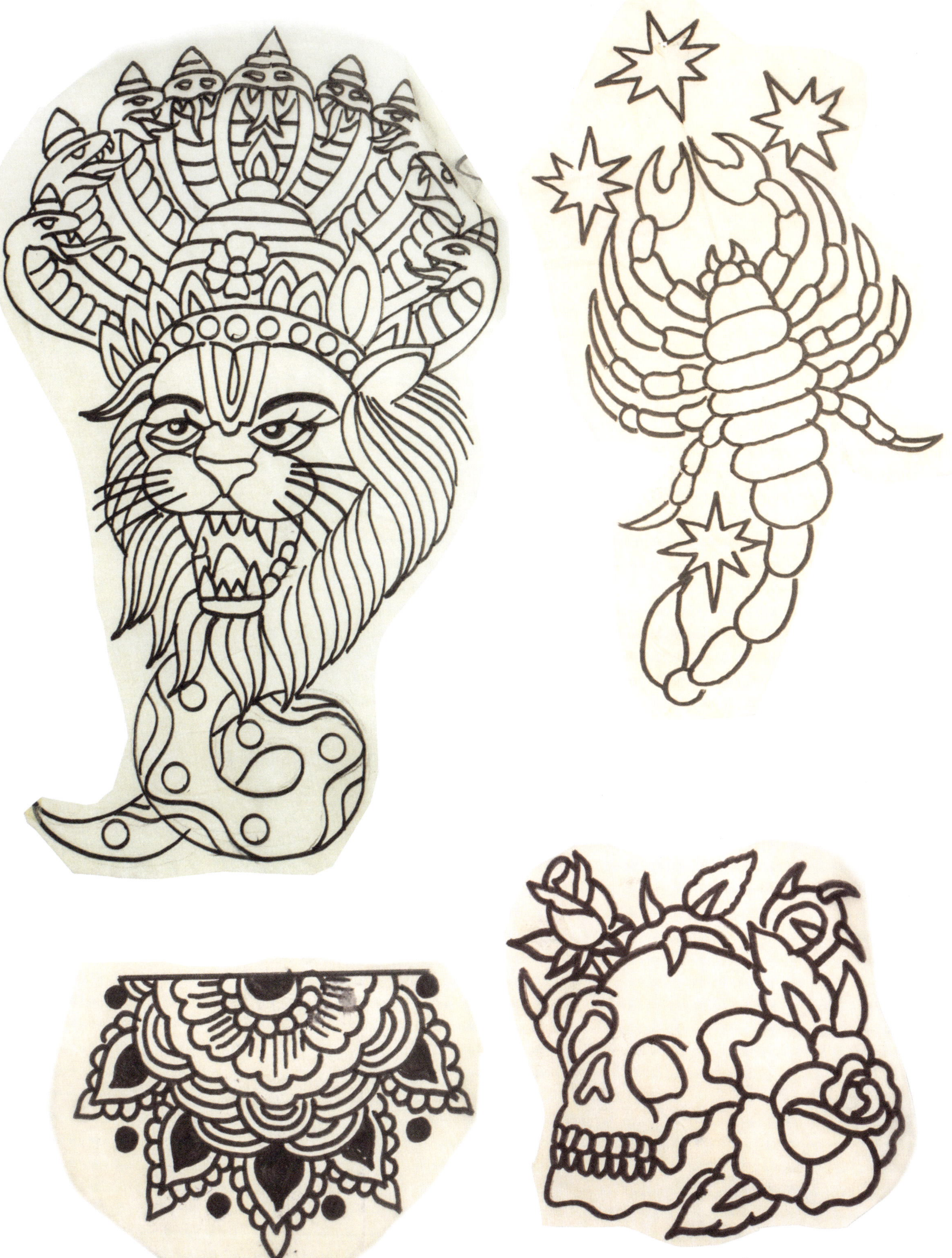

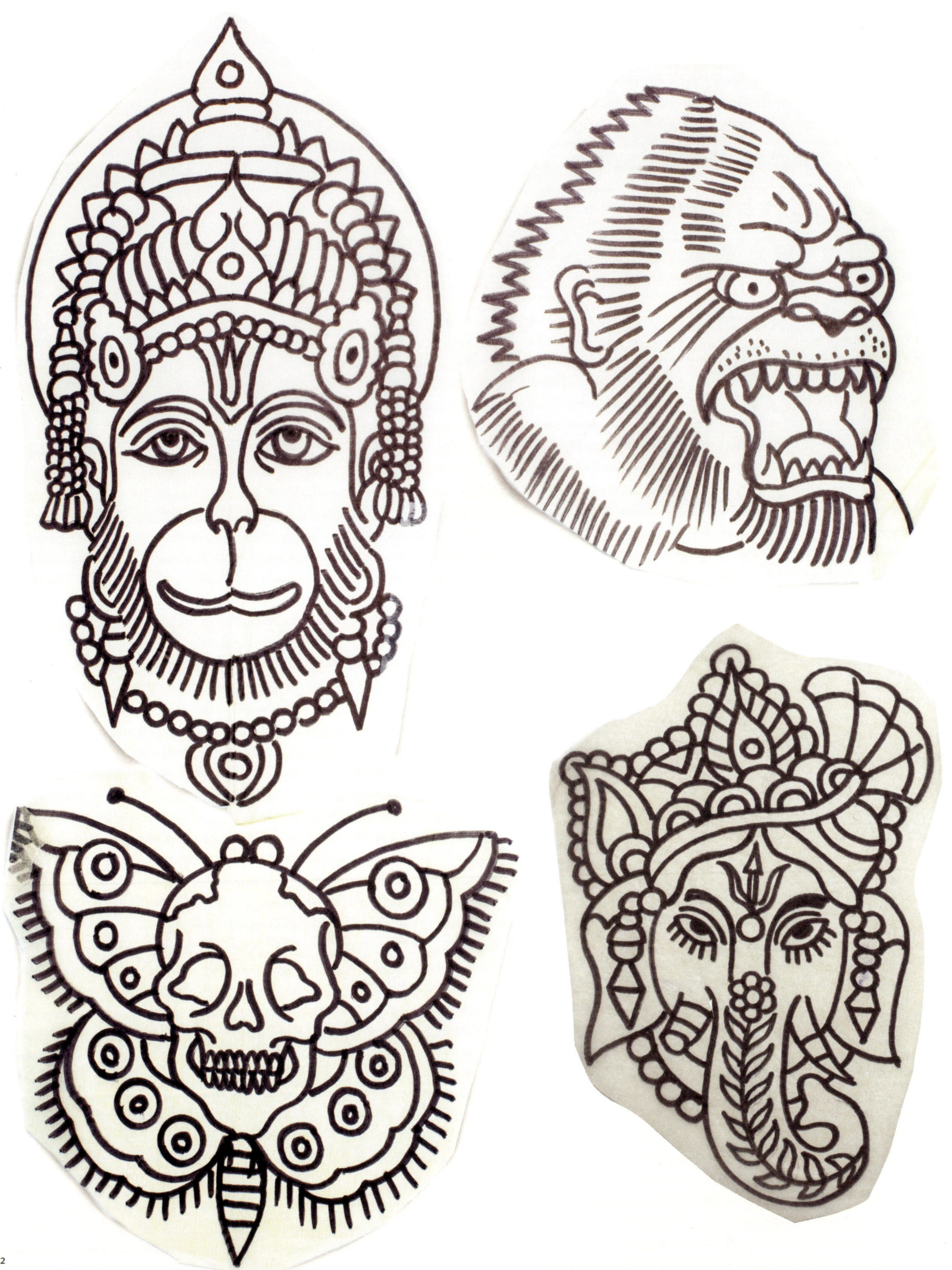

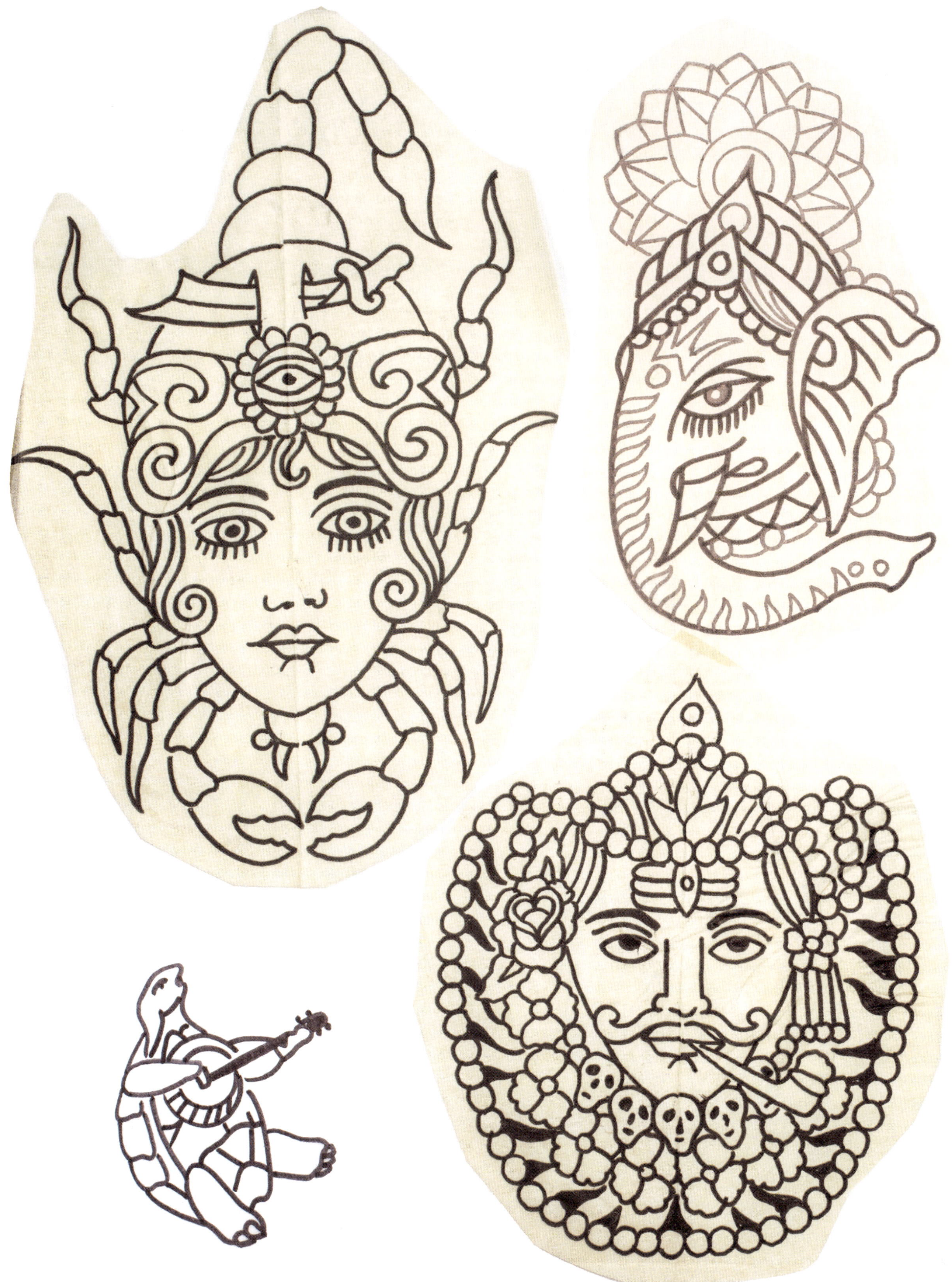

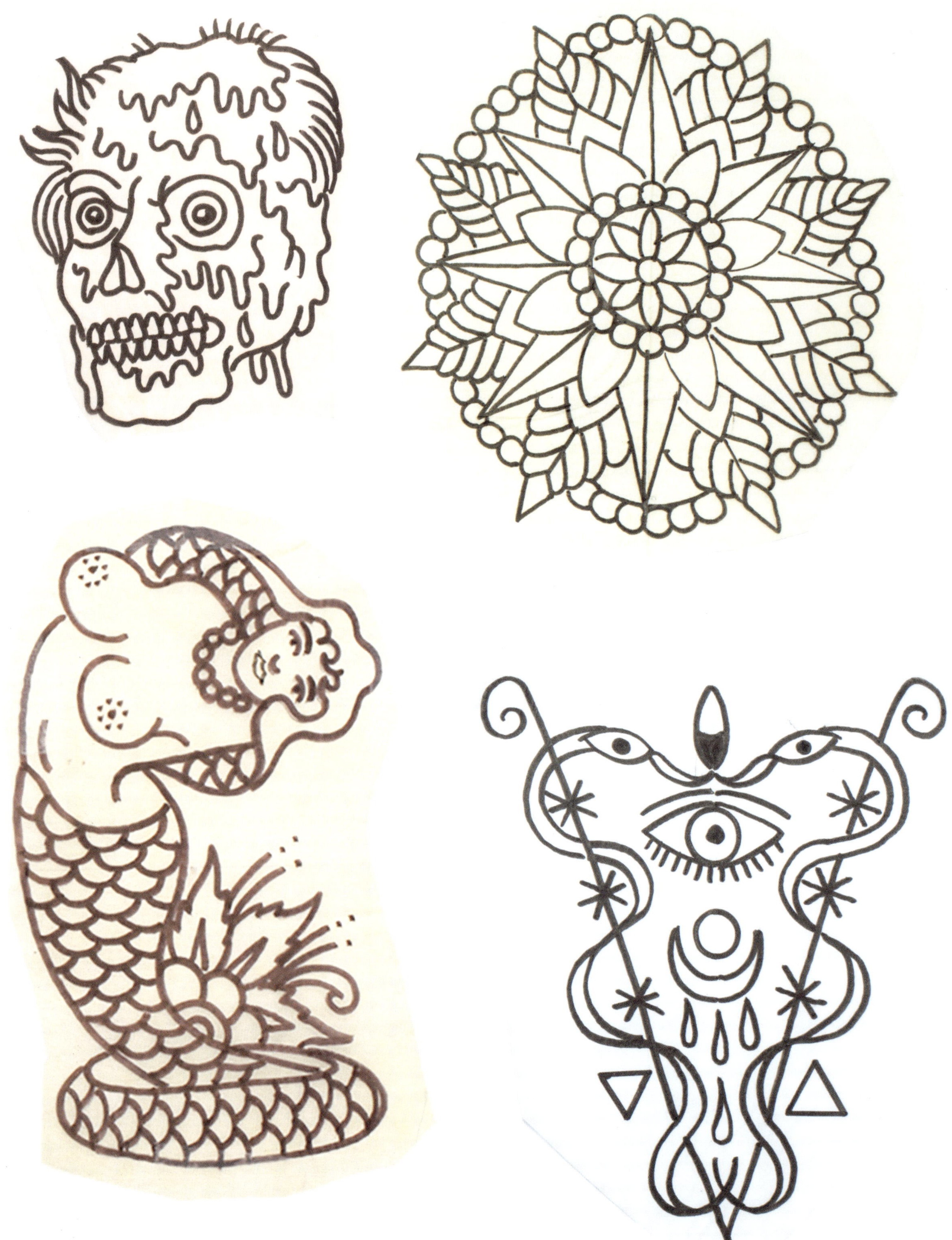

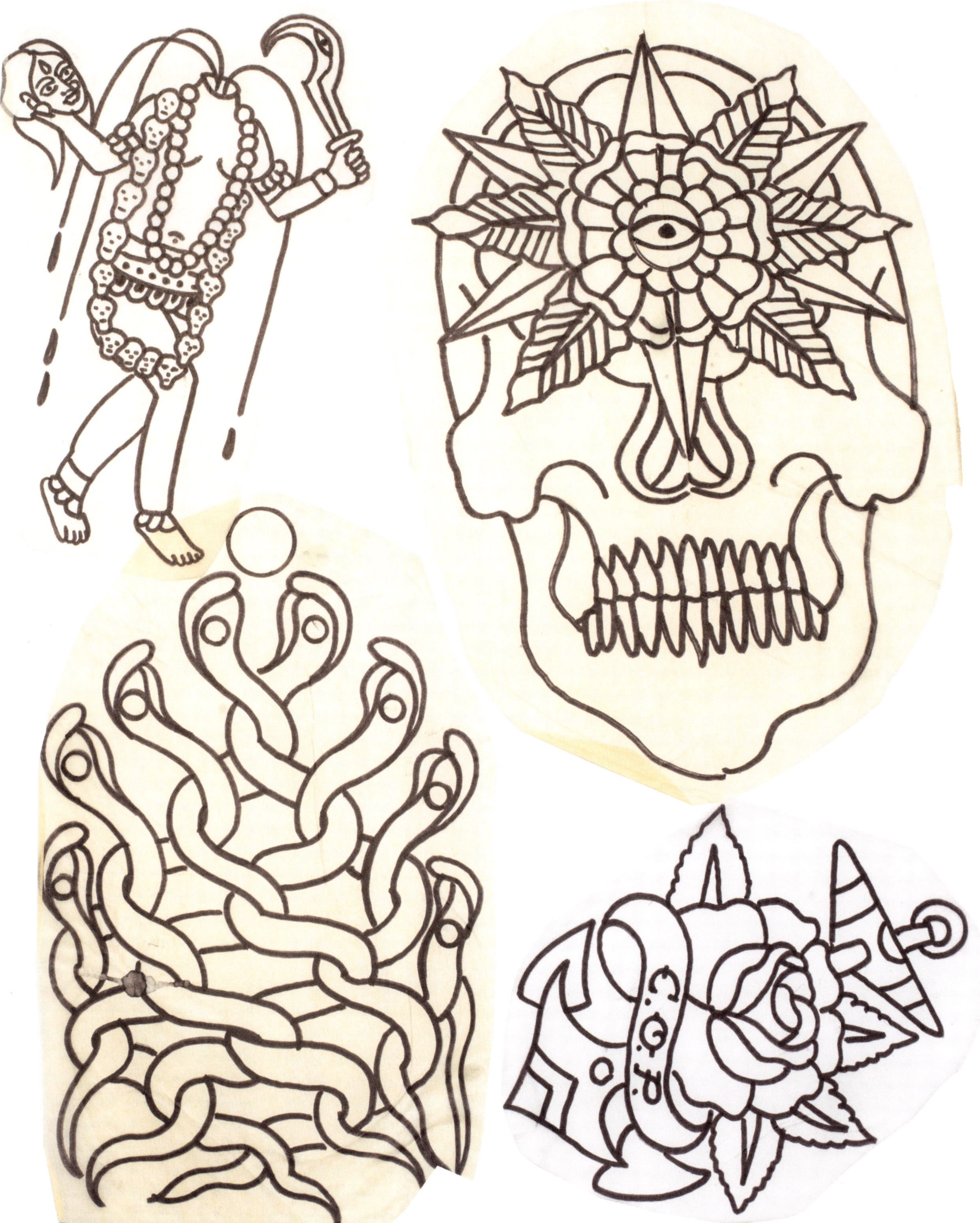

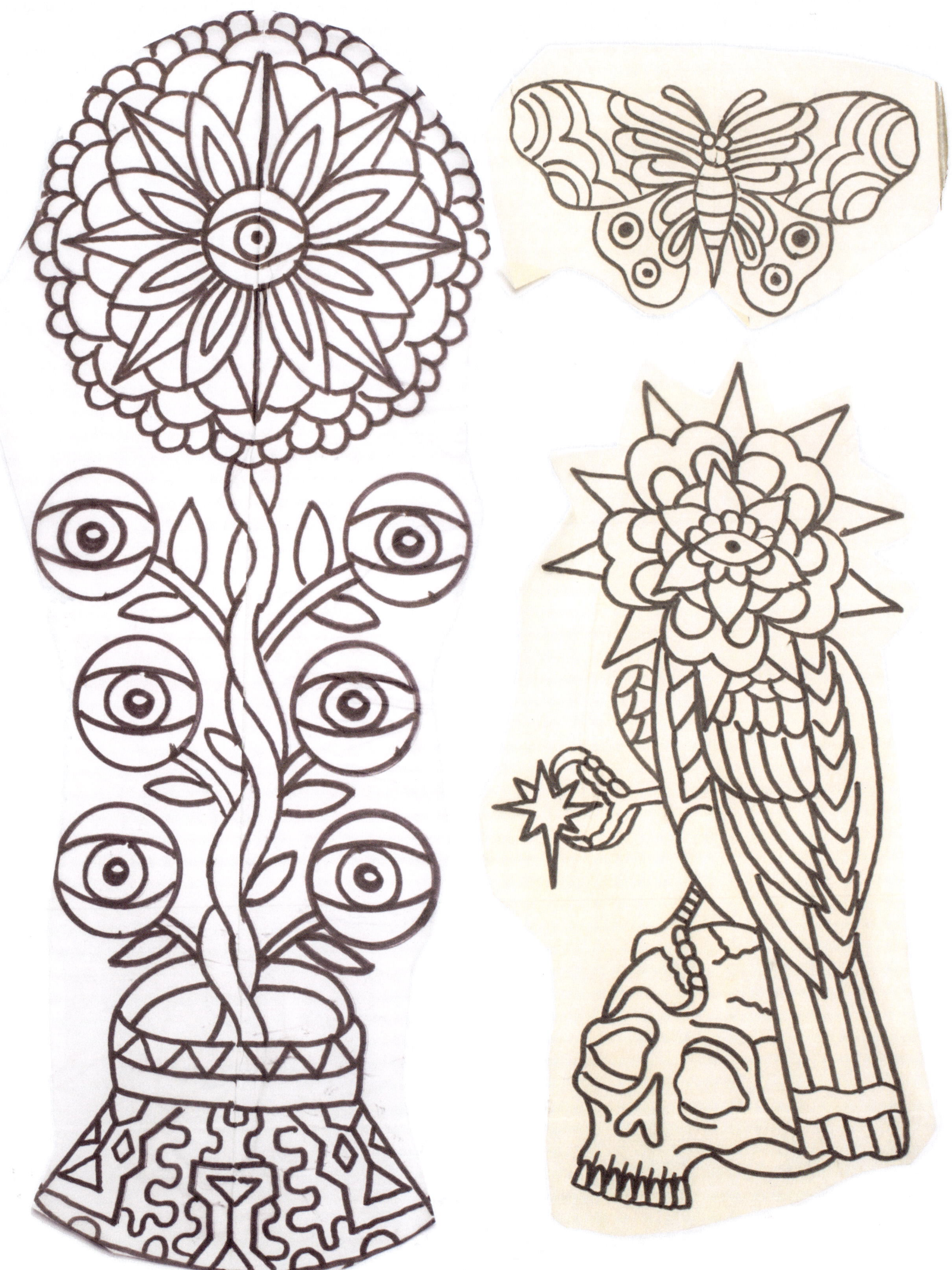

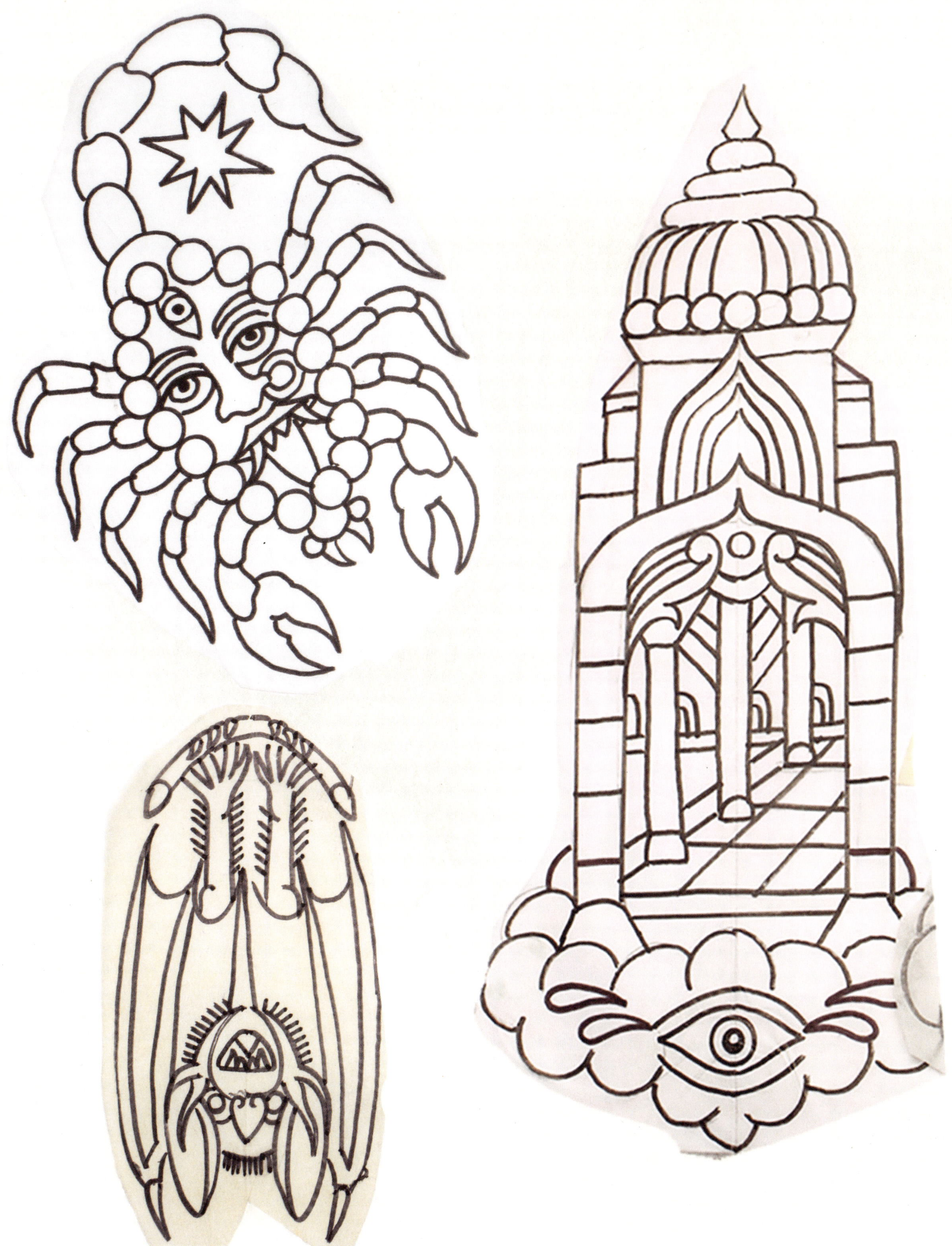

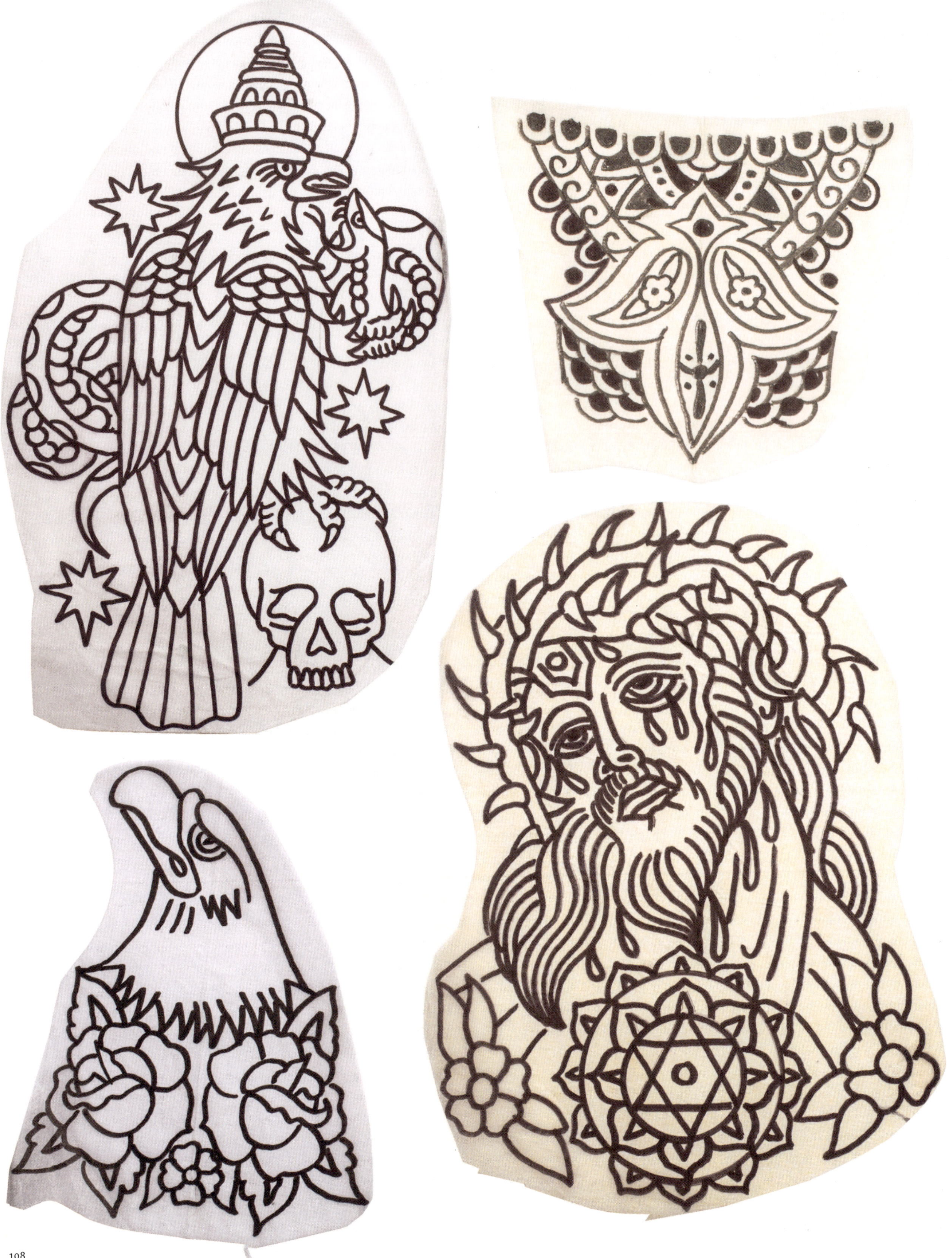

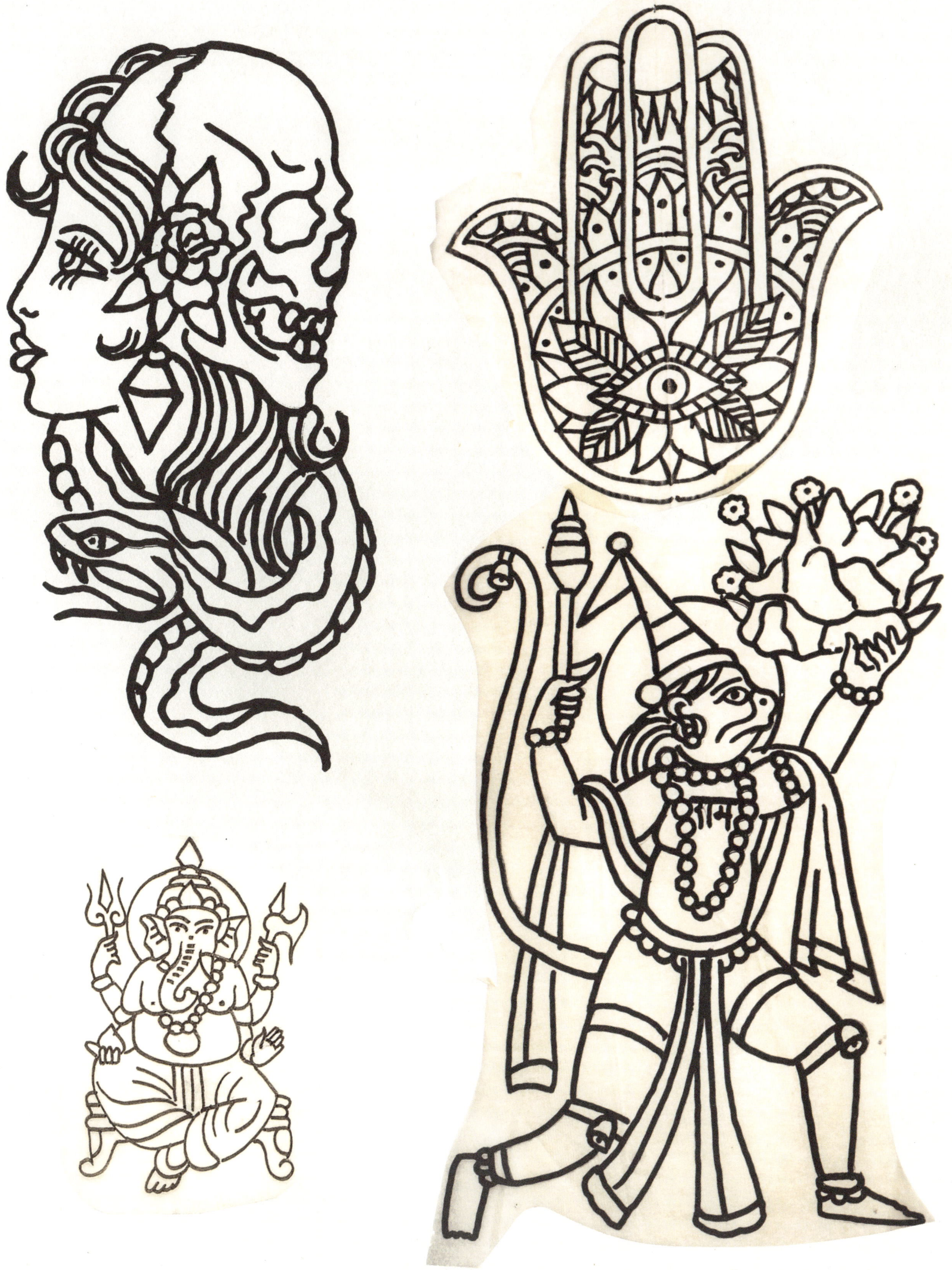

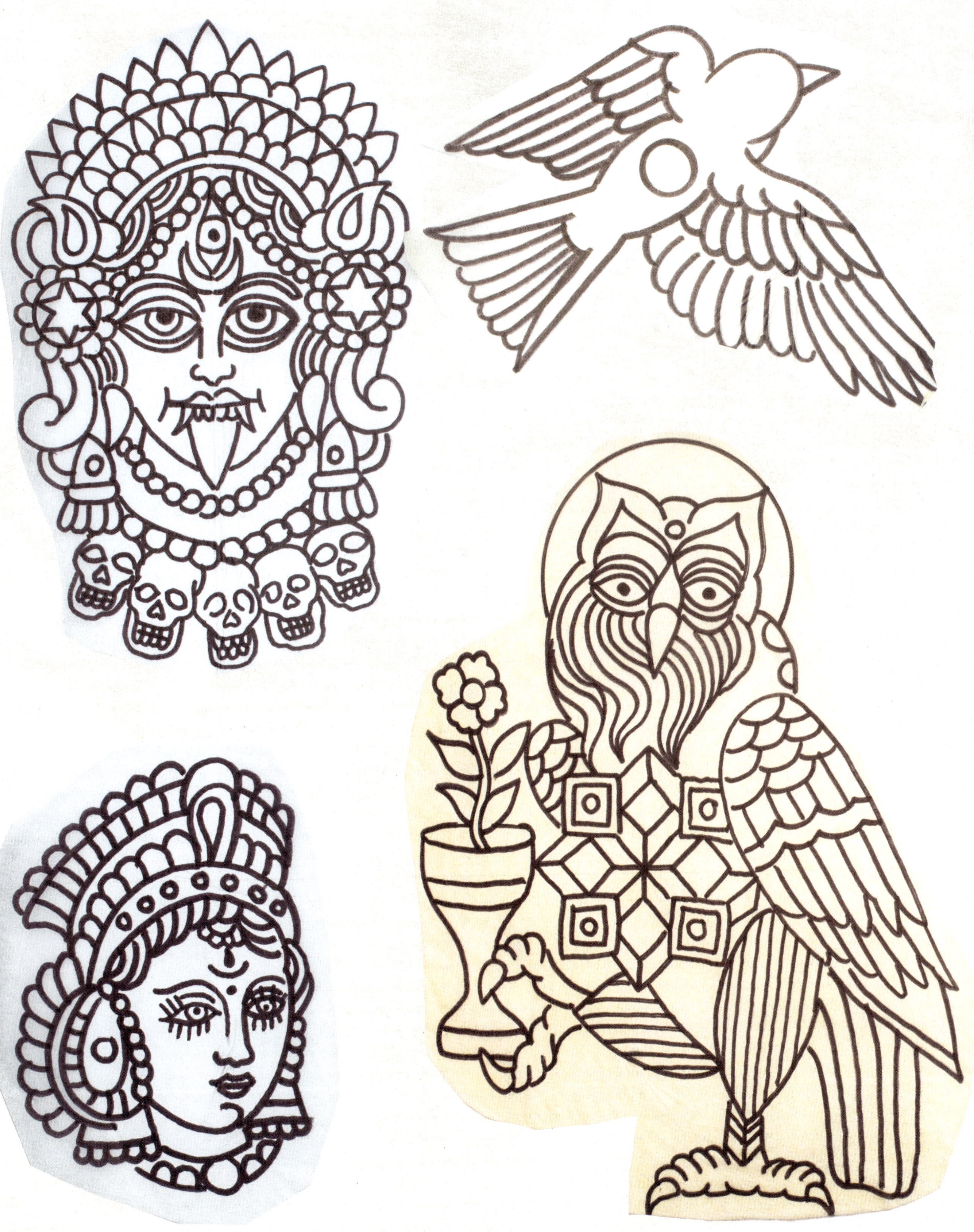

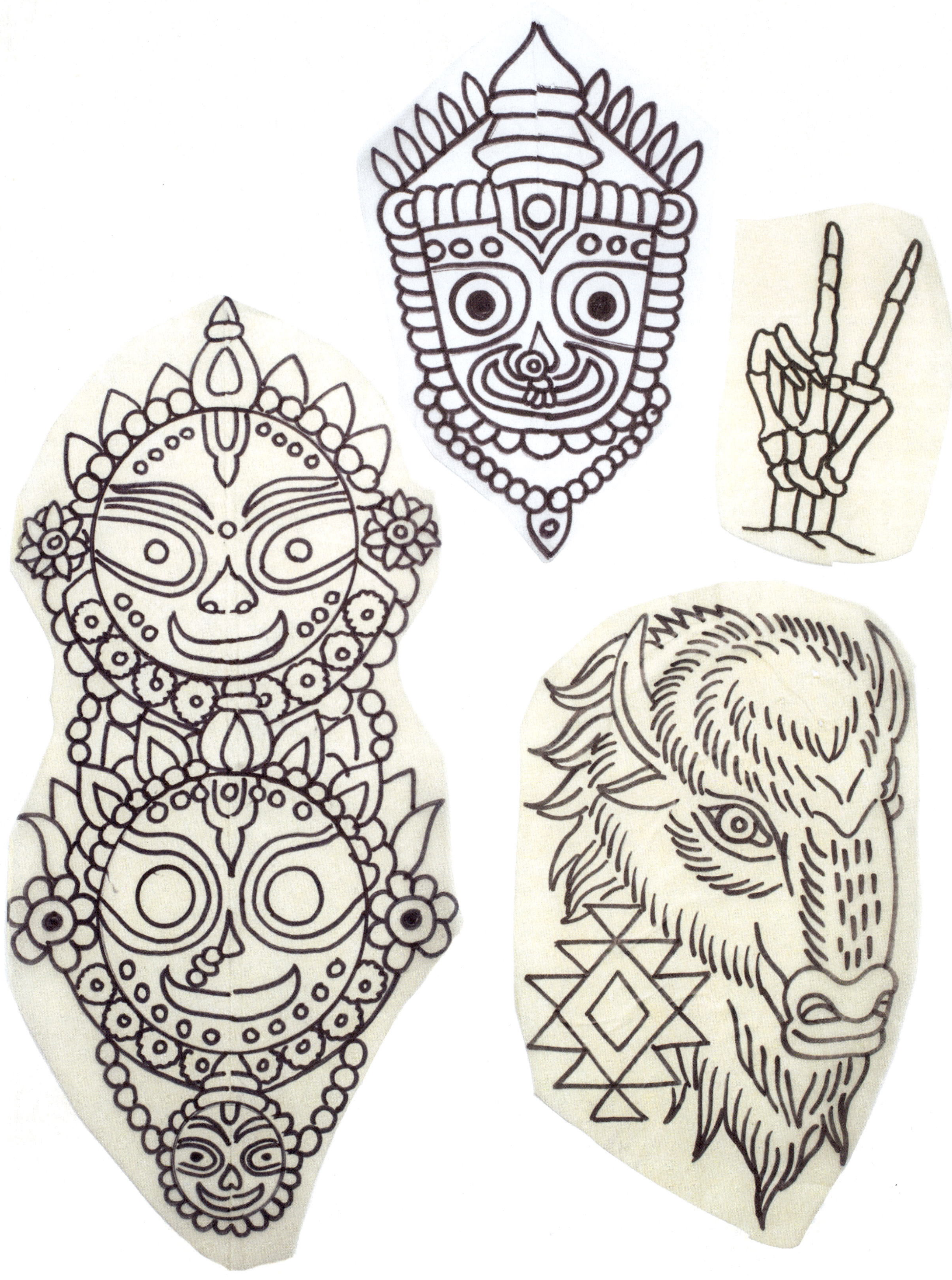

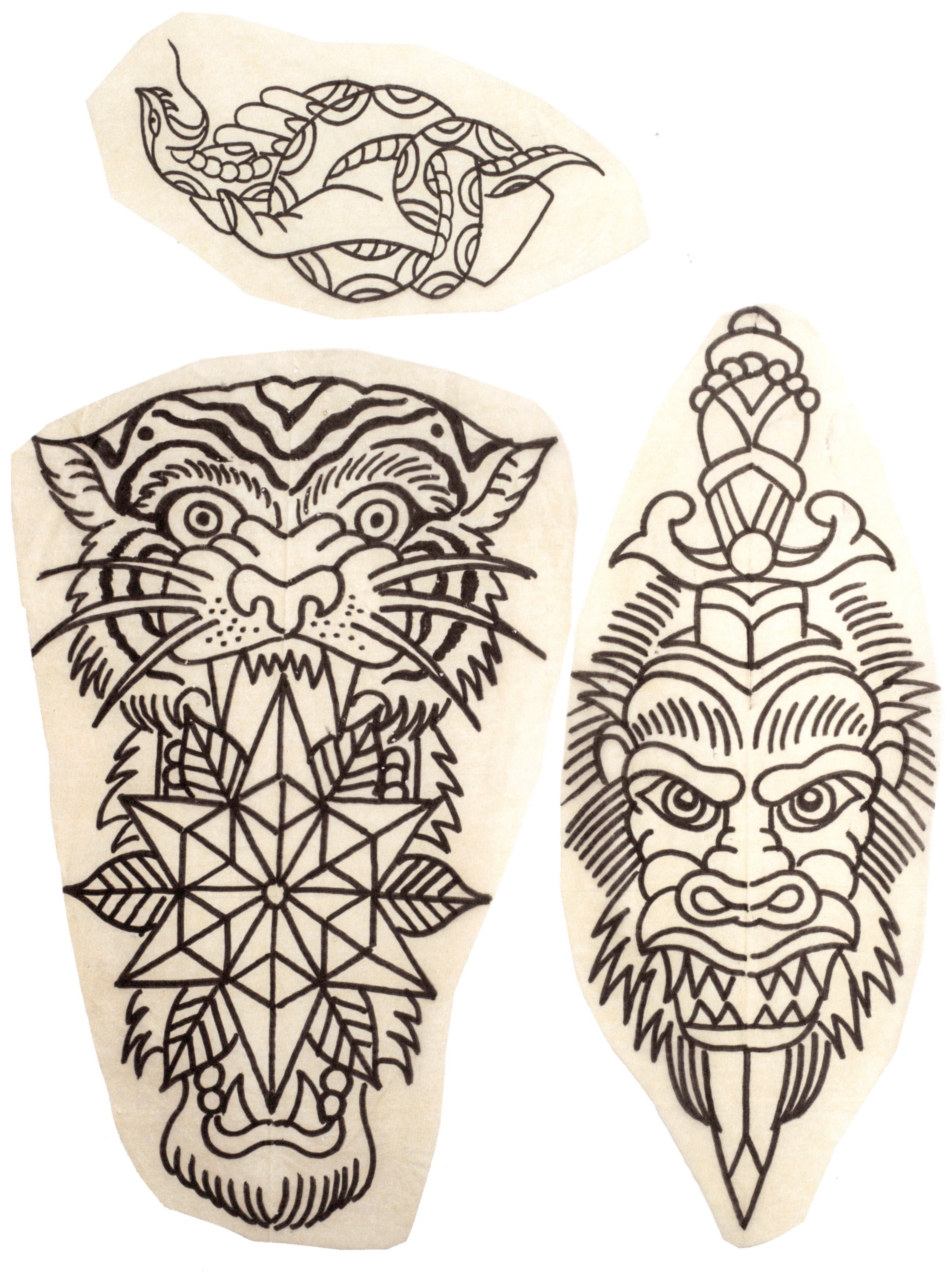

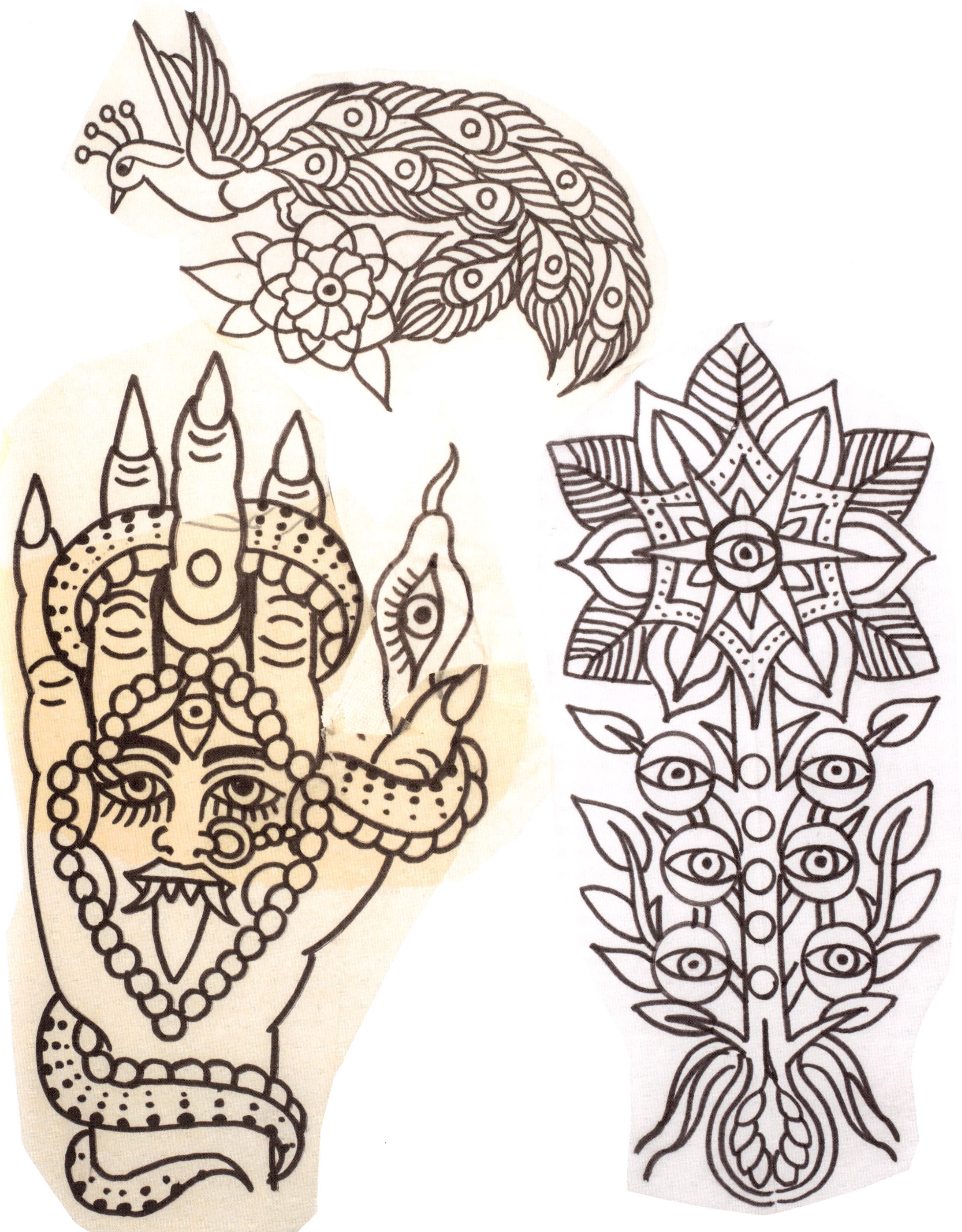

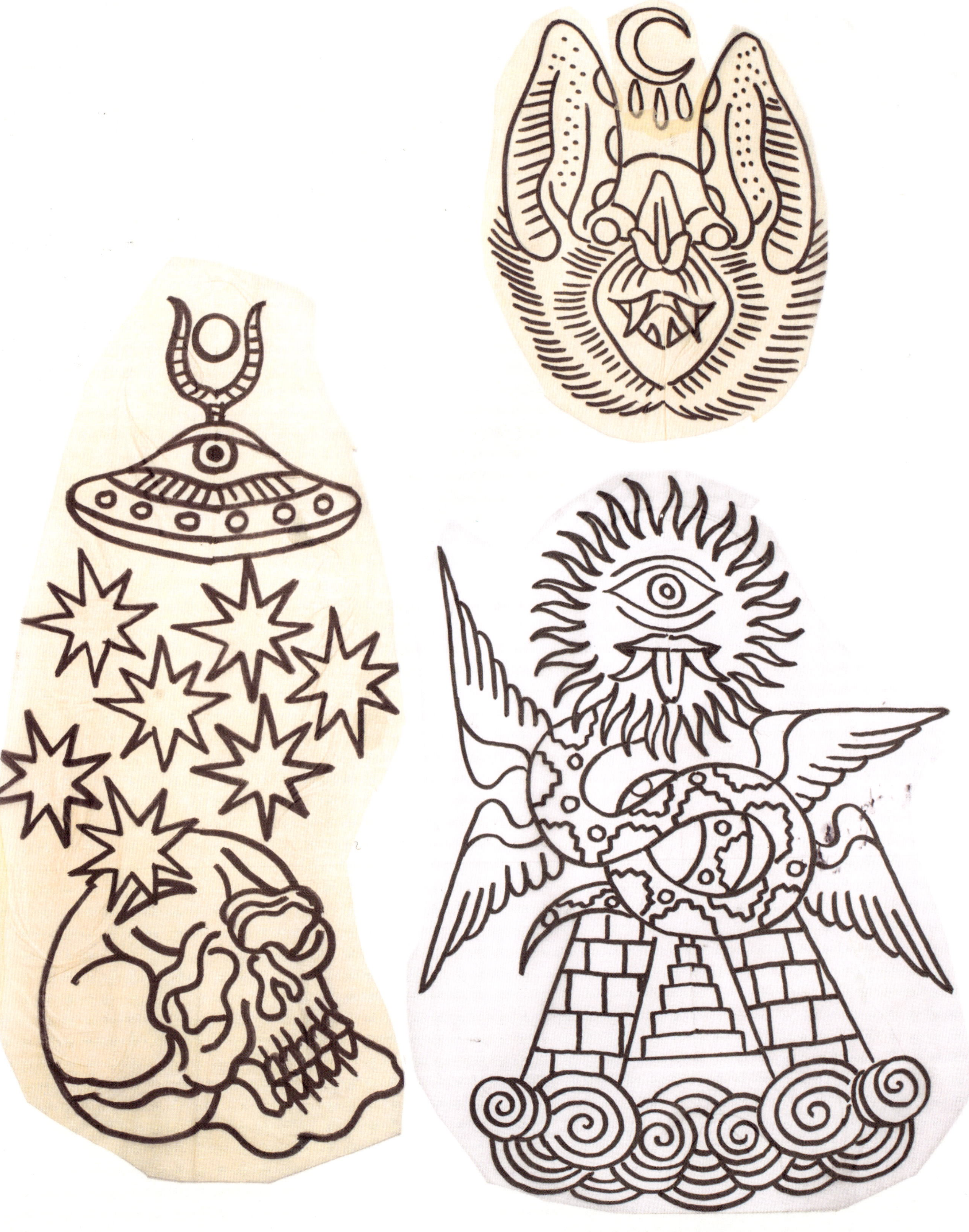

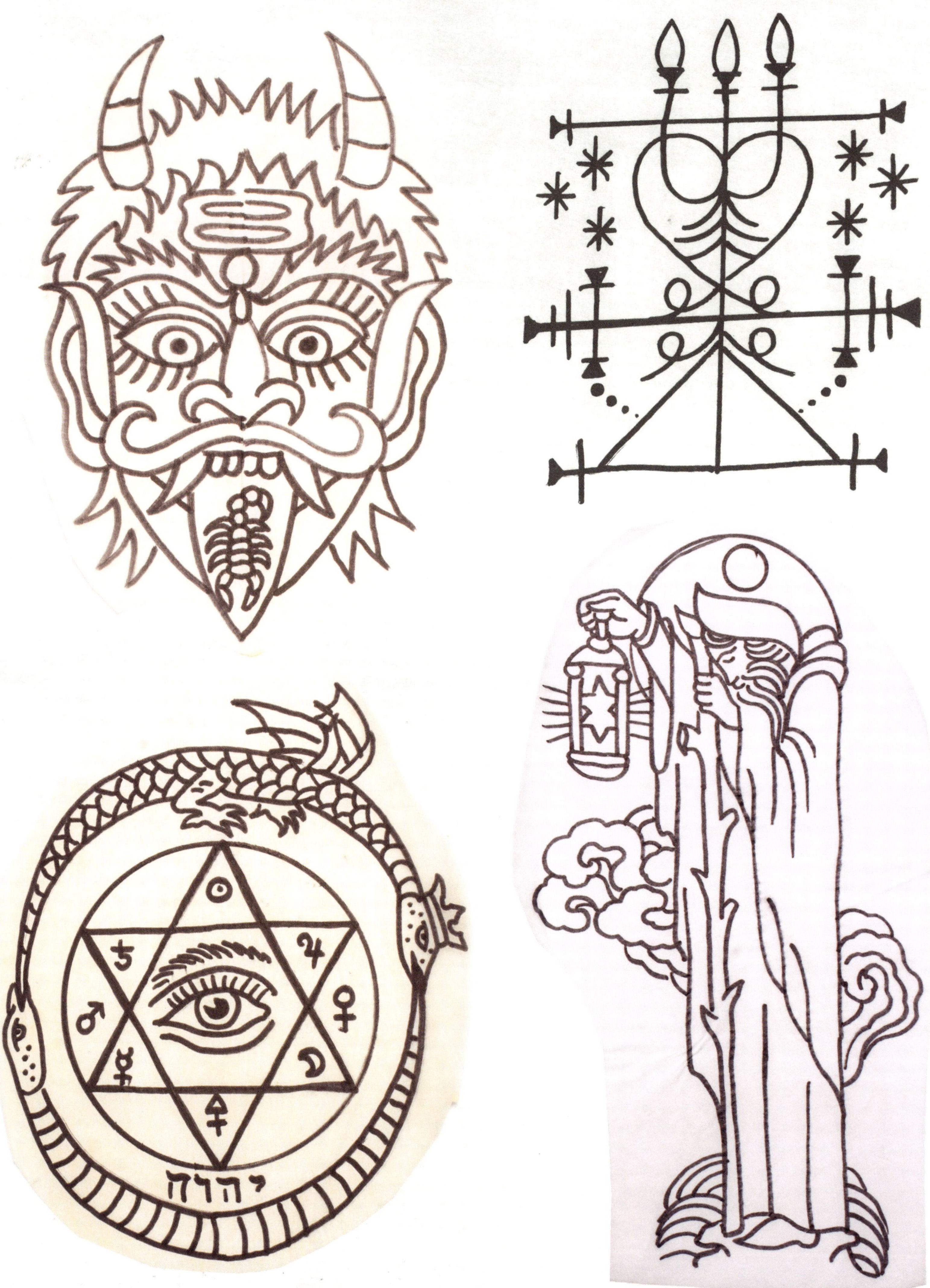

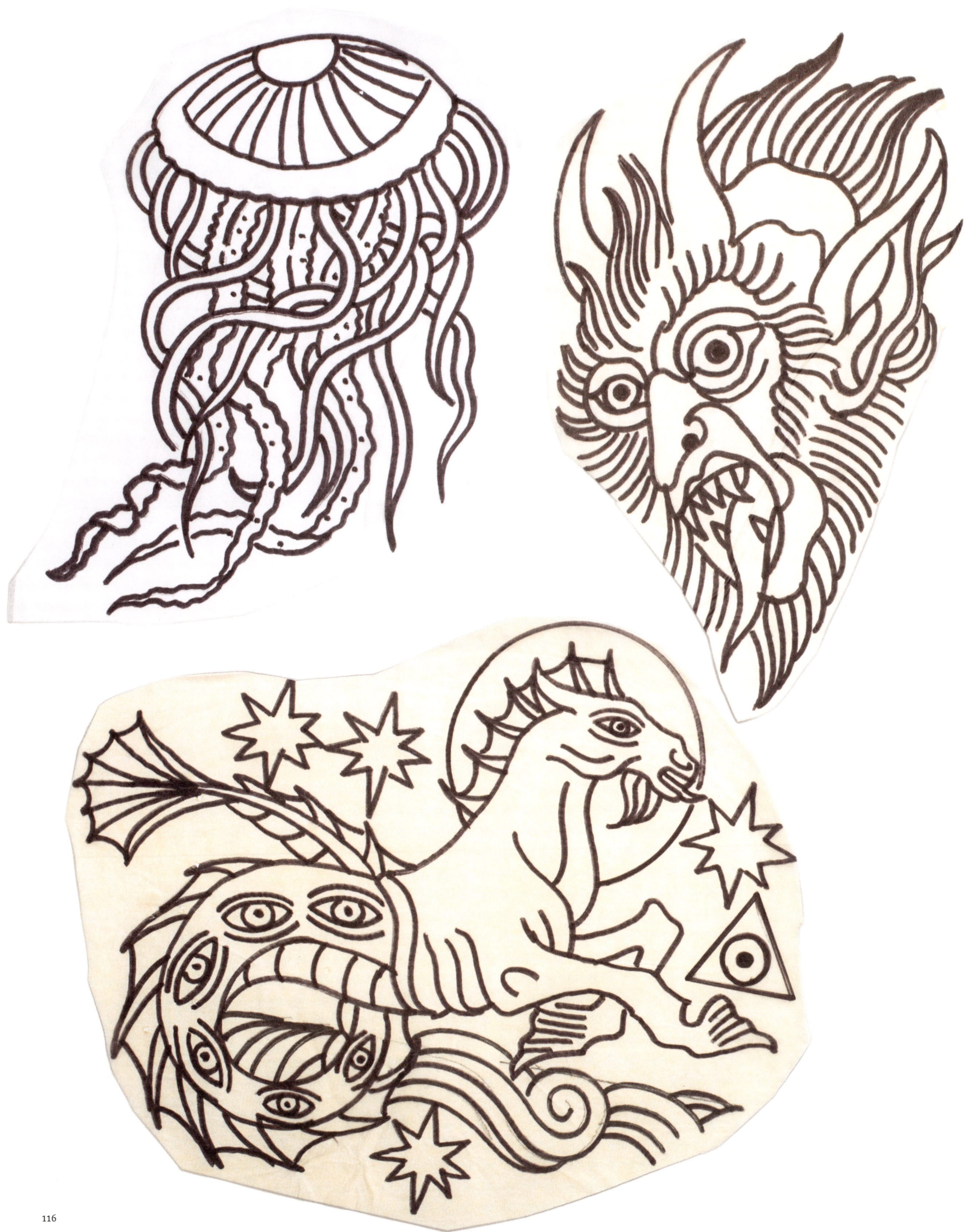

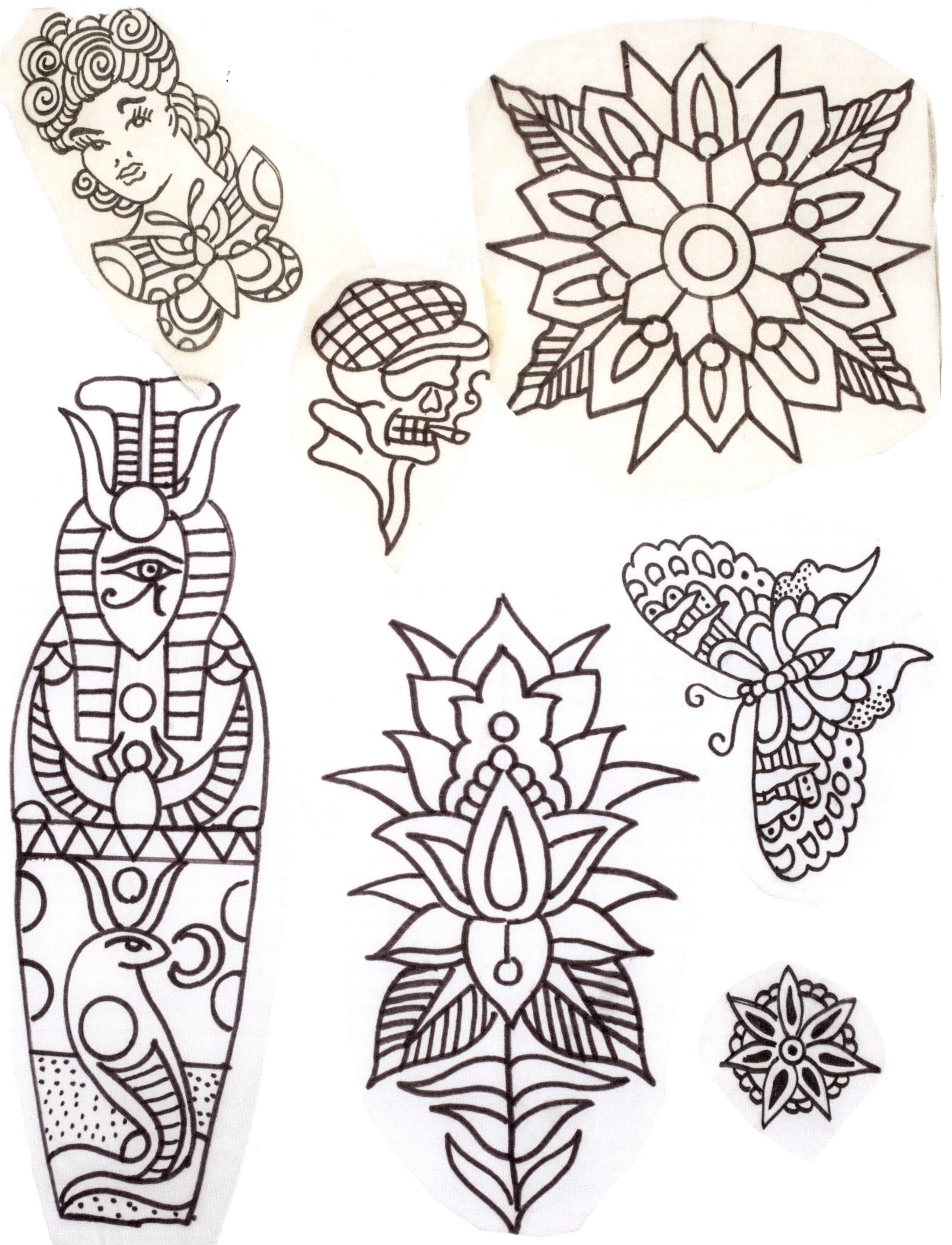

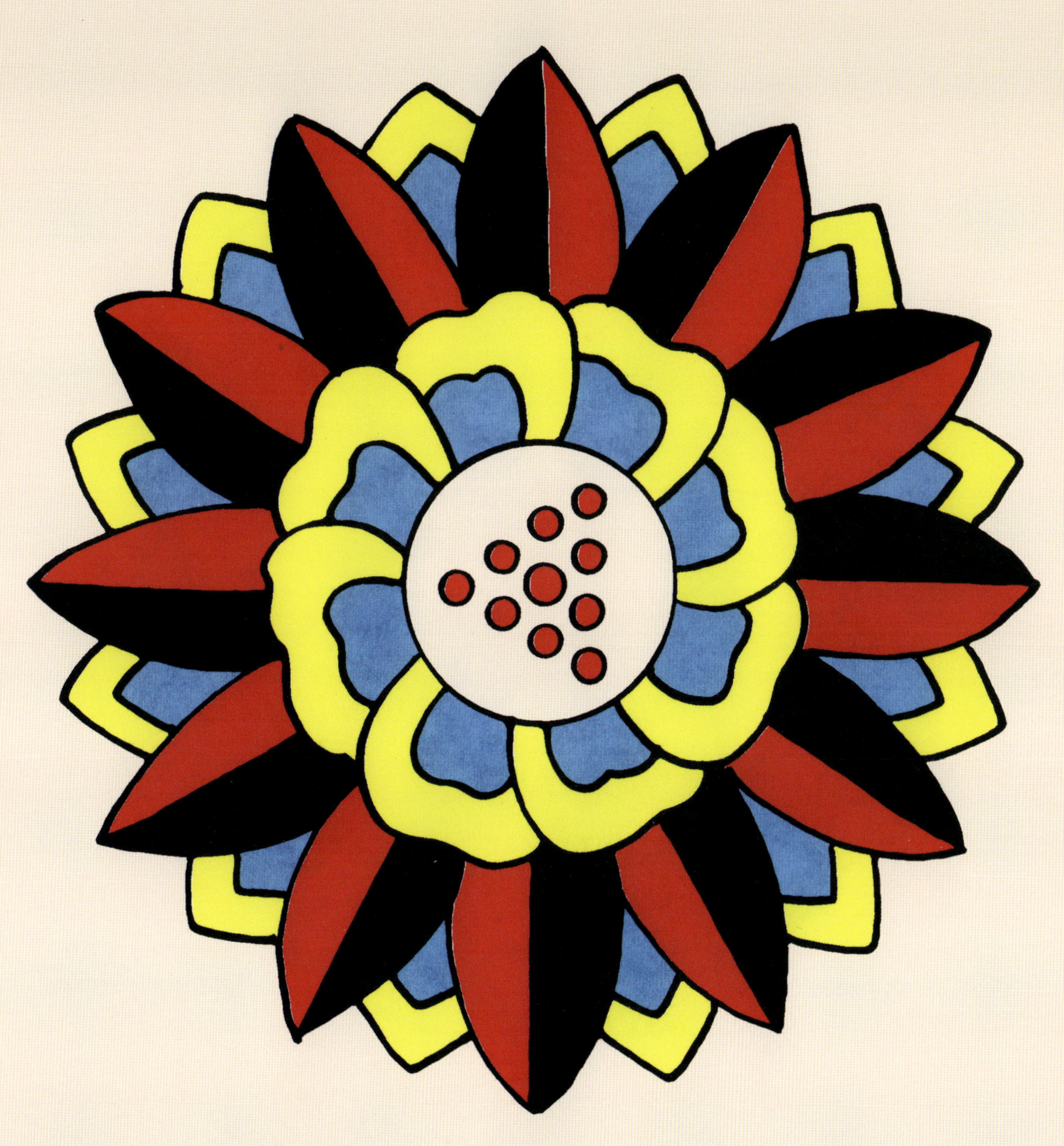

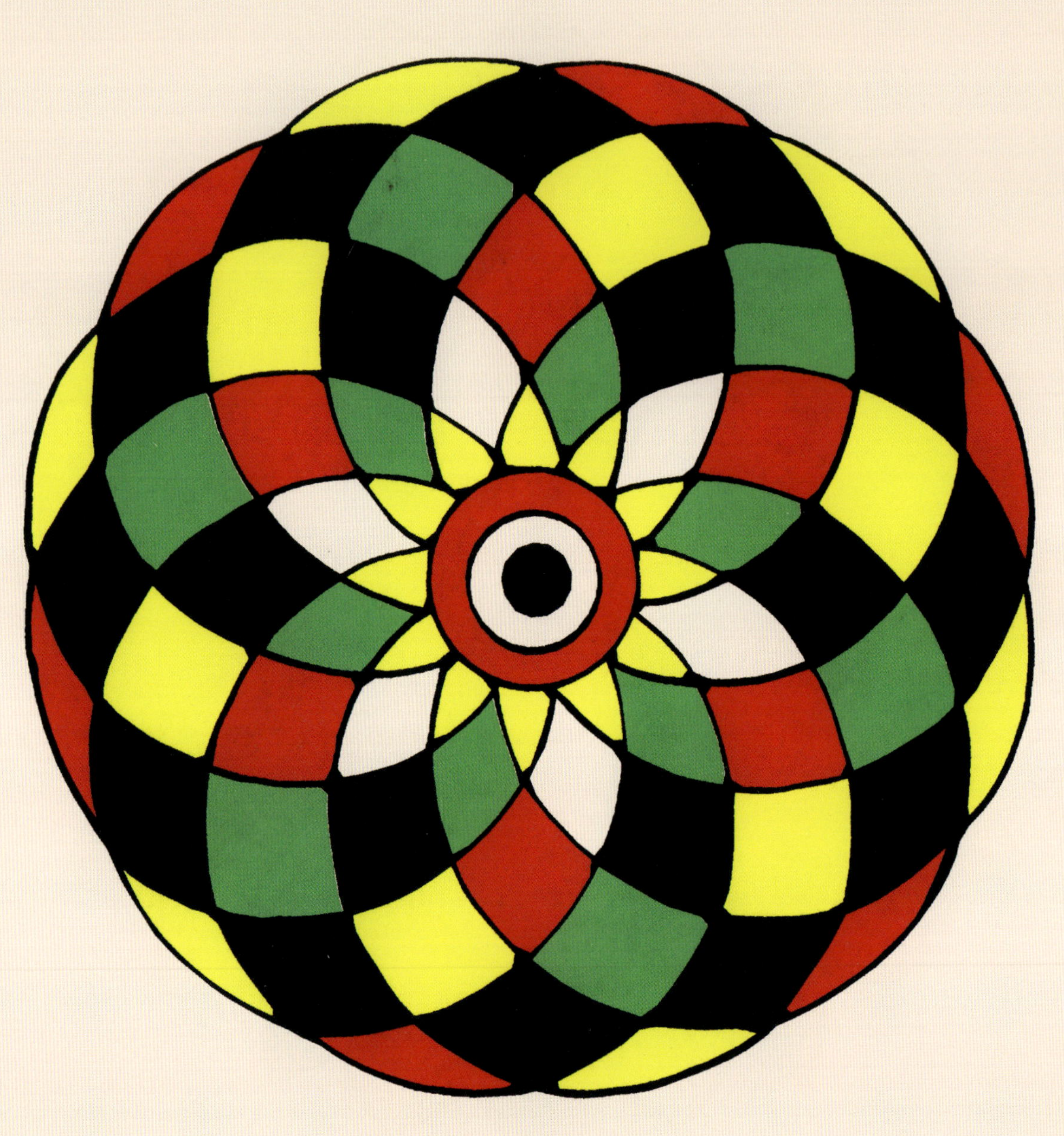

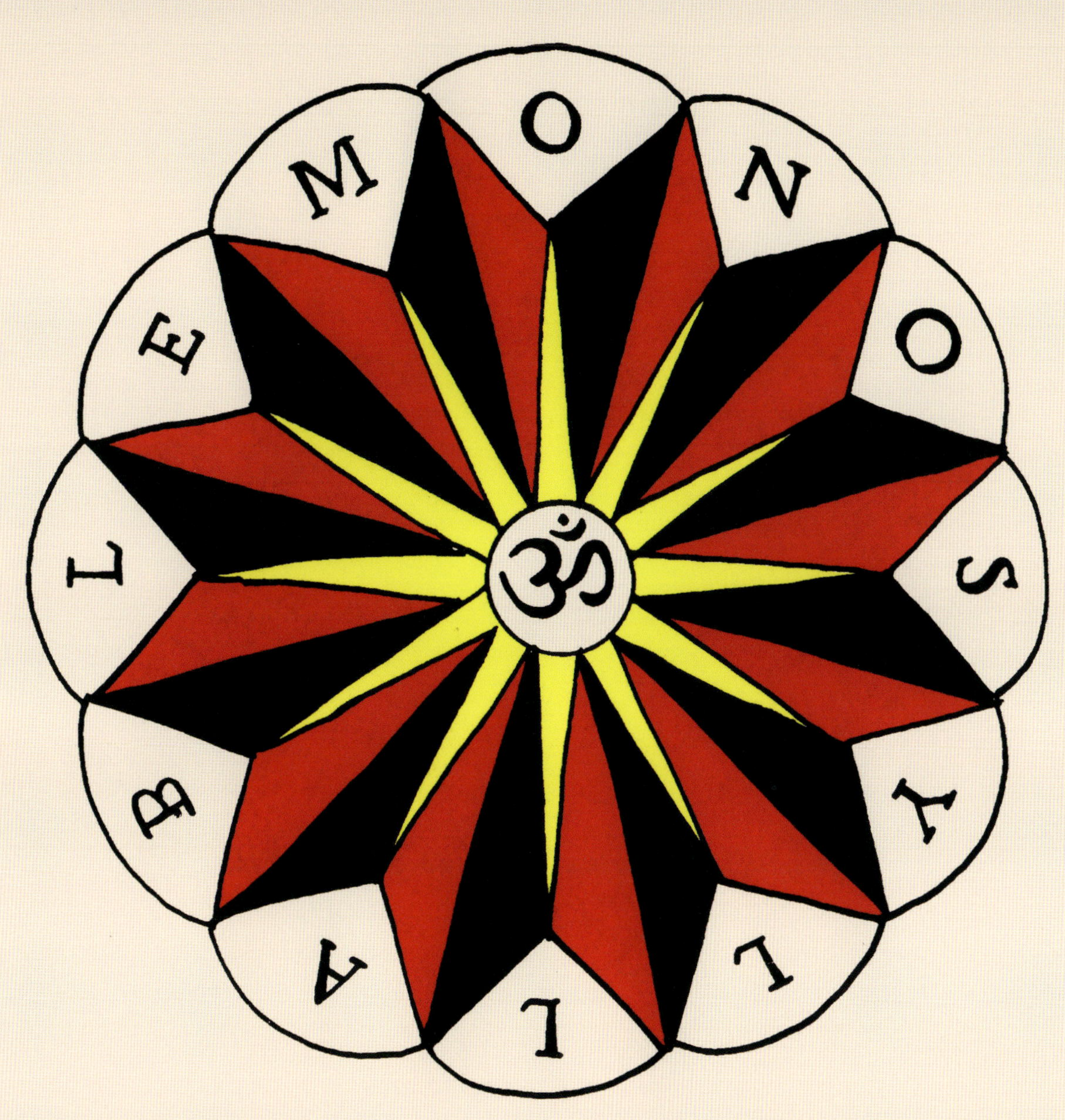
L E M O N O S Y L L A I B E

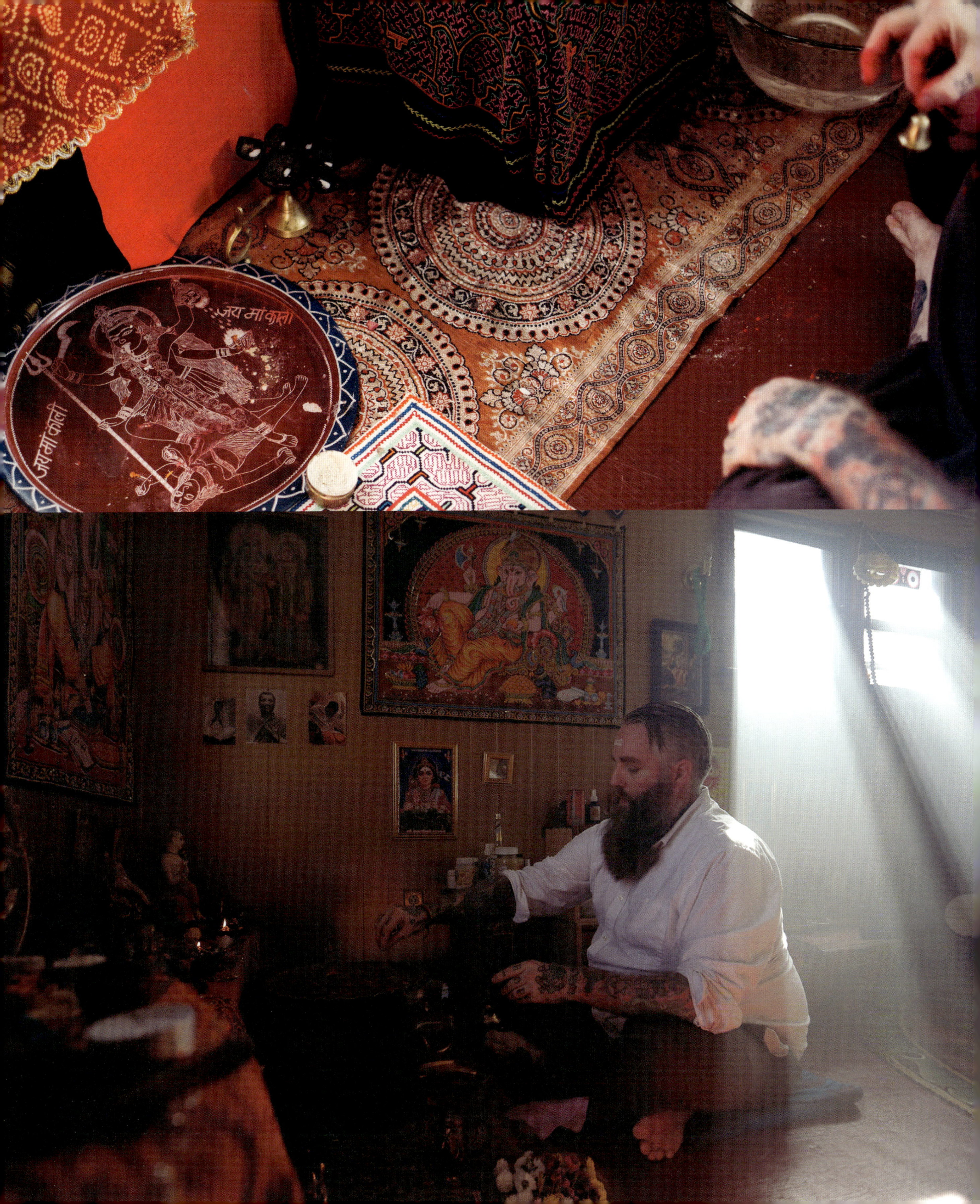

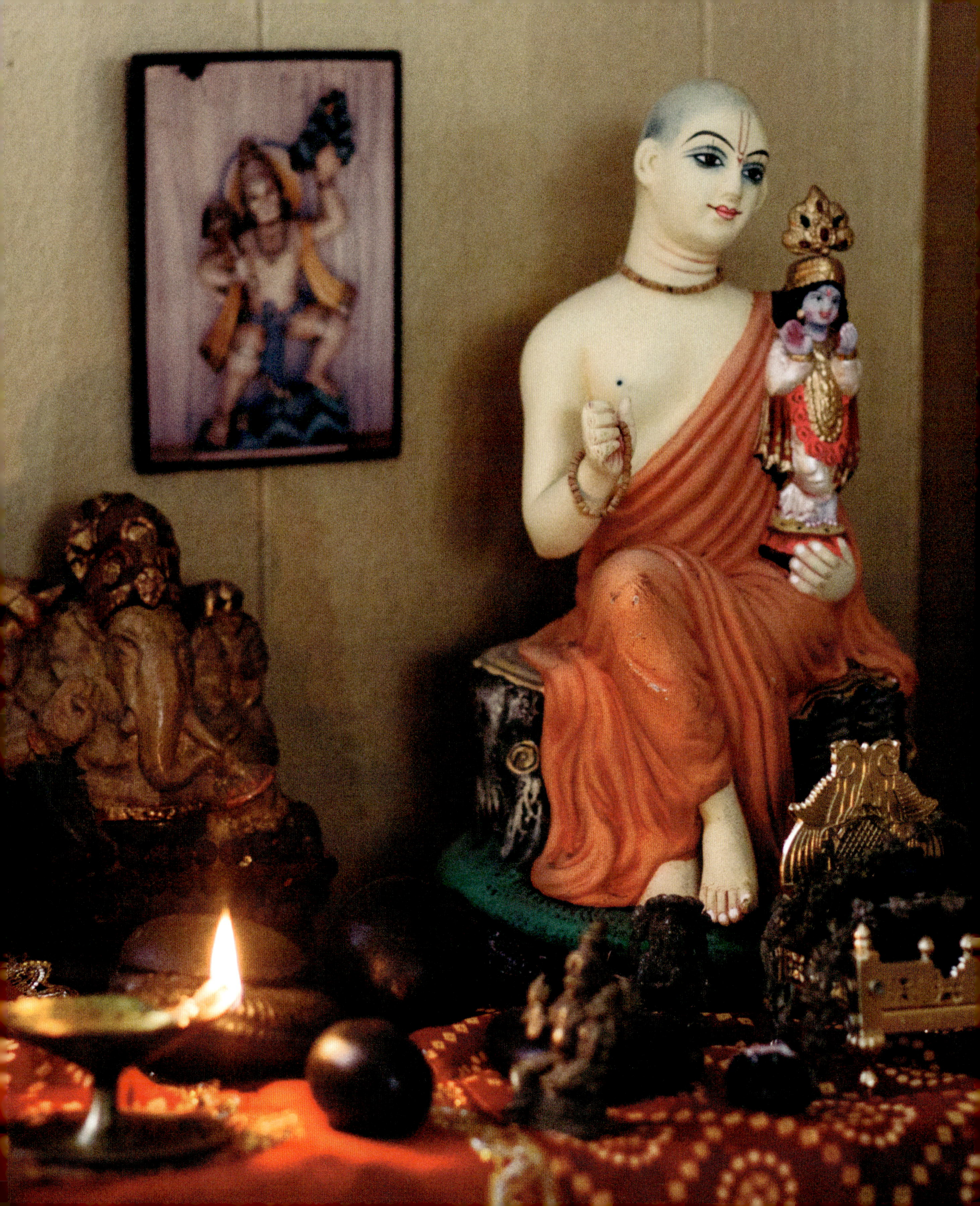

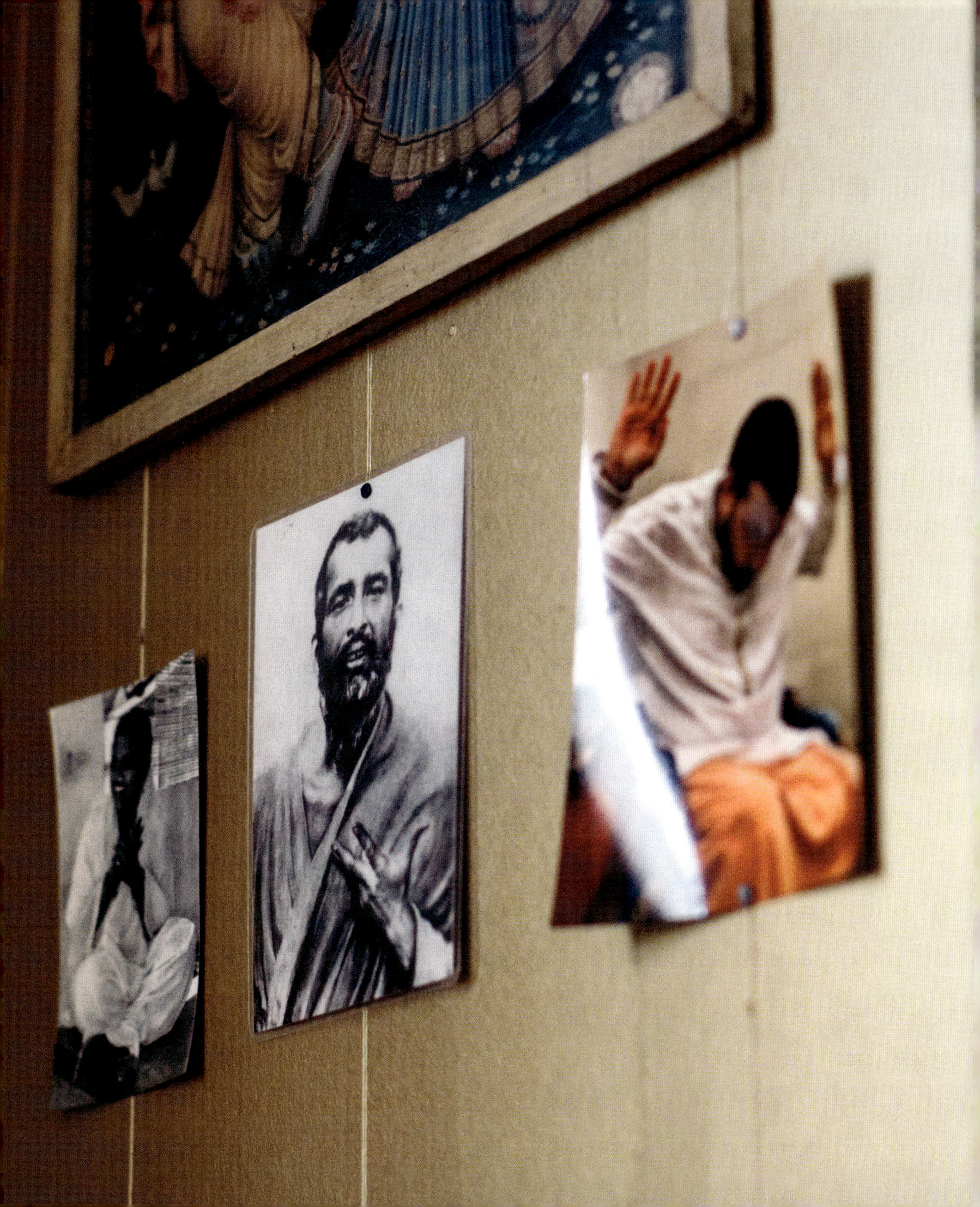

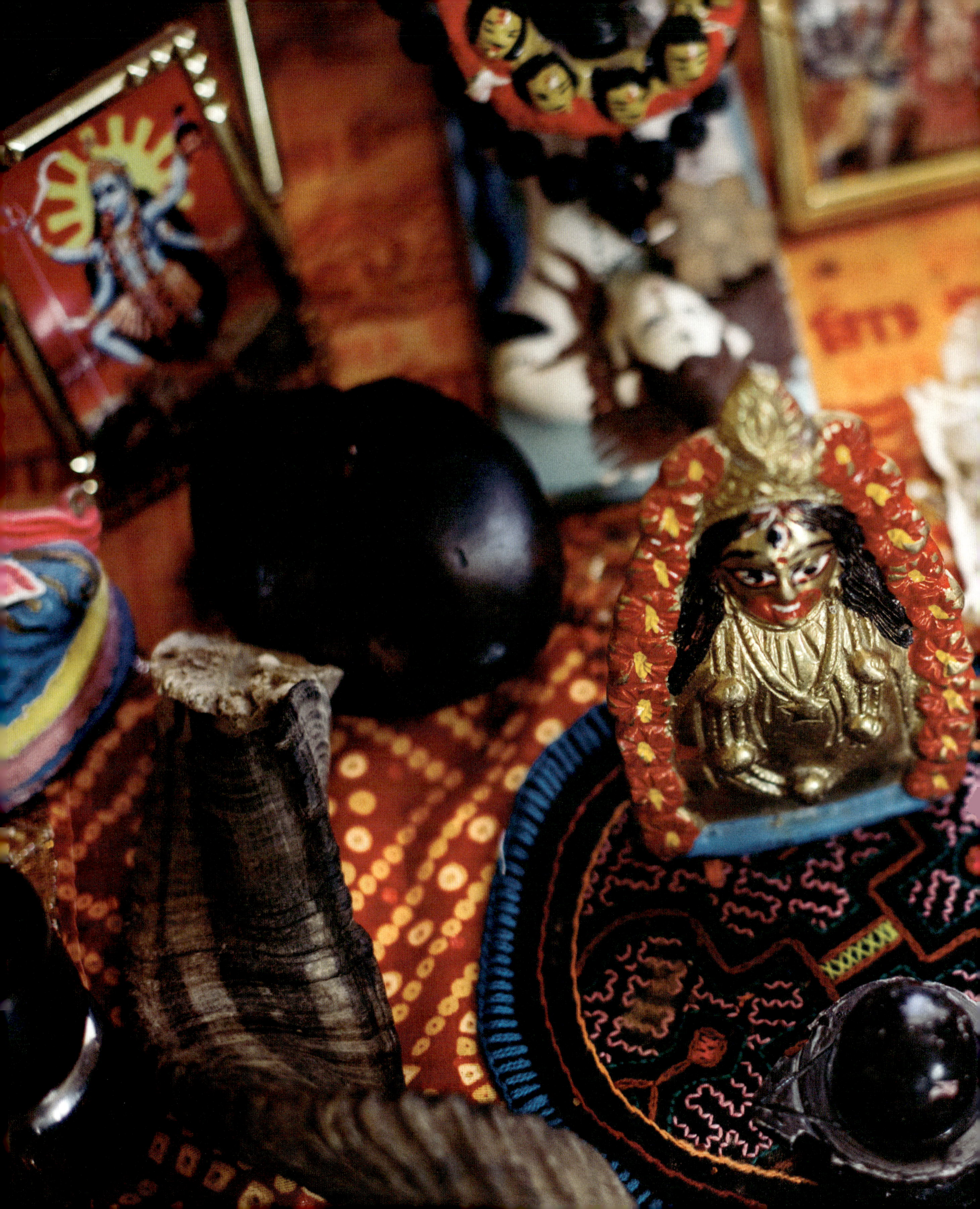

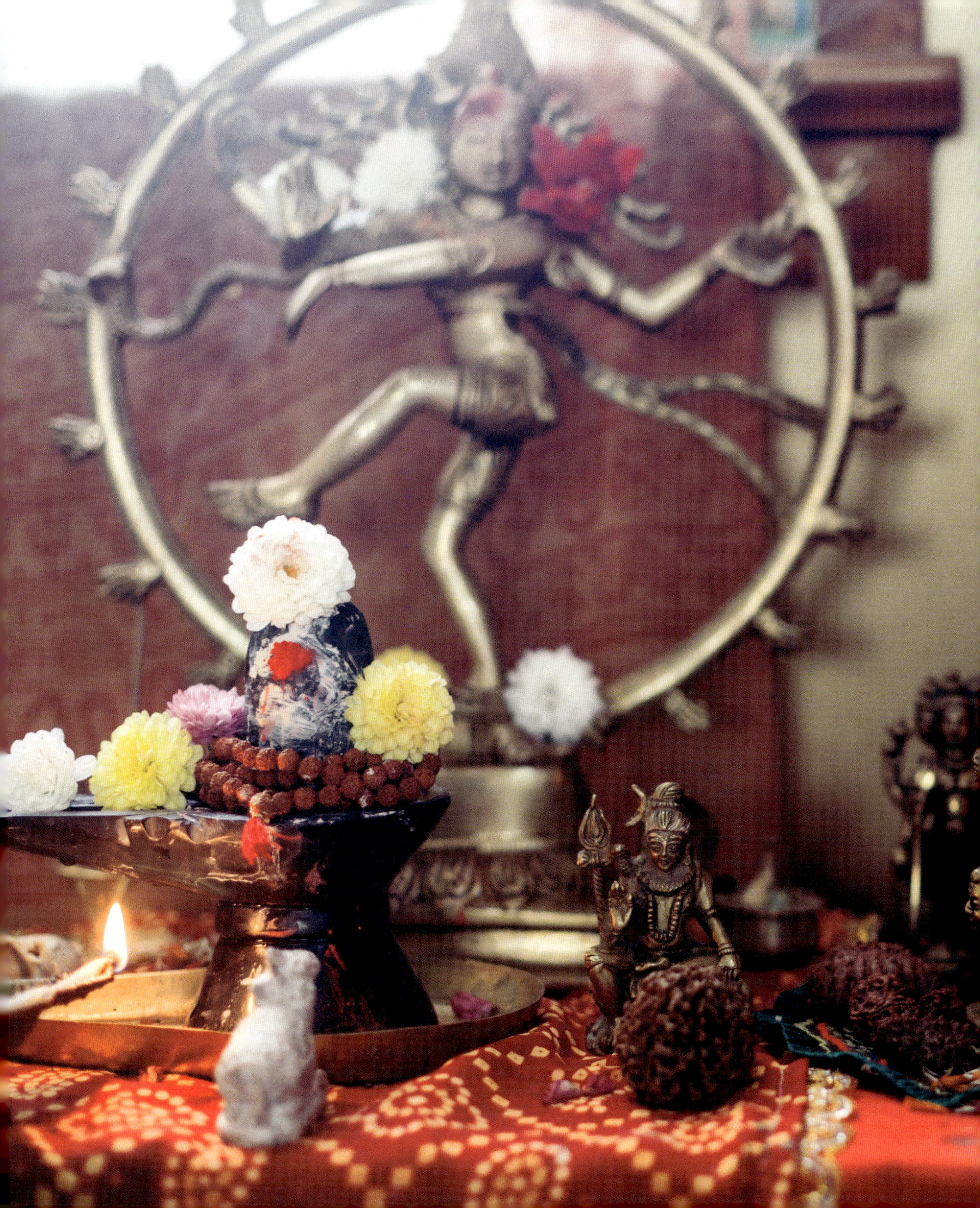

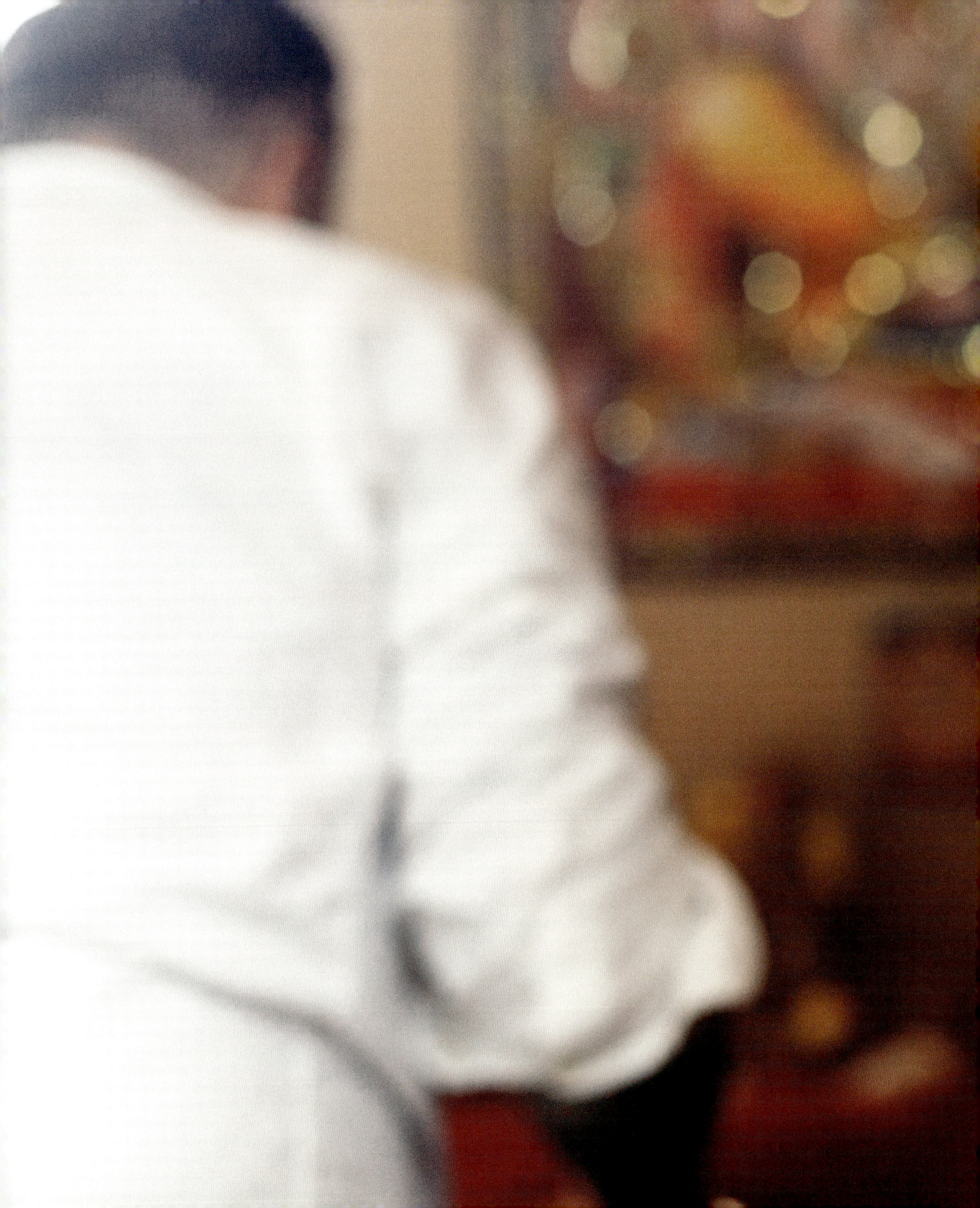

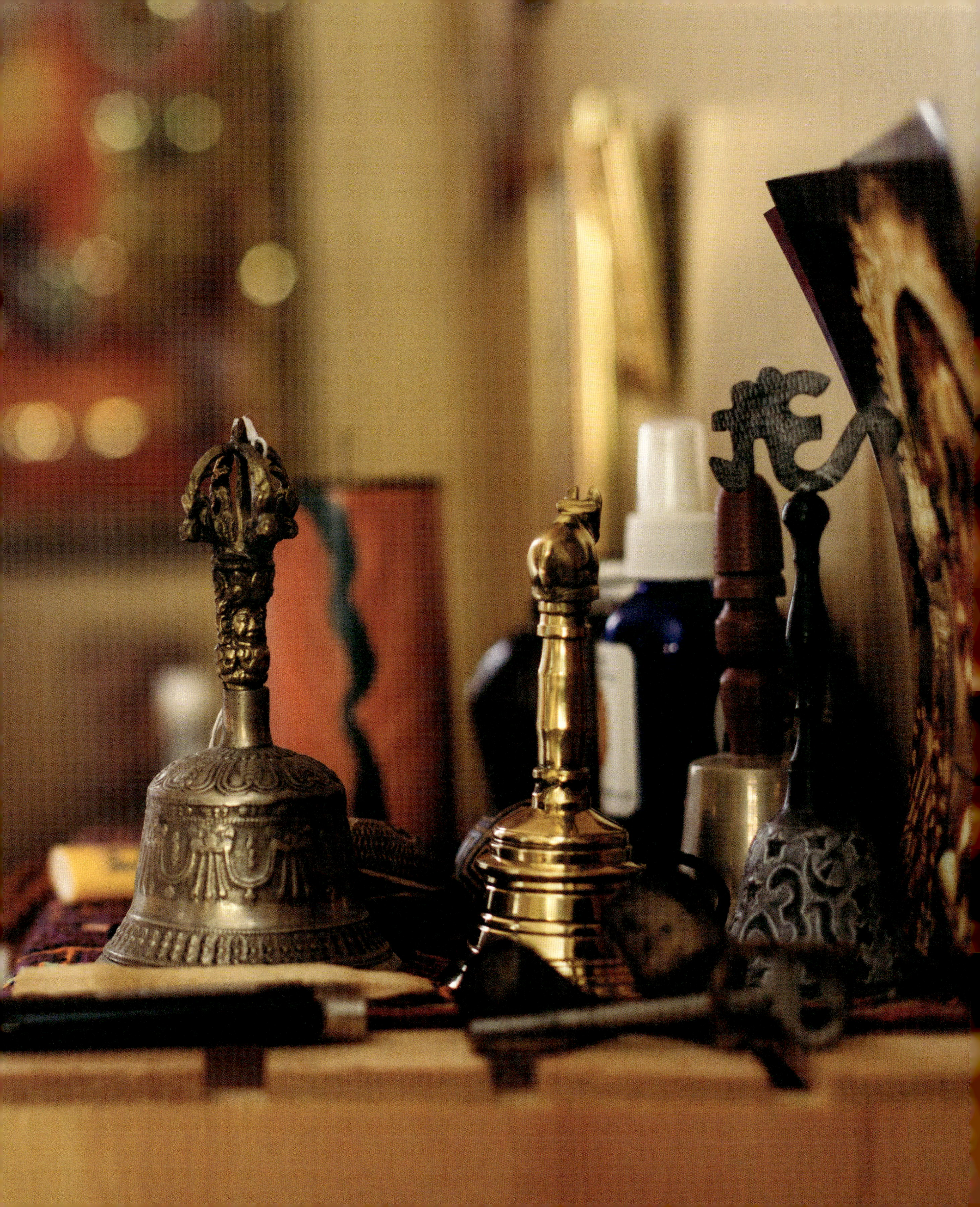

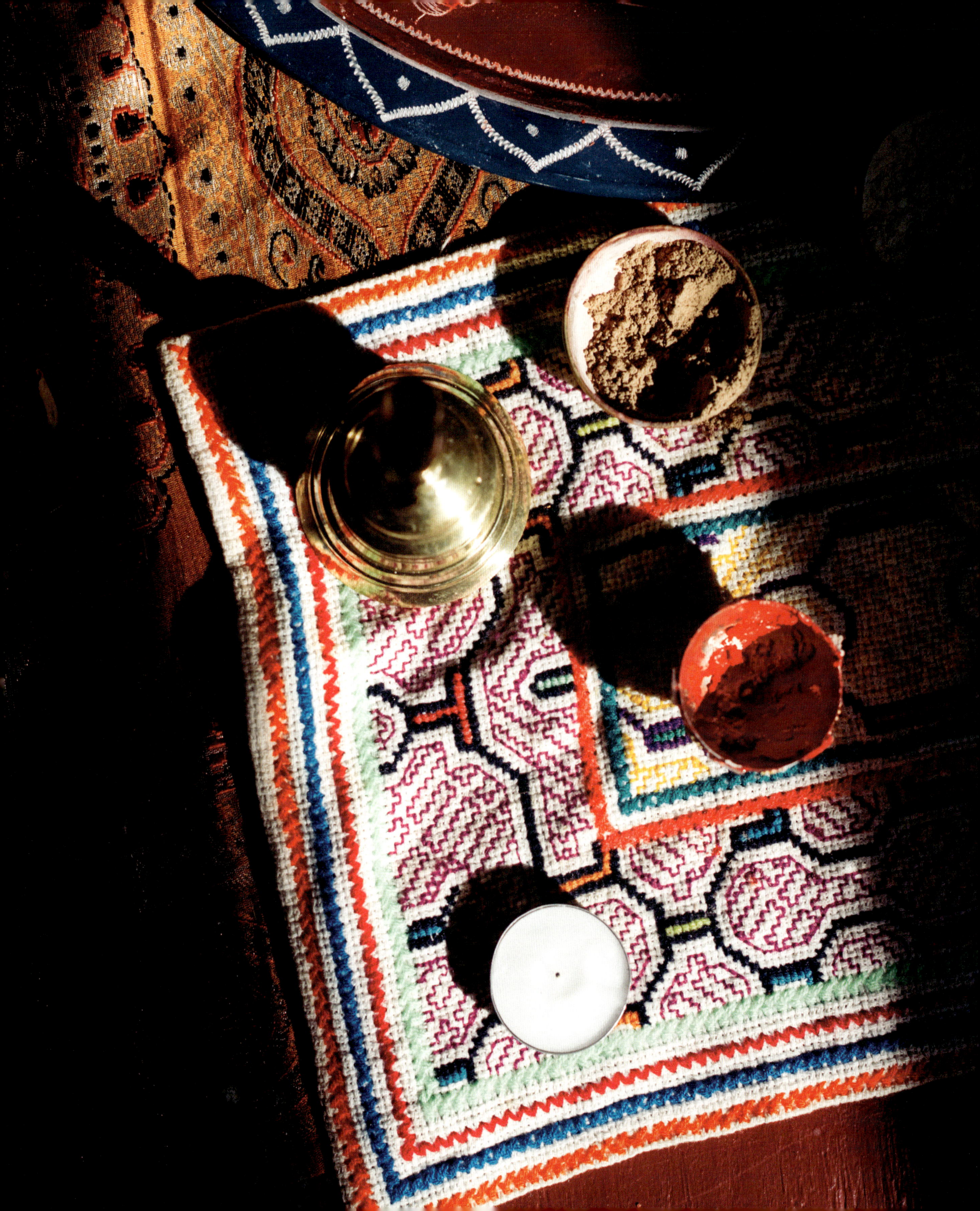

UNDIFERENTIATED LIGHT:
A CONVERSATION WITH
GENESIS P-ORRIDGE

Without exception, I think every one of my friends is cooler than me in one way or another: some of them more daring, some more instinctually kind, some more able to express themselves with clarity, and some simply more true to themselves than I allow myself to be. But Robert - Bink to all of his close friends - is all of these at once. It was so simple and immediate when we met as twenty-five-year-olds: of course we would be friends. That total urge to burn away all vanity that moves some people to a discipline of daily running and others to drunkenly sing, some to count their breaths and others to read voraciously: Bink and I had this thing in common. And still today, we share our thoughts and feelings without restraint. We excel at sitting together in silence. Both entirely and intuitively disinterested in all things we think foolish and habitual gigglers, we make each other laugh a lot.

So when we met in Manhattan on a July morning for Lebanese eggs, it was crazy how uneasy we both felt. I am notorious for being chronically early, but that day it was Bink who set the time and place, and I was astounded to learn that we were two-and-a-half hours early, just blocks from our appointment. Of course the day that Genesis suggested we come over was the one day that entire year that I had already planned to be in New York and had the afternoon free. We were so intimidated to meet her, the living, breathing thread through so much counterculture and avant-garde history. This is the person that invented industrial music with Throbbing Gristle, was the founding member of the art performance and musical collective COUM Transmissions before that, created powerful pastoral pop visions with Psychic TV, and continues to produce a dizzying array of art, film, and musical projects. Not many get called a "wrecker of civilization" by a member of the British Parliament. With her travels to Nepal and longstanding history with different religions, no one else made more sense to talk to about these paintings.

Bink and I sat in the park in quiet, and I repurposed questions that I had asked someone else as a sloppy plan B in the event that the interview stalled. We walked a long ways to a bookstore and browsed slowly and still had time. We got a coffee and sat bouncing our knees and sighing. We kept saying that we were going to buy flowers, but not quite yet, we didn't want to carry them that far, we'd get them soon. And then all at once we were late and pushing fast along a Broadway sidewalk thick with tourists. We'd moseyed in a giant circle since breakfast and were now, with just ten minutes to spare, as far from Genesis's apartment as we'd been all day.

We jumped in a cab that sat still in traffic. Our nerves intensified when we hopped out of the cab near the appointed address to find a bodega. We were so agitated that it felt like an epiphany of Copernican proportions when Bink finally said, "I'll go ask the guy at the counter."

Around the corner, the buzzer: "G. Orridge." We were buzzed in without a single syllable of nicety—no "Come on up," or "Eighth floor." We accidentally took the elevator down into the basement. We rode it back up and knocked and Genesis called out, "It's open," and never turned around to even peek at us when we entered. She was working at her desk and mumbled hello. We sat on the couch, and after a while passed in silence, she mumbled some frustrations about a minor banking irritation, revealing more detail than one commonly expects upon a first meeting. With a sigh, she then announced that she had to go buy some orange juice. She put on her leather jacket and left us there on her couch, still without so much as a glance at us. Bink and I sat in silence for ten minutes in a stranger's apartment, eyeing her bookshelf from afar, but never daring to stand up and walk over to it.

Upon her return, we cleared our throats and laid the paintings out on the coffee table.

Tim Kinsella
January 2016

Genesis P-Orridge [Looks at Sri Ganesha.] Oh, Ganesh.

Robert Ryan Yeah, that's Ganesh. I have him first because he's the Lord of Beginnings.

gp He's like Eshu-Elegba.

rr Is he the first deity you would approach?

gp Yeah. There always has to be an offering to him before you do any other ritual. He's the only one who knows where all the others are, where they are residing. He's also the Lord of the Crossroads. People say that he's evil, but he's not; he's a trickster. Westerners think that chaos math and quantum physics—which are both tricksters—have a negative moral cast, which they don't. It's the nature of existence: it is fluid and chaotic and it can't be defined.

rr And if you approach it with an open heart, it can work for you instead of being an evil thing.

gp Absolutely. That's why we use the number twenty-three. That's what we've used it for: as you go through life with an open mind and open heart, the universe does seem to become more and more friendly, and things that people call synchronicity happen more and more often. The universe becomes friendly with you. It starts to aid in your decisions, but really, you're aiding yourself by focusing inwards and getting more and more clear about what it is you really mean when you speak, what you really mean to do. We call it the "of-course factor."

rr I'm born on the twenty-third.

[We all laugh.]

rr It's always coming up and it's always something I've paid attention to.

gp Burroughs was the one that turned me on to it. In his notebooks, as he went along, he would notice that there were more and more and more twenty-threes cropping up—more hotel rooms with the number twenty-three, more receipts from cafeterias with twenty-three dollars. So he had the same belief: that you can create the equivalent of a friendship with what other people think of as "coincidence."

rr And it's funny that you mentioned that it's more about learning about yourself. That's what all these Hindu rituals are about. It's not about worshipping a man with an elephant head. It's about recognizing that spirit within yourself, with each one being a symbol of your evolutionary path and your spiritual path. It's conditioned from the moment of birth.

gp Before you're even out! They now know that fetuses smile, even laugh inside the womb. Now what is a baby laughing at before it's even appeared out here? The ridiculousness of existence, obviously. The cosmic joke. So there they are listening and hearing sounds and people assume they don't know what the sounds are. But we believe tones in and of themselves can give meaning. We read our poetry all over the world. And a lot of our poetry is complicated, yet we can read poetry in Austria and Russia and Australia and Scandanavia and Iceland and Africa and people respond to it in the correct way emotionally. So the tones must be communicating, because they don't know the words. That was interesting to learn—that no matter how complex the idea, you can transmit it just by saying it with belief.

Tim Kinsella Do you feel that's true with color and form, too? If someone was to see these paintings and not know the traditional story that it represents, is there something inherent to these images that would transcend the tradition?

gp We believe so.

rr I believe so.

gp There are certain similarities that crop up everywhere. The trident appears everywhere, from Greek to Roman to Hindu to Tibetan to Native American traditions. It's everywhere. What does that mean? It means it's a nonverbal cue of some kind. Obviously it's a very important one for every culture to have honed in on it.

rr Swastikas, the cross as well. How do you feel about the swastika? How Hitler hijacked that symbol. Do you think it's important to take that back? To liberate it from a negative force like that? It's such a powerful symbol and such an important symbol.

gp It is. That's always been a difficult one. Why should forty years of human history in one small part of the planet dictate how everybody interprets a symbol that's ancient? It shouldn't. But again, it's ignorance in the West; it's the same as when they say about Santeria, "Oh they killed chickens and turkeys and ducks and goats." Well, what happens at Thanksgiving? How many millions are slaughtered, and more at Christmas for Jesus? But do you do it yourself? Do

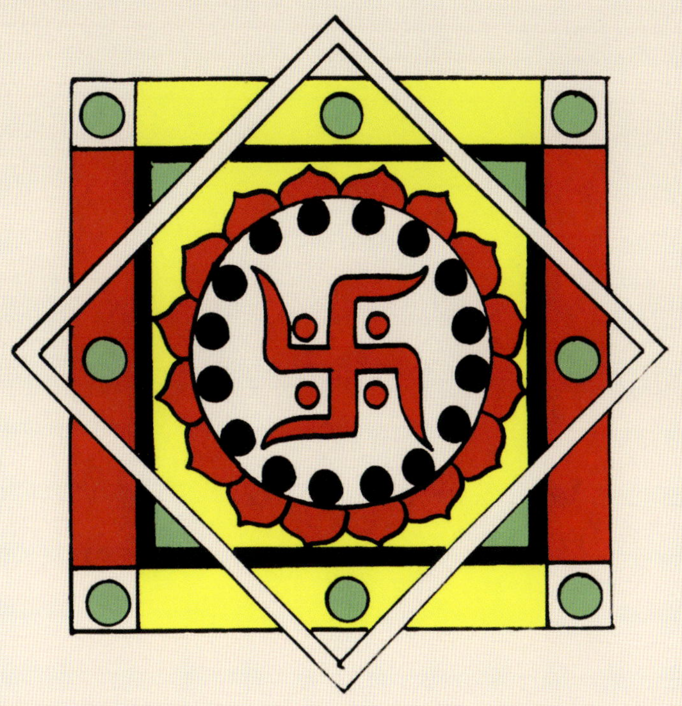

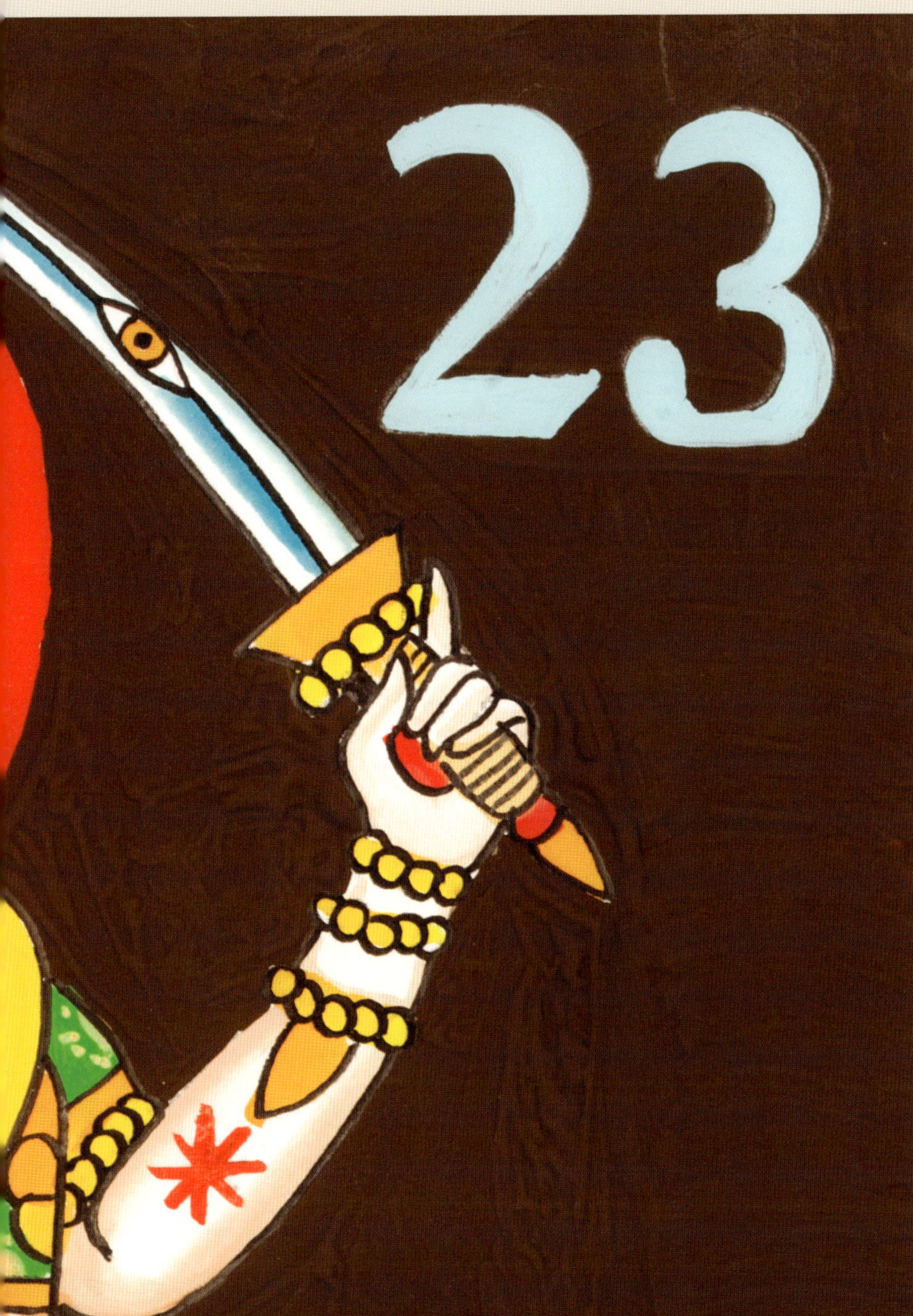

you bless the animal? Do you say, "We are sorry for taking your life but we will try to have you come back in a higher state," and then eat it and take responsibility? No. They've divorced themselves from the meanings of their own rituals.

rr No, they have a butcher do it and it comes in a nice package.

gp And they don't have to think about it, which is completely against the point. You're supposed to think about it. When we were in Benin and saw the religious ceremony with the chicken, they cook it and they eat it because they can't afford to lose a chicken. They're so poor, so it's a big decision to make a sacrifice. And unless it's to cure a really bad illness, you eat it. You have to.

rr It's the true meaning of the word sacrifice.

gp Exactly. So many people think pluralism is somehow primitive, but it's not. It's actually a sophisticated system. It's the oldest system in terms of a structured system of thought. Hinduism is closer to the story of the universe and how it was formed than any other religion.

rr Even that has been hijacked by the priest craft. When it was a folk religion, given to the people by the Rishis through the use of the plants and agriculture, I think it had a lot more resonance in the heart than it did with caste or governmental systems. Do you see a shift in attention now? A lot of people talk about it, I hear it a lot, and I'm not quite sure if I do or not … but I do see an awareness starting to spring up.

gp We're really torn as well. We've been giving lectures for years now. We talk about psychic phenomena, different religious beliefs, things that we have witnessed that go beyond rational Western thought. Ironically, even though we've been called the most evil person in Britain, we talk about kindness, compassion, and forgiveness. We used to get maybe thirty to sixty people, now we get three hundred to four hundred. And they're really listening, because we will often do a two-hour nonstop talk off the cuff and they don't leave; it's totally silent. That has nothing to do with me; it's just this hunger that has developed amongst a lot of people who are dissatisfied with all the purported answers from captivism and fundamentalism of every kind. They know that it's not satisfying, they know it's not the truth, and they know it's not telling the story of what this might be. This is a very mysterious thing to be a part of, this apparent physical world. And we're here very briefly, unless you believe in reincarnation. It's a blessing to experience anything with your senses. The sensory existence is just one of the most miraculous, fantastic things. And for people to be distracted by all these toys, all these crises and pressures and structures, is a sin, if there is such a thing. That's a sin: taking people away from their chance to be liberated from ignorance and fear. Fear is the basic weapon of all power structures. Its main application is for someone who is different, or some kind of people who are different. Something "other" to distract people from what's really happening to them.

rr It works both ways. I see it in this country now: we have the Islamic fundamentalists. But the Islamic fundamentalists have the infidel: Westerners. They're both playing into this illusion of difference, of separation.

gp We used to work with this Apache shaman back in the '80s. He was black. A lot of people don't realize that there were black Native Americans, but they mingled. He was from a clan of shamans and they would teach other shamans. They were like the PhDs of shamanism. They were living on this small piece of land where they would mine for bits of tin and this and that. Then they came across uranium in the '60s. And one day when all of the grown men of the clan were in the mine, it blew up and killed them all. The government took back the land, saying it was too dangerous for them to live there, because they wanted

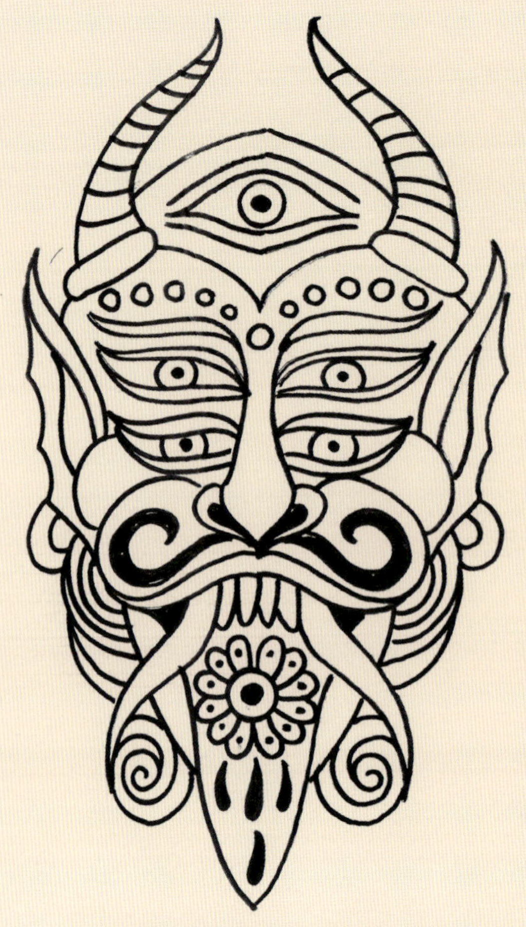

all the minerals. He was then adopted in the suburbs of Los Angeles. They were all orphans, so they spread them out to "good Christian families." Can you imagine how weird it would be sent to live with right-wing Christians in LA? In the late '50s, early '60s? After a few days of him living there, the father said, "I need to talk to you. Why do you keep urinating in the garden?" And the kid said, "Well where else am I supposed to do it?" The father said, "You use the toilet." And the kid said, "What's the toilet?" So they showed it to him and he said, "Oh, I saw that, but it's clean water, why would I do that in the clean water?" To him, that was too precious. You don't piss in pure water.

rr You piss in the dirt.

gp It makes you realize how far apart we are in our perceptions of simple things.

rr How counterintuitive, too.

gp I asked him about death, and he said, "We don't have a word for death. The nearest would be 'separation.'" We thought about it and realized that when you put concrete over the earth that's fertile, you're separating it from the life that can grow in it. And you start to see how many things we do that separate us from natural processes. Then

this kid went to school and he was told by the art teacher to do a painting with the color green as the main aspect to it. So he sat there and looked at the paper, and everyone else was painting away and he was just staring at the paper. The art teacher came up and asked, "Why aren't you painting anything?" The kid said, "I don't know what green is." The teacher said "Green! You know, red, white, blue, green." And the kid goes, "I don't know what those mean." And eventually after a discussion, the young shaman said, "Oh I see, you mean the color of the grass when the rain has just fallen and it's really bright." Or maybe he mentioned the color of the leaves on a certain tree, but everything was a natural connection and really accurate. There are infinite greens.

rr He's looking at the world through undifferentiated light.

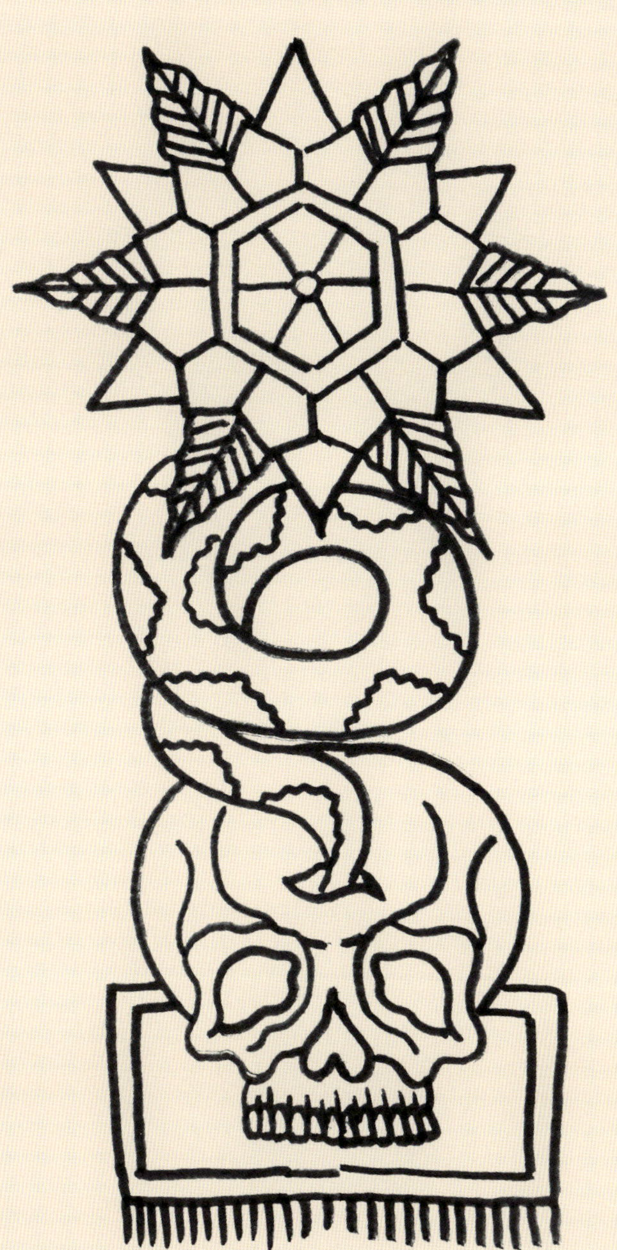

gp Yeah. They're bringing everything down, restricting even the encouragement of perception to the lowest possible form. "There are six colors and black and white." They don't even explain that white is everything reflected and black is everything absorbed. We got really lucky in school. After the age of eleven, they didn't even admit that art existed, they didn't teach you anything other than painting and drawing. But my art teachers thought that we had some talent and so when we were fourteen they gave us the key to the art room and let me use it anytime during lunch or after school. So we became self-taught at painting.

rr You were so lucky because you weren't instructed.

gp The irony of it was that eventually the school created an art prize for me when we left. We got an art prize for a class that didn't exist. We got a book on Dada and surrealism as the prize.

rr Were you influenced by the early Dada stuff?

gp Especially the collages. Those collages just blew my mind. We tried to copy them at first. We've still got diaries from then. You want to see what I was doing in 1960?

[Laughs.]

rr You've traveled so much I can't believe you still have all this stuff.

gp It was in storage. *[Retrieves diary.]* This was in '66. So at first we were just trying to copy little weird things. That's what I looked like as a teenager *[shows picture]*. Especially the Dada collages; those collages just blew my mind. We tried to copy them at first.

rr A hippie! Were hippies "hippies" at that point?

gp We called ourselves freaks. We still do collages *[flips through diary]*. Look at that: an African shaman.

Of course everything was going to be OK. Genesis handed me her teenage diary and motioned that I should flip through. It was a dense and colorful tcollage of drawings and writing, photos and quotes cut from magazines. All the common signifiers that we talk about as adults with long histories of investment into these issues - conformity and rebellion, spirituality and the drive to really live - were being investigated by Genesis when she was just a teenager, before hippies were even called "hippies."

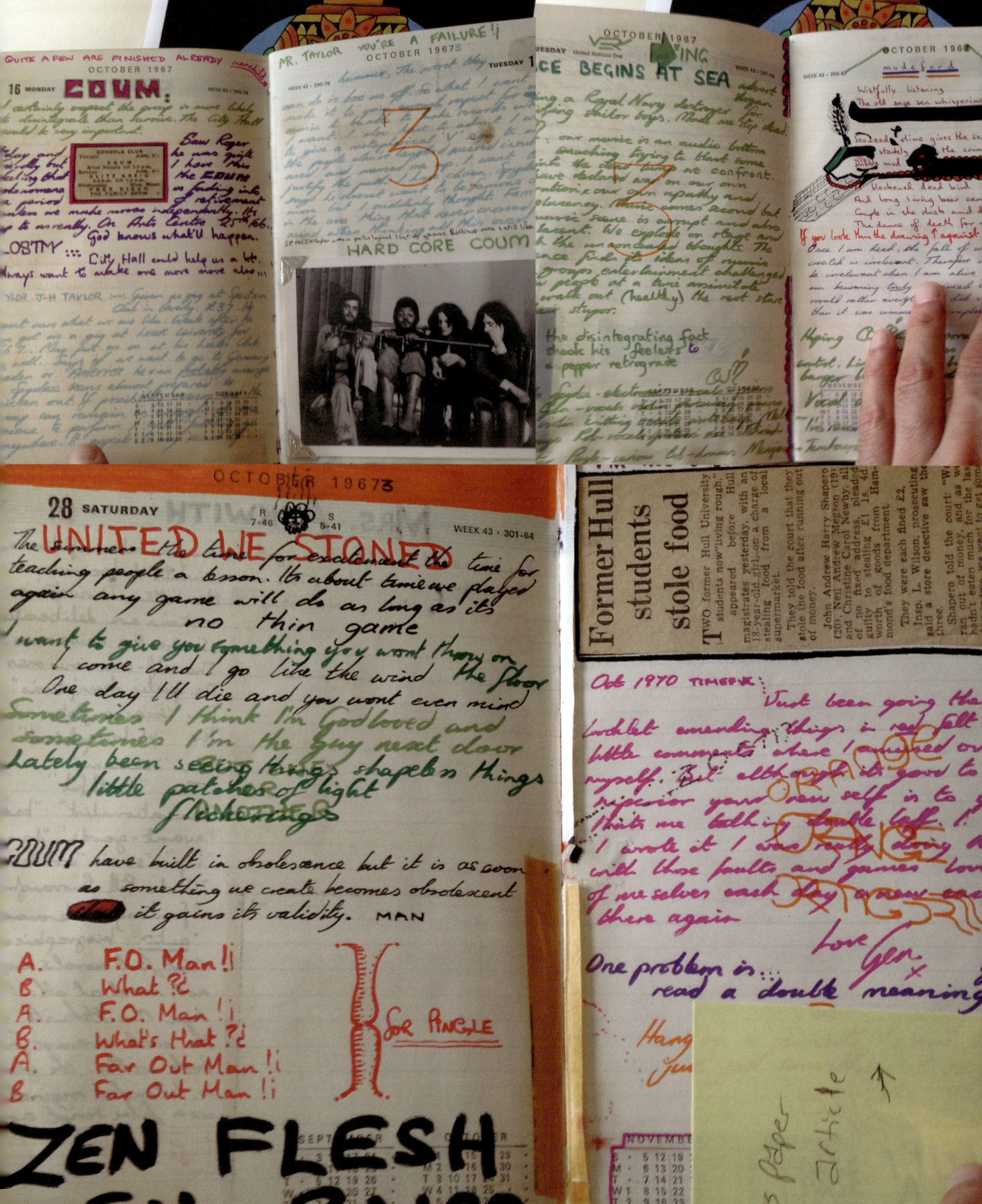
QUITE A FEW ARE FINISHED ALREADY
OCTOBER 1967
16 MONDAY COUM:
MR. TAYLOR YOU'RE A FAILURE!
OCTOBER 1967
3
HARD CORE COUM
OCTOBER 1967
...CE BEGINS AT SEA
3
OCTOBER 1967
mudeford
Wistfully listening
The old sage sea whispering
OCTOBER 1967
28 SATURDAY
WEEK 43 · 301-64
UNITED WE STONED
no thin game
for PINGLE
A.   F.O. Man !i
B.   What ?i
A.   F.O. Man !i
B.   What's that ?i
A.   Far Out Man !i
B.   Far Out Man !i
ZEN FLESH
Former Hull students stole food
Oct 1970
One problem is...
read a double meaning
Love Gen

rr The Eastern philosophy or Eastern thought was present from this early on with you?

gp What happened was when I was a kid … I used to have asthma really bad. I would be too sick to get out of the house, so I would read. My father would give me books, and one of them was [Heinrich Harrer's] Seven Years in Tibet. I was ten, and we became totally enamored with this culture. We thought it was incredible. And from then on we tried to get everything we could find on Tibetan Buddhism, Zen Buddhism, Hinduism, and so on. My father's policy was, "If you can read it, then you can read it." He never censored what I read, which is incredible.

rr Did he have any kind of religious or spiritual leanings?

gp No. He was in the war in the very beginning, and I think you lose your sense of religion when you see that. He did become a Christian in the last two or three years of his life.

rr That happens to a lot of people.

gp You're right. A lot of people do that when they are facing death. He was dying of emphysema. Whatever works, you know? I'm not going to say anything positive or negative about that. It's a terrible way to go, so I'm sure he needed comfort of any kind.

rr It's fascinating to me that through asthma you discovered Buddhism. Because Buddhism is all about the breath.

gp I got rid of my asthma through meditation. When we got asthma attacks we would always panic. As we got older and we read more, we decided to focus inward and not panic. Go somewhere else that was calm. And at first it would be four or five days that we felt really ill. Then it would get shorter and shorter, until it was a day. And then it wasn't a panic at all. So by the age of seventeen, we were playing sports in school. They had been giving me cortisone, which at the time was a new wonder drug; they didn't know the dangers of it at that point. So the doctor told me I didn't need to take my pills anymore because I wasn't having asthma attacks. This was on a Friday when he told me. On Saturday we started feeling a bit weird. Sunday, we felt even more strange and couldn't breathe properly. Then Monday, I told my mom I couldn't go to school. She went downstairs and she heard a big thud. My sister ran up, thinking I had dropped or broken something and was going to enjoy getting me in trouble. Apparently, I was on the floor, unconscious, turning blue.

Then there's a series of beautiful of-course factors: of course a doctor had just moved into the house opposite ours on our street, and of course he was late for work that day, and of course that weekend he had just read a magazine article that said that one of the side effects of long term use of cortisone and other steroids is that it destroys your adrenal glands. And so he just guessed and put it all together and he ran across the road and did the whole Pulp Fiction thing—bam! – with adrenaline and they took me to the hospital. And we remember this bit: we remember floating above me in the ER and the nurses and the doctors trying to decide who would tell my parents I was dead. I'm thinking, "I'm not dead! I'm fine, I'm here!" But we don't remember getting back in the body, which is really frustrating. Next thing we remember is waking up the next morning with an oxygen mask, still alive … theoretically. My mother said the first thing we said when they took the oxygen off was, "Fuck! What is this? What is all this stuff on me? What the fuck is going on?" She didn't know I swore until then. [Laughs.] The doctor came and explained what had happened. Your adrenals have two cortices. One of them is fight or flight, and the other one releases small amounts all day long that trigger other organs to work. And that's the one that got destroyed by the steroids. All my organs were shutting down one at a time, keeping the heart going the longest.

rr So your body wasn't getting any adrenaline anymore?

gp No.

rr That's crazy. Was it a withdrawal symptom from the medicine?

gp No, it was permanent damage.

rr Wow, so if you hadn't been taken off these drugs you would be dead. That's powerful. Was that your first shamanic or out of body experience?

gp Yes. It was very powerful. The doctor came to see me and said that it was such a new development with these drugs that I could go on to lead a normal healthy life for a long time or I could drop dead any day.

rr How old were you at the time?

gp Seventeen.

rr That's a heavy message to carry at seventeen.

gp We just sat there all day and rationalized it and thought it through. We had already decided we wanted to be a beatnik bohemian, traveling the world looking for wisdom … fuck it! What's the worst that can happen? We'll starve to death? Fuck it. I just needed to do what I really wanted to do because I didn't know how many days I had. What a great gift! That's how we looked at it. What a beautiful gift to tell us not to take for granted any time that we got, to use it wisely.

rr That diagnosis could be given to anyone at any time, though.

gp It's true, but I think for most people it's just not that vivid. We were lucky we got it in such a vivid way that we got the message. Later we read about the Sufi saying "Live every day like it's your last day and that it's the day upon which your life will be judged." And that's how we try to live. We don't always succeed, obviously, but that's how we try to live. That's when it all really took off, focusing on what we had already experienced and intuited on different levels but deciding that that truly was the only thing of infinite value.

rr It's crazy to view that from the outside. You started by meditating, focusing on your breath, then you have this moment of clarity when you were outside of your body, and then brought back and set on the path. Total initiation.

gp We got lucky. It's nice to hear someone who views it like that because not everyone does.

tk [To Robert] Do you have a moment like that?

rr I did almost drown when I was sixteen. That definitely changed my view on everything. I was surfing in the wintertime and I misjudged the size of the wave. I thought it was something I could handle. It was just me in the ocean by myself and confronted with the ultimate fear. I started paddling in, and I almost made it to the beach when a wave crashed behind me and held me under for what felt like an eternity but what was actually about thirty seconds, and I woke up on the beach. I realized then that I needed to get my shit together. It was also a step into my adulthood, when I learned to stop looking at things like a child and to start trying to live my life.

gp That reminds me! We were looking through some papers, we didn't remember where they came from. A friend of mine wrote this essay about childlike perceptions. It obviously turned up for you because it turned up last night. She actually wrote her PhD on Hermann Nitsch and me.

rr You're in good company.

gp We ended up meeting him. We went to meet him at his chateau in Austria and drank his wine and watched videos of him playing with entrails. Really cool.

rr What was your connection to him in your past?

gp We got asked to do an art history book in 1975. We moved to London from the north of England and got to know the editor of a magazine called Art and Artist. The editor was asked to do this book that was going to be a catalog of the thousand most important artists of the twentieth century. We had been writing reviews and articles for the magazine under fake names. So the editor asked if I wanted to help with the book. That was my introduction to Hermann Nitsch. We were already doing COUM at the time and that editor asked if we were inspired by him and everyone was like, "Who the fuck is Hermann Nitsch?" We didn't know

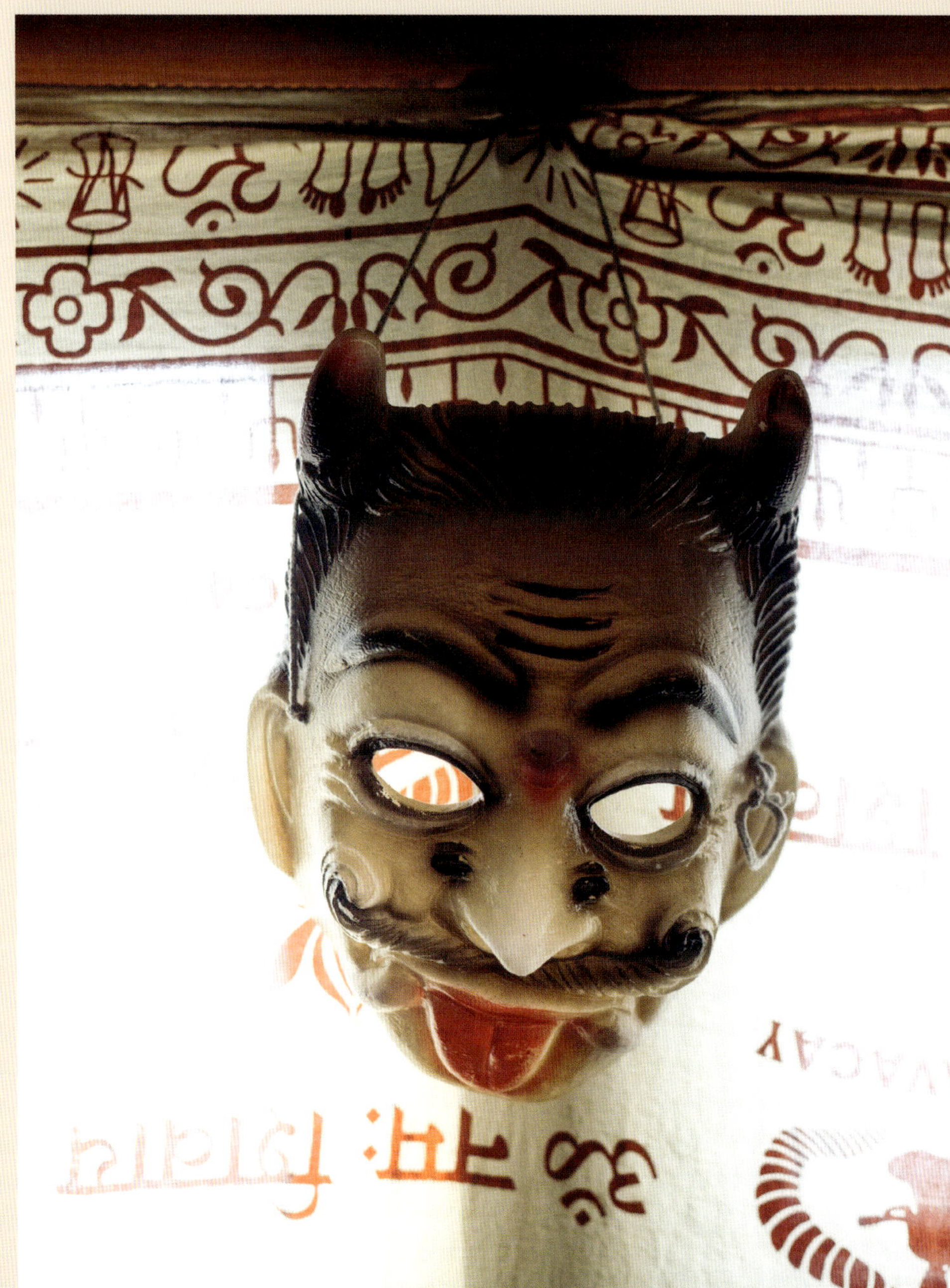

anything about the art world. We were a bizarre little commune of freaks. But when I saw his stuff, I just fell in love with it. So I wrote to him during the book, and we had some correspondence. Years later, a friend of mine knew I wanted to meet him, and I know he knew about me because of that PhD that was written about him. So I was flown out to Vienna, and I hung out with him for a few days and we became buddies.

rr It's interesting because you weren't inspired by him, but he was making that type of work at the same time. It's like the wheel: it kind of happened all over the place and no one person invented it. Do you think there are hot spots or energy portals?

gp That's why we've always said that there was nothing remarkable or special about us and industrial music. It was inevitable that would happen. It might have been called something else, we just picked up on it because we've learned to observe the undercurrents really well from years of practice. We were always looking at the semi-visible signals in popular culture and used them to determine what was going to happen next. For example, you do tattoos. It was me that suggested to [V.] Vale to do Modern Primitives and RE/Search. We were visiting one day and he was doing Search and Destroy. We thought it was too disposable. So we basically suggested doing this series of books, and you collect them all until you have this encyclopedia of the weirdest and most wonderful information. To his credit, he immediately got it. So the first one we worked on was William Burroughs, Brion Gysin, Throbbing Gristle.

The next one was industrial culture, and by the next one he was trying to figure out what to do. We had started getting pierced and tattooed, which at that time was really underground. There was only one person in the whole of Britain doing piercing, and that was Mr. Sebastian. He happened to have met Fakir Musafar and Sailor Sid. We knew Rob in Holland, so between us, we knew most of the key people. So we said to Vale, "Look, this is going to be huge." And it was. Now there's a tattooist or a piercer in just about every little village around the world. That's what we call cultural engineering.

rr That's what I was going to ask you about. Did those perceptions kind of come about organically?

gp That one kind of did. We just got into it because it gave us a whole new perspective on the body and liberating my sense of who controls my own skin. Just as women should be allowed to control their bodies, so should everyone. Why

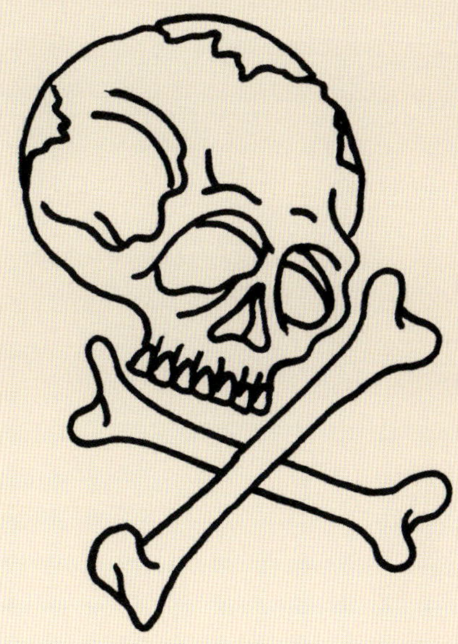

aren't we being given this information? Why are we always told it's gypsies and criminals? That just doesn't make any sense. You start to realize that suddenly, all over the world, people are tattooing and piercing and modifying their bodies. Why? A sense of tribalism, of having like-minded people around you to support you. This is a good thing. It wasn't because we were clever; it was because we felt the pulse correctly. He put the book out and it sold however many thousands of copies that it's sold now.

rr That Fakir Musafar interview is mind-blowing. It's incredible. It was a peek into something that no one had ever seen before. It was really powerful to me, reading it for the first time.

gp For a lot of people. We're very proud of the part we played in that. It's just really disciplined observation with yourself. It's like what you were saying earlier about sigils, and how they are about observing yourself and really understanding what you truly need to become, what you need to be. You can apply that sort of rigorous thinking to culture. And once you begin that process, it just builds up and builds up as other people recognize the echoes of what they've been thinking and join in the energy that's pushing it until it's everywhere. Cultural engineering is totally feasible.

My feeling of the moment is that the zeitgeist is communities. The only way for us to survive as a species is to have think tank communities. Not completely off the grid. Western magic is all about the individual becoming empowered, and what do you do with power but control other people? That's a bit sick. The lesson with individual power is that it's not enough unless everybody else is benefitting, too. The true message is that you have to start with everyone else and help them rise up to their potential and give back, otherwise what you've done is wasted and worthless. It has to be about the species, and the picture we give is very simple. If you start to remember the human species is one great big organism, and every one of us is one bit of it, what does an organism do when it's damaged or wounded or sick? It gets together all of its resources to try and heal the wound or get the right nutrients to the part of the body that needs it. It replenishes and heals itself. If we were all to think of our species the same way, we would inevitably apply all the resources we have to wherever there is suffering, and healing is needed. Then we would be liberated from war and totalitarian capitalism, and we could turn our species into what it is really here for. And as Brion Gysin said so astutely years ago, we are meant to go forward. We are meant to go into space. That's the only thing that makes any sort of sense for the future.

rr I think when you introduce a lot of these culturally engineered ideas, it's tough when they start to become commodities. You mentioned that happening with industrial music. I deal with it with tattooing. I feel that there is magic involved: it's an ancient practice, there's a little shamanism involved. There's also currency, and now there's a level of celebrity involved. It's really risky. It could take away from it. Maybe it has taken away from it in a lot of ways. But I feel that the practice is so strong—of marking your body—that it has the power to overcome that.

gp Now that everyone and their mother has a tattoo, is it still special? Yes, of course it is. The way you perceive it, use it, and learn from it is your responsibility, but that doesn't negate the power of it.

rr It never does, right? Same with music?

gp Industrial music is a difficult one for me. We don't listen to industrial music, let's be frank. But out of the blue last year, we got an email from Trent Reznor asking us to do a remix for his new album. And we said of course. I don't know if you know this, but we were in a lawsuit with Rick Rubin back in the '90s.

rr I didn't know that.

gp In 1995, we were in LA in Harry Houdini's old mansion with Love and Rockets. It turned out that all the electricity was plugged into old sockets and it caught on fire. So about 6:00 a.m., my T-shirt girl was running around screaming, "Wake up, everybody, the house is on fire!" We were at the top of the house, so somehow we got out the window safely.

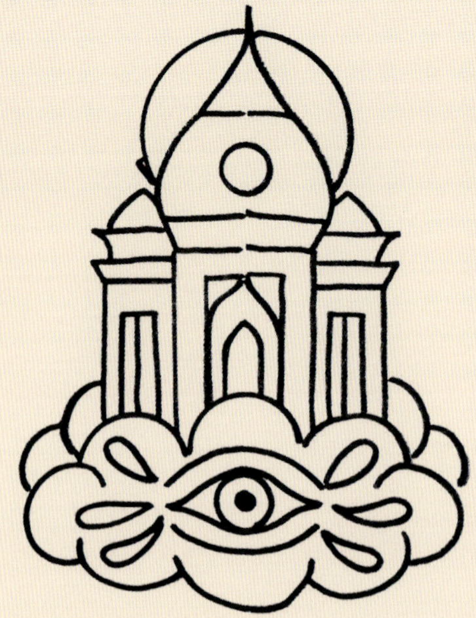

The door started to melt. So we grabbed at a tree, but it was dead and the branch broke. So we fell backwards, and all you say when you fall into the void is, "Oh shit." *[Laughs.]* We fell backwards and landed on concrete steps. One of my hips was broken, which is still numb to this day due to nerve damage. Ribs were broken, my wrist was broken, and my elbow exploded into thirty-six pieces. Lady Jaye came out to LA, and I spent my convalescence at Timothy Leary's house. And from his garden you could see the Tate house, where Trent was recording the famous album at the time. A few weeks after the court case that we had won, we got a letter in the post from a woman named Dianne, which read, "You don't know me, but I'm the juror who worked at the LA zoo. We all felt like we got to know you and Jaye so well during the court case and we were really glad we could help you out as much as we could. So here's a cassette: I look after the howler monkeys at the LA zoo and I recorded them waking up this morning just for you." So we took the cassette—and this is 1997—and put it in a drawer and kept thinking that one day we would find a really good use for it. Last year we used it all the way through in the background for Trent Reznor's remix. *[Everyone laughs.]*

rr Full circle.

gp That's also the other thing: patience. You got this beautiful talisman from someone you don't really know but has come to care for you by just witnessing you in a stressful situation. And they have come up with the most perfect gift they could give you, and you think, "One day, that's going to be really important." That's what you have to learn with patience: to recognize the value of things but not rush into how they are going to be used. They'll tell you when it's ready. Twenty years later, it fit perfectly with the rhythm of the song.

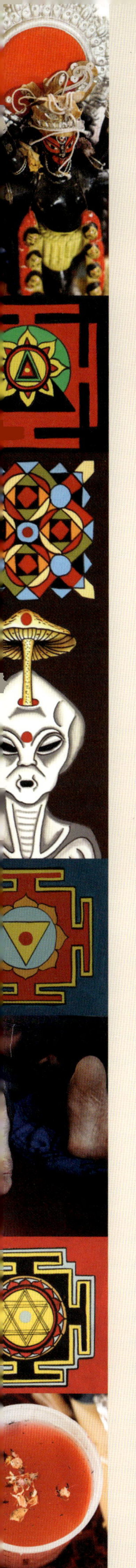

rr It's real magic. It's so beautiful that she was so enamored with you both.

gp She said the whole jury felt that way. It was so nice to receive because it's really stressful being on the witness stand for days with people trying to make fun of you.

rr In that setting too. It's harsh. You are in judgment. Speaking of juries and trials, in your travels, did you ever have any contact with the Manson family?

gp I got a letter from Charlie.

rr I'm fascinated with that energy. I feel like it was kind of an inevitable lesson on how power can get corrupted or out of your hands. Like you were saying before: power only gets you so far. It gets you to the gates but not through the door.

gp You only get through the door if you open it for everyone else. Here's Charlie's letter to me: "Gen, you must be a retarded person. Or maybe you are in another universe." I'm in another universe? He thinks I'm weird! *[Laughs.]* So let's play the song with the howler monkeys.

We all sat quiet together and looked at the ceiling and looked at our toes and listened to the song, nodding our heads. You can imagine Nine Inch Nails accompanied by howler monkeys. But can you imagine that sound and it actually sounds awesome? Howler monkeys really do sound quite a bit like their name implies. And of course it would be a pioneer of "industrial" music who knew to insert the field recordings with only the slightest of modifications, if any—maybe the monkeys were slowed down a smidge.

gp *[Looks at Ardhanarishvara.]* That's the male and female! What is it called again?

rr Ardhanarisvara. Shiva and Parvati together.

gp You know what that means to me. This is the ultimate point of evolution. The apparent corporeal existence of anything is the reunification with self-knowledge. That's what the Big Bang is to me: a moment of absolute revelation. However, that shattering leaves us with the responsibility of reunifying ourselves in a nondamaging, compassionate way. Eventually that has to mean the end of either/or, male/female, biologically, at least. The unfolding of both has to be the ultimate state, and that state would eventually lead us to the spiritual state. No contradictions, no conflicts: ultimate reality, ultimate balance.

rr This painting is actually what made me want to talk to you about these paintings You're someone that has actually lived this. Many people use it as a symbol, but you've adopted it and are living it.

gp We met this guy, Timothy Wyllie, who was one of the founding five members of the Process Church, as well as John Lilly. It's interesting that John Lilly, after a certain amount of experimentation, became both empathic with dolphins and also started trying to grow breasts. And started dressing in female clothing. And so did Timothy Wyllie, and so did we. We believe every chemical intoxicant has a spirit. And ketamine has a pandrogyne spirit. It's just too specific that three seriously questing minds have found the desire to dress like, and to become, both. So this *[points to the painting]* is the divinity of pandrogyny and of ketamine. We've never found it to be in any way negative. The trips are very short, about twenty to thirty minutes using it the way we did, which was injecting it into the muscle.

rr This image came to me through ayahuasca. Which is also funny, because it's the ayahuasca and the chacruna together. Neither one does anything for you until you put them together, and it's the same with the male and the female, Shiva, Shakti. One needs to activate the other, and if you have too much of one or the other, it's useless. You're not suppressing any part of the self, you're balancing them out with the others. With suppression you get psychosis.

gp You also have to be very good at self-observation and be honest with yourself, because you're out of balance. When you're leaning too much in one way for whatever reason— you want to fuck somebody, you're scared, you've been tricked into your own ego—and you start to use these maps, you can avoid all of those pitfalls. You can reach a place of balance and calm.

rr That's all we really want, right? This one is kind of the same. *[Pulls out Shiva and Parvati.]* Balancing the fire and the water, the sun and the moon. Then the serpent is always present, too.

gp In Africa, it's a python, but it's really just a serpent. And again, it's everywhere, whispering wisdom and knowledge. Why is that bad? We have been telling people for a long time that the only way forward for art is for it to become spiritual and devotional and mystical again. The great art of the Renaissance was all attached to spirituality. Obviously it used Christian imagery as camouflage, but it was much deeper than that. It was alchemy. And the great artists were clearly playing games with that, with symbols and metaphors. The only future for art now is to be discussing the extension of life. Otherwise there's no conversation. Sentimentality, authenticity of a description of a way of life, mysticism, devotion, spirituality … they're all big no-nos in the art world. They don't want to be confronted with meaning.

rr *[Pulls out Radha and Krishna.]* So here we've got Radha and Krishna intertwined again, the male and the female. Here we have music, too.

gp Do you play music as well?

rr I do. I play a lot of different flutes. I play the harmonium.

gp Do you want to try this? It's like a trumpet.

For a couple minutes, Bink blows blasts and groans into a thigh-bone trumpet as Genesis and I watch and smile. It sounds like an elephant mixed with a scream, mixed with a piece of dry wood rubbing against wood.

gp It's hard, it's one of those instruments that you try for an hour or so and then you'll get the resonance. It's three hundred years old.

rr So, Krishna and Radha—it's the lovers' embrace. Devotional love. In hearing you talk about Lady Jaye and your relationship, this one kind of resonated with me. True, unconditional love.

gp That's been an amazing journey, too, with the film [Marie Losier's The Ballad of Genesis and Lady Jaye]. The number of people that come up and say, "I've always believed in absolute, unconditional love, but I've been too afraid to really relax into it. I'm always scared of being hurt." We always say, "You'll probably get hurt anyway, so why not just do it?" And some people do say that they're going to change the way they are in their relationship because they've seen the film. People would talk to Lady Jaye and ask her what she wanted, and she would say, "I just want to be remembered as a great love affair." That was the truth; that was all she cared about. Absolute love.

rr And everything else was a manifestation of your love. *[Pulls out Chinnamasta.]* Here we've got Chinnamasta. She's taking off her own head to nurture her attendants, her devotees.

gp Who is this again?

rr This is Kali.

gp I didn't know she took her head off.

rr This is one of the Mahavidyas. Each one is an aspect of her personality. It's one of the most esoteric forms of Kali worship. But to me it was really moving that she would cut off her own head to nurture everyone. It's such an arcane and heavy image for people to worship. It's obviously the trinity, with the three bloodstreams.

gp Who are they?

rr This is Lust and Desire. And Love is stepping on Lust and Desire.

gp Because true love is sacrifice. The blood sacrifice. When I think about all these neo-Christians who quote the Old Testament, I want to ask them if they actually heard the message. God is not here to destroy us and punish us and make us miserable for eternity. God is love, baby. God threw

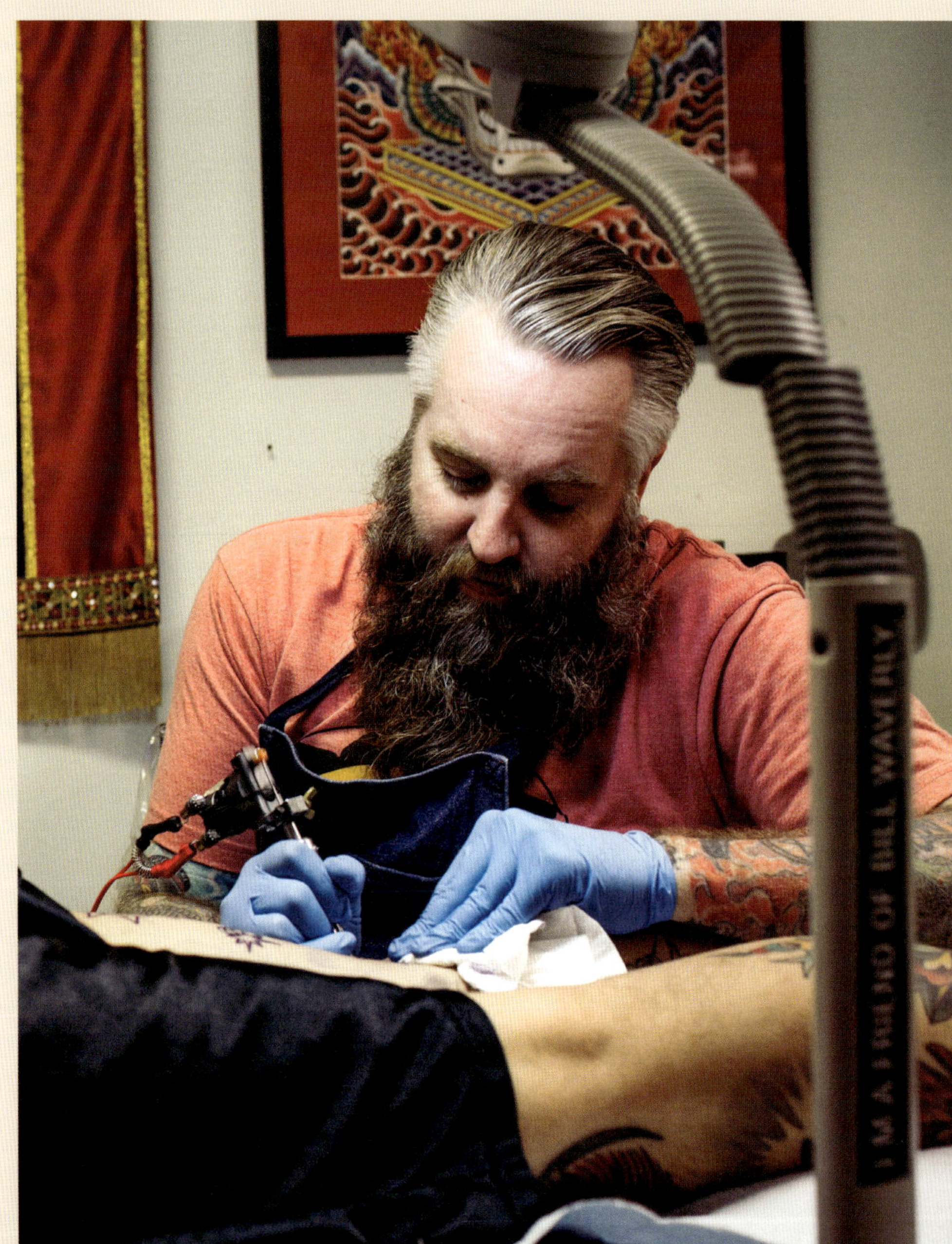

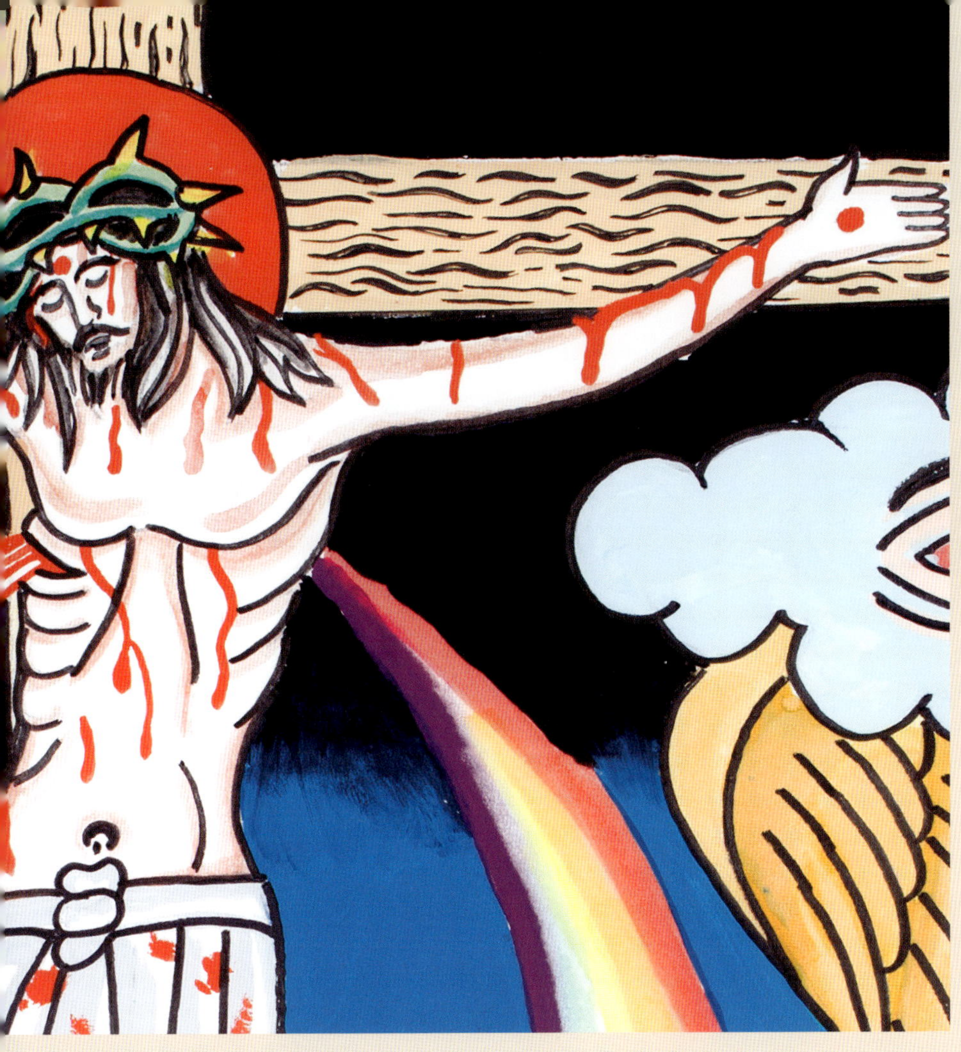

rr We all go on the cross at some point in our lives.

gp I've been on political crosses as you know, sometimes losing everything we had, but trusting in the vision enough to know that we would be OK. At first the Tibetans in Nepal said, "You can stay free for as long as you want." And we come here and Winona Ryder's parents looked after us for months. My whole experience in the United States has been being supported and nurtured and cared for by people. Not the normal political vision that we are taught. And to me that is the spirit of the United States: the original reason for America was not to get rich quick, it was to take care of each other.

rr You came to America under religious persecution?

gp I did.

rr That's amazing. I never looked at it like that. You are living the true American dream.

gp We were welcomed.

rr Pilgrims.

gp It's beautiful, though. *[Looks back at the painting.]* The colors are so beautiful. Are they done on canvas?

rr They're done on board. It's gouache and watercolor on board.

gp That explains the style of your tattoos.

rr I've tried to bring this Eastern iconography through this American traditional style of tattooing. It's kind of taking off. I see other people doing it, and I don't think I was the first person to do it. But I'm starting to see it more and more. I'm doing one Kali tattoo per week. People are resonating with it. It's powerful. I'm also trying to take a step back and approach it as respectfully as possible because it is such a powerful image. *[Pulls out Dattatreya.]* So this is Dattatreya: Shiva, Bhrama, and Vishnu all in one body. The trinity, the trident, as you said before.

gp Are you with me on this idea that they've all grown from the same story?

rr I think so.

gp They have to. Different environments that people lived in and the way things occurred gradually added to the

---

out the people with money and the high priests and told them they didn't need a temple. God lives inside every one of us.

rr *[Pulls out Crucifixion.]* Crucifixion. Sangre.

gp I like the rainbow. Is that coming from Jesus as well?

rr Yeah, it's coming from the other side, kind of nurturing the followers and people who are truly devoted. I wanted to ask you about Christ. Not about Christianity, but about Christ as a person. The cosmic Christ.

gp Well yeah, we use the cross and it factors heavily into our cosmology. We see him as a misunderstood figure, mainly misunderstood by Christians who don't really know the story. They don't know that they're following a renegade Jewish cult. They don't know any of it. They don't know that the four gospels were written by people who were never there, two hundred years later. Then they were edited over and over again for political reasons. It's always the same message behind it all. Whether he was a human who took on the role of being a symbol or whether he was truly a symbolic being, it doesn't matter. The story is that you have to give for everyone. It becomes not about individual power but about doing for everyone.

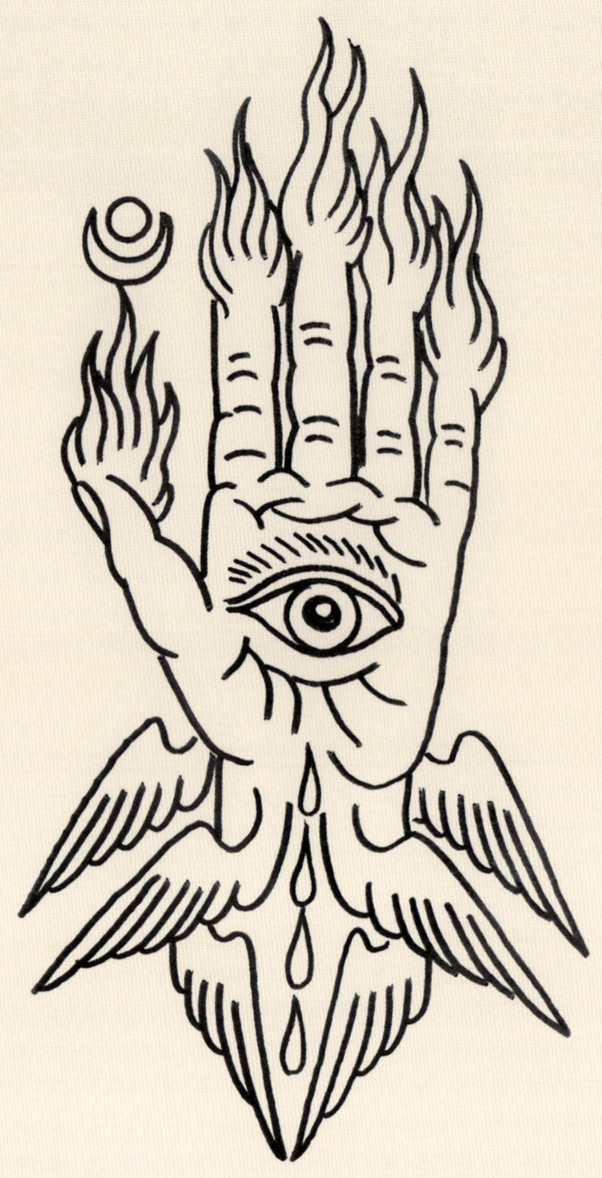

detail in different ways, but there's a story at the bottom of it all.

rr The African system you were studying, do they have a trinity?

gp That's a really good question. We don't know the answer. In Benin, the first night we got there, we were sitting in the town square drinking beer, and in the distance we saw a very tall, thin person in the shadows wearing robes that seemed to just be floating. We blurted out, "That must be a high priest." Everyone turned and looked and couldn't see anything. The next day our translator said, "Would you like to come and meet my family?" So we walked in and there's this tall person that I had seen the night before. He's six-foot-eight and is the high priest of voodoo of that whole area, and the father of our translator. His first words to me in Fon, through

his son, were, "You had a twin but she died. And she was wearing those gold earrings." I said, "Yes." And the night after that, we were already doing a ceremony so Lady Jaye's soul could be transferred to this doll, so she could be with me all the time.

rr What an amazing gift.

gp Then we started trying to find out more about this twin cult that exists in Benin. No one would talk about it on the first visit. In the rest of the world, there are about four twin births per thousand. And in Benin it's twenty-five to forty per thousand. Finally the high priestess agreed to talk to us, at the end of the second visit, and we asked why there are so many twins. And she said, "Because they know they will be loved whether they live or die." You talk to them, you feed them, you take them everywhere you go. There's no shame, there's no sadness, there's no guilt. Their spirit is still there and with you and you just carry on. At the same time we were there, there was a twin festival. The first week is for the twins that died, the second week is for the twins that are living. They let us take part in all of that as well.

rr That's one of those of course moments, because when you went you weren't going for this, were you?

gp No, not at all. We were going to go to another festival and look at the costumes.

rr Love is such an important catalyst for all these things that are happening right now.

gp It also goes back to one of Jaye's favorite phrases: "See a cliff, jump off." Never be afraid.

rr [Looks at Durga.] There you have Durga, the divine mother, in a very peaceful, benevolent form. I like that we have these different forms of her. Just like any mother: there's the tender and the chiding and the wrathful, you get all of those degrees.

gp Do you think these deities are constructed around human behaviors for us to recognize ourselves more vividly? Or do you think they exist beyond us because of so much belief that it made them manifest?

rr I think they were given to us from the beyond to help us with our everyday lives and to get through the illusion of life. That's my belief. I'm not saying that's how it is, but from my understanding, they are gifts for us to advance our spiritual evolution.

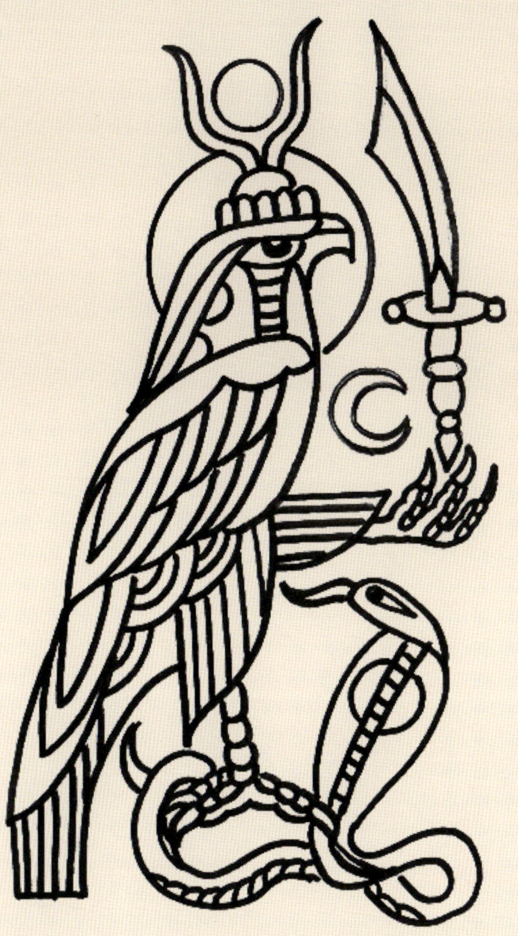

gp Isn't it sad that the West has lost that? The deeper desire for real wisdom, instead of worship, the seeking of the deepest revelation and the nature of existence. Beingness.

rr You can get into the separation of wisdom and knowledge. Because there is a thirst for knowledge, still. Anyone can get knowledge. But the wisdom comes in how you apply that knowledge to your life.

gp That's a bit of the full stop with Western magic: do you use that knowledge for your own ego and power, or do you use it to open it up and reveal the true next phase? Which is wisdom. We've seen so many people fall into their own egos and power. So many people did it to be strong.

rr That's why I was asking about Manson. I feel like there were some magical things happening with his group and it got away from them.

gp Definitely. Sadly, he believed in his own hype. The poor guy never had a chance. If you read the testimony he made, "Your Children," which was never allowed to be heard by the jury, it's really good. It's as if all the things that happened somehow gave him a moment of visionary transcendence, where he did understand some of the basic dynamics of existence. But he was seduced by his own trip. There's no place for violence and murder and greed. That's when it becomes thuggery.

rr I went to the place where he was born. It has the largest burial mound in North America that's still intact. Also, they found when they excavated the burial mound, that the markings on all the graves were runes. They weren't Native American. Apparently the Native Americans wanted nothing to do with this area. Like you said, it was a hot spot. It was a power center, and I think he was a manifestation of that energy that just got corrupted over time. Especially being institutionalized.

gp Just because someone has done something abominable doesn't mean that everything they speak is irrelevant. You should always look for truth regardless of where it's from. Our society doesn't have a system when someone has shamanic tendencies, where they are put under the wing of wise old people and they are trained—why they're having visions, why they're seeing things as they are. People give them explanations and maps they can use to make sense of it. But in the West we have thrown all of that away.

rr Now we medicate them or lock them up.

gp People like Jimi Hendrix or Brian Jones or Janis [Joplin] were pulling down some amazing energy. But no one was there to help them understand it, and they burned out. No one took care of them.

rr Brian Jones is an important one to me. And I know he was to you. Did you know him?

gp Only met him once. Met all of his sons several times, and Linda, who had one of his sons.

rr Was there a connection to the Joujouka musicians?

gp Yeah, I mean the Joujouka musicians lived with me and Jaye for a year. And of course, Brion Gysin was connected with them. The guy who murdered Brian Jones confessed. The first thing that people did after he was murdered was not to call the police or an ambulance, but to call the Rolling Stones' publicist, who lived in London. And he drove all the way from London and collected all of Jones' stage outfits and any reel-to-reel tapes they could find and burned them all in the garbage, and only then did they call the police.

rr Why?

gp Because Brian had started a band with Jimi Hendrix. And had demo tapes. I have a copy if you want to hear it. *[Looks in a drawer and pulls out the first tape.]* Wow, first one. Obviously meant to be there. Everything is popping out for you today. So Jimi Hendrix and Brian Jones had recorded demos. I saw the Stones in Hyde Park after he was dead and they were terrible. Can you imagine if, at that time, there was a supergroup with Brian Jones, Jimi Hendrix, the singer for Manfred Mann, and Mitch Mitchell? There would have been no Rolling Stones as we know them.

rr I can't believe we are about to hear this. While we're waiting, maybe we could look at this painting.
[Pulls out Ashta Nagas.]

gp Oh my goodness, scorpions! "It's in my nature," the scorpion said as he killed the frog. *[Laughs.]* Scorpions freak me out.

rr These hang outside of people's homes in Nepal. They'll hang them outside their door with a little bit of cow dung and a certain grass. It's a protector. I've seen it in Nepal quite often. It was in a hotel room I stayed in.

gp I don't recall seeing it, but I bet now when we go in October I'll see it everywhere.

rr These are the poisons that Shiva had swallowed for the sake of humanity. This is the churning of the earth and the poison was created.

gp So what happened when the poison was swallowed?

rr Turned his throat blue. His name is Neelkantha, "the blue-throated one." The gods asked him to do it. When they were churning the ocean, some poison was created and had gotten away, so the gods asked Shiva to swallow the poison. If it had gotten out, it would've destroyed earth.

gp The intertwining just suggests to me the connectedness of all different disciplines and stories which in the end all lead to this revelation. The serpent, the python, is an essential part of this whole process. It's DNA, it's kundalini, it's fear of knowledge. It's sexuality, too.

It's interesting that in Nepal, it's the naga. In Christianity, it's the serpent, and in Africa, it's the python. The snake is essential to whatever the original story is.

rr It's funny, Joseph Campbell used to say that humans blame the serpent for the errors.

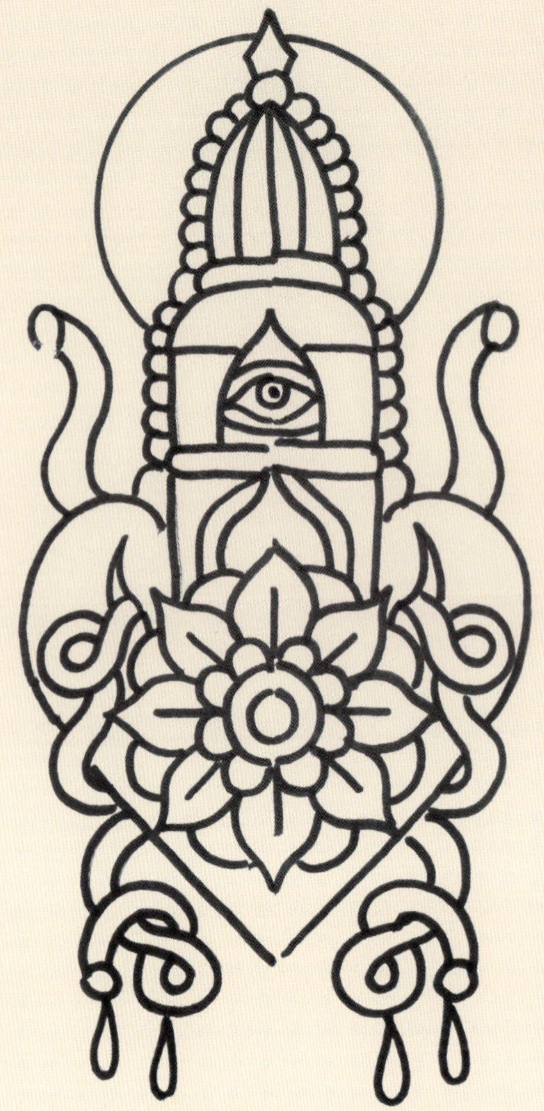

gp Wisdom is wisdom. It's your responsibility to do with it what you will.

We hushed as Genesis clicked the tape in place and hit play. Six or seven minutes passed.

So much secret knowledge and lost history had been discussed this afternoon, and now the Jimi Hendrix-Brian Jones supergroup just made perfect sense. It was the popular form of its era, rock music, and it was the pinnacle of its potential, and it was fated to be forever unknown.

We sat in silence for a moment when it finished, and no one commented on it.

rr *[Looks at Muruga.]* This is an interesting one. This is Shiva and Parvati's other son. This is Muruga, and he's the god of war. He has the spear, and I think the spear is about cutting through the ego. The peacock is standing on the serpent, taming the serpent energy. He's always youthful, too. He never grew old. He's worshipped in the South, and in the North, they worship Ganesh.

gp So complex, this system. Have you ever thought about looking for Western equivalents of some of these?

rr Here and there you see it. I mean the Star of David, that was a yantra, used by the Indians way before. "As above, so below."

gp *[Looks at Maha Kali Ma.]* I think a lot of people look at that and get freaked out by the heads and skulls and the blood and all that.

rr That's all ego. The dismantling and cutting through your ego.

gp And regeneration. You've got to let go of all that, the physical body.

rr It's so important with the pangender. Letting go and taking away the notion of predetermination of what you are supposed to be.

gp As Jaye said, it's not about gender at all. Pandrogyny. Some people say they're a man trapped in a woman's body, some people say they're a woman trapped in a man's body. We just say we're trapped in a body. That's the great conundrum of existing: the mind is the real you, and the real you can exist outside physical and linear time. *[Looks at Opening the Heart Temple.]* Are these decapitated snakes?

rr No, these are ventricles of the heart. I had the idea of a heart temple.

gp They look like worms. We like worms. We came home once and found all these worms in the garden that were having sex with themselves. We had to take a lot of Polaroids of that.

rr I had the idea of opening up the heart and having the temple inside your heart as a place to worship.

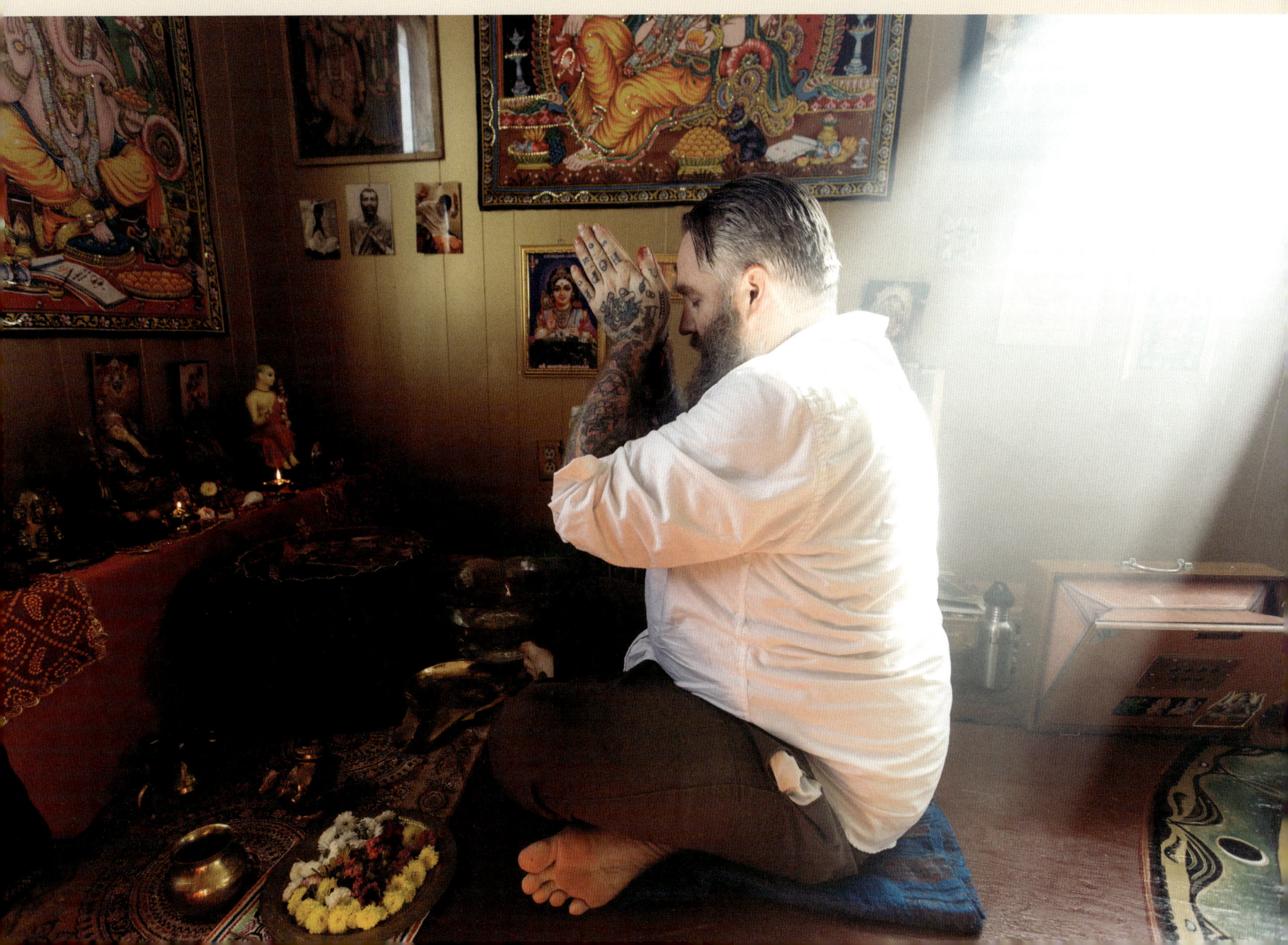

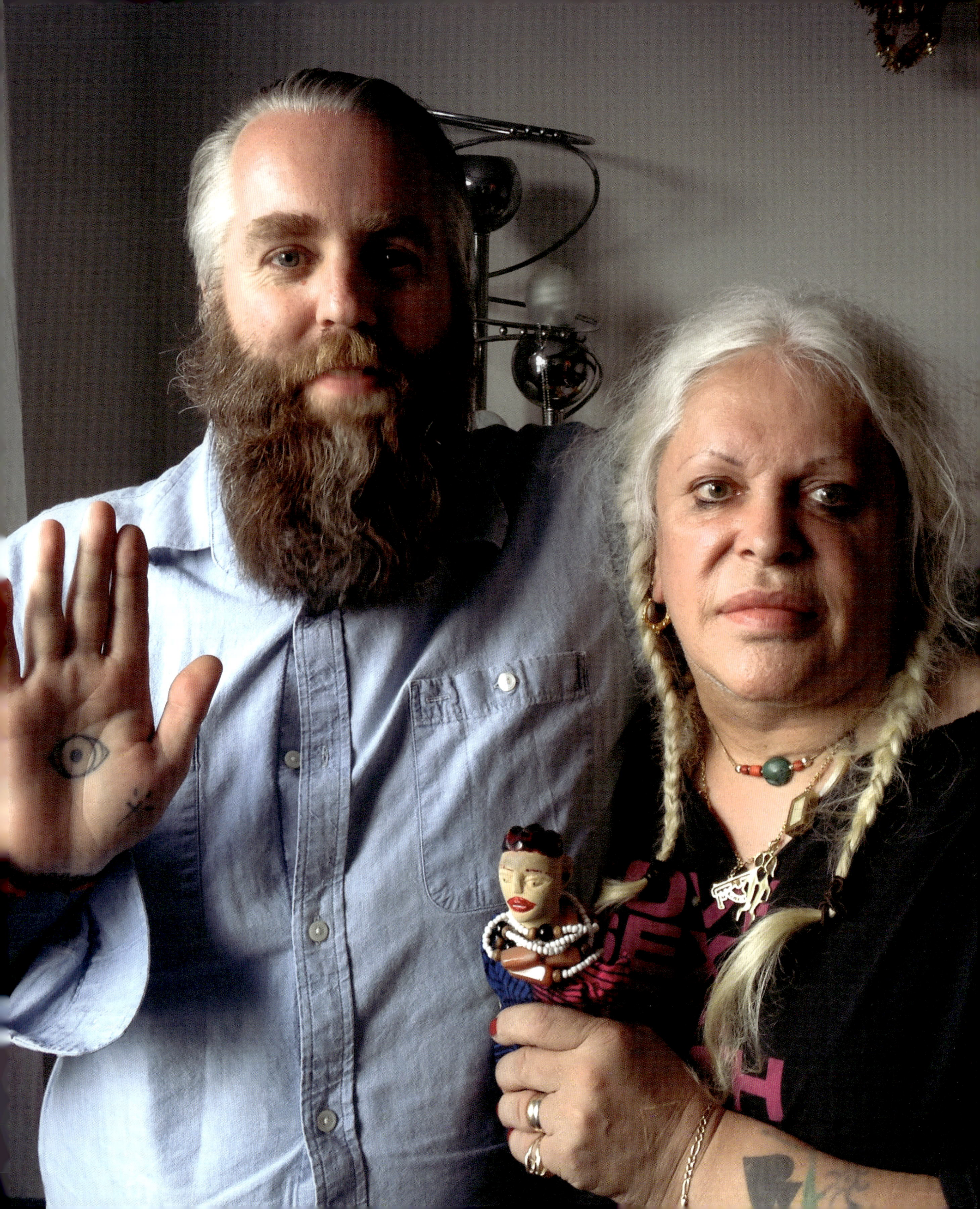

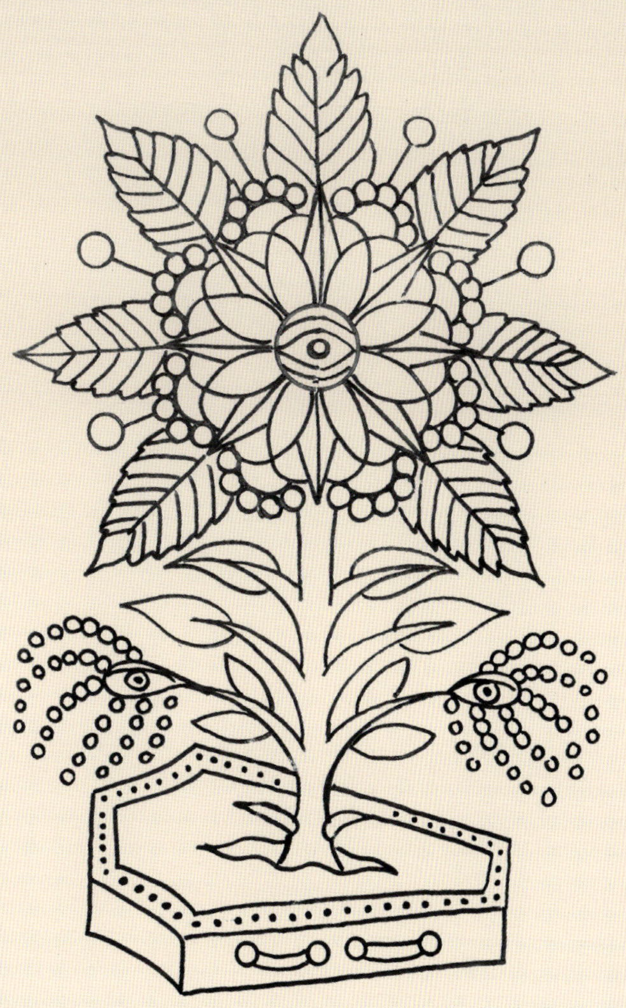

gp What's your relationship with the mushroom and that sort of visionary experience?

rr I think it's important and I think it's one of the gifts. I feel that stratus around the gods and halos are representative of mushrooms originally. I think the idea of Santa Claus and him coming through the chimney because he couldn't get in the door because they were snowed in, and he would come to bring mushrooms to the people. I do think that they were instrumental in culture at some point. I still use them. They are powerful teachers. I think they're alien.

gp That's what I was just going to say to you. You picked up on it. I was going to ask if you thought they were alien creatures.

rr I think they are.

gp An alien form of life here on earth. There's a huge one somewhere that's like twenty miles long. If you think about it as one conscious organism, then it's the largest organism on earth. It's in Vancouver.

rr What else could they be there for, if not to give knowledge?

gp They grow out of dung. They eat rotten things and create visions. How beautiful is that? From nothing comes something amazing.

Genesis leashed her small dog and we all walked out together. In the elevator, she was viscerally kind to her neighbor, a middle-aged man who was visibly uncomfortable with her. We all walked her dog in the small park adjacent to her building and exchanged niceties and tallied friends in common, almost like now, after the conversation, we were all being introduced for the first time.

Bink and I said thank you and good-bye and wandered the Manhattan streets aimlessly for a good long time without saying anything. We sat and ate pizza slices, watching the rush hour commuters hurry along the sidewalk in front of us, feeling either dazed or clarified, unsure of which.

IMAGE INDEX

Robert Ryan would like to thank: Genesis P-Orridge, Ryan Martin, Freddy Corbin,
Sara Stadtmiller, Autumn Spadaro, Meghan McAleavy, Andrew Fingerhut,
Eddy Deutsche, Ryan Begley, Thom DeVita, Nick Bubash, Ed Hardy,
Scott Harrison, Daniel Higgs, Mike Schweigert, and Tom Yak.

Special Thanks to Tim Kinsella and Ben Fasman for their tireless work on this project.

This book is dedicated with love to Swami Kodi Thatha
and Swami Rudra Abihishekam D.D.

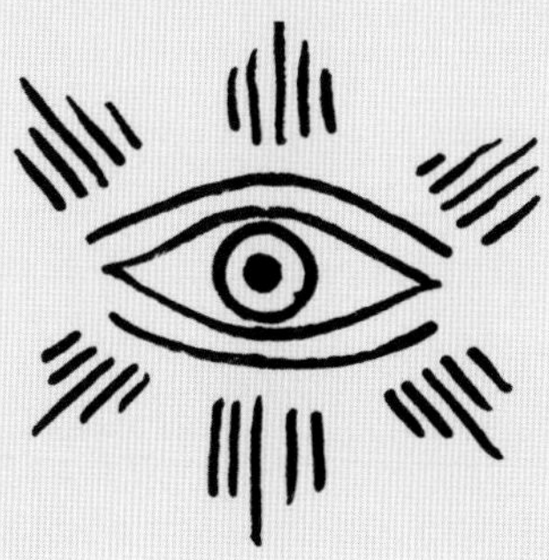

The editors would like to thank: Ryan Lowry, Mitchell Wojcik, Ben Poster,
Laura Ferrara, Meghan McAleavy, Rebecca Fasman, Edgar Bryan, Andrew Berardini,
Jeff Bradbury, Nick Colella, Allison Attwood and the whole crew at Great Lakes Tattoo,
and everyone who loaned us paintings from their personal collections to shoot.
Impossible without the time and thoughtful consideration of Freddy Corbin,
Ryan Martin and Genesis P-Orridge.

Endless gratitude to Tim Breen for bringing this book to life with style,
and Naomi, Jason and everyone else at Featherproof.

Most importantly, this book exists because we have been and continue to be
excited about Robert's work. Without him letting us into his life and opening it up,
none of this would've happened. Thank you doesn't really cut it.
We hope you like it, Bink.

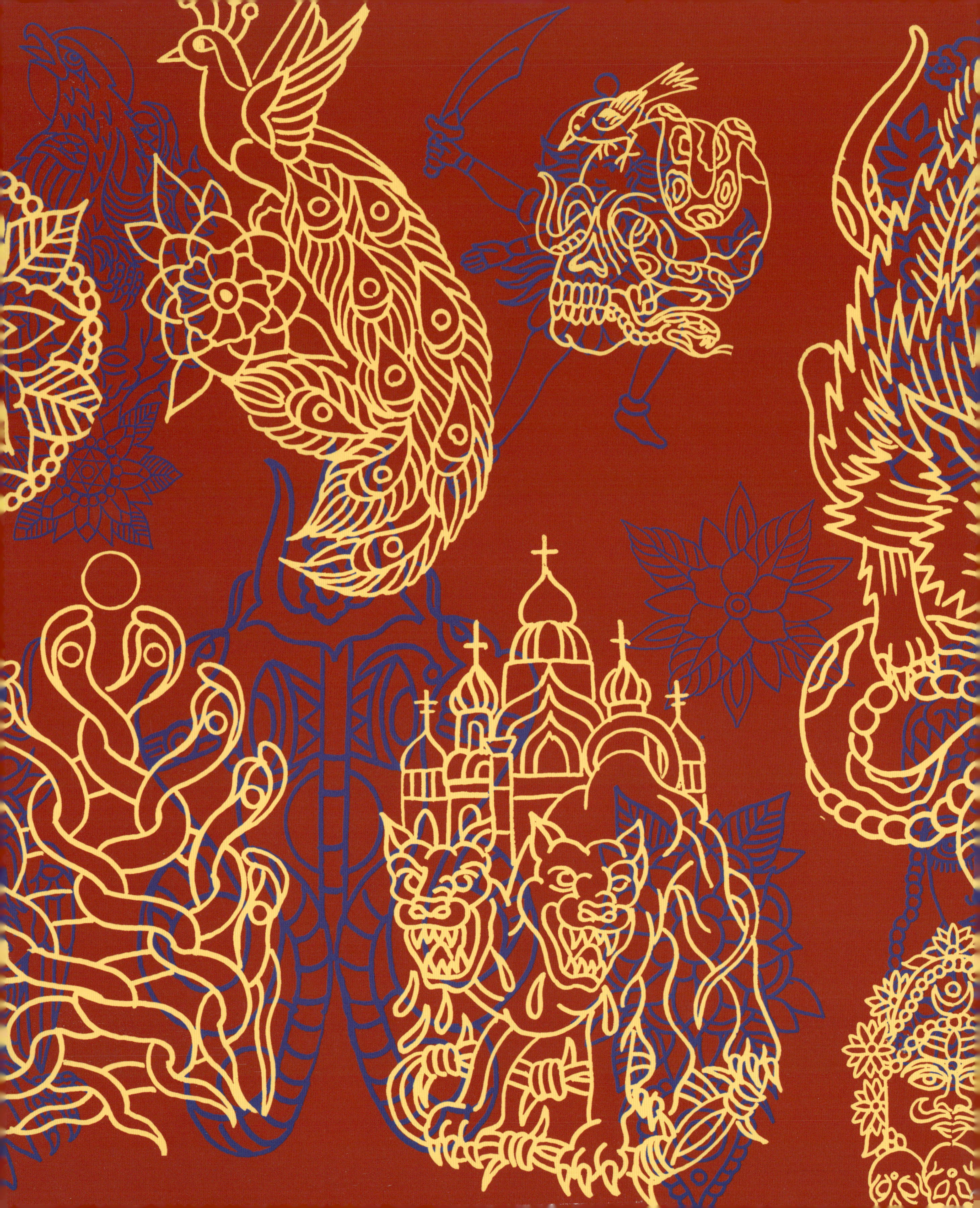